WORLD WITHOUT DESIGN

World Without Design

The Ontological Consequences of Naturalism

MICHAEL C. REA

CLARENDON PRESS · OXFORD
2002

OXFORD
UNIVERSITY PRESS

Great Clarendon Street, Oxford ox2 6DP

Oxford University Press is a department of the University of Oxford.
It furthers the University's objective of excellence in research, scholarship,
and education by publishing worldwide in

Oxford New York

Auckland Bangkok Buenos Aires Cape Town Chennai
Dar es Salaam Delhi Hong Kong Istanbul Karachi Kolkata
Kuala Lumpur Madrid Melbourne Mexico City Mumbai Nairobi
São Paulo Shanghai Singapore Taipei Tokyo Toronto

with an associated company in Berlin

Oxford is a registered trade mark of Oxford University Press
in the UK and in certain other countries

Published in the United States
By Oxford University Press Inc., New York

© Michael C. Rea 2002

The moral rights of the author have been asserted

Database right Oxford University Press (maker)

First published 2002

British Library Cataloguing in Publication Data

Data available

Library of Congress Cataloging-in-Publication Data
Rea, Michael C. (Michael Cannon), 1968–
World without design : the ontological consequences of naturalism / Michael C. Rea.
p. cm.
Includes bibliographical references and index.
1. Naturalism. 2. Ontology. I. Title.
B828.2 .R43 2002   146—dc21   2002020083
ISBN 0–19–924760–9

1 3 5 7 9 10 8 6 4 2

Typeset in 10.5 on 12 pt Minion by Kolam Information Service (P) Ltd., Pondicherry, India
Printed in Great Britain by Biddles Ltd., Guildford & King's Lynn

To
Alvin Plantinga
and
Paul Viggiano

Acknowledgments

WORK on this project was supported by a General University Research Grant from the University of Delaware, a grant from the Pew Evangelical Scholars Program, and a fellowship from the Center for Philosophy of Religion at the University of Notre Dame. I thank all of these institutions for their financial support, and I am especially grateful to the Center for Philosophy of Religion for the opportunity to spend an enjoyable and productive semester in residence. Thanks also to Rowman & Littlefield Publishers, Routledge, and Blackwell Publishers (respectively) for permission to reprint small bits of the Introduction to *Material Constitution: A Reader* (1997), most of 'Naturalism and Material Objects' (2000), and almost all of 'Theism and Epistemic Truth-Equivalences' (2000) in Chapters 4–6.

Many friends and colleagues have helped me to bring this project to completion. I owe a special debt of gratitude to Michael Bergmann, Crawford Elder, Robert Koons, Trenton Merricks, and Joel Pust, each of whom provided extensive and very helpful comments on the entire manuscript. I would also like to thank Fred Adams, Robin Andreasen, Chris Boorse, Jeff Brower, Andrew Cortens, Judy Crane, Tom Crisp, Terence Cuneo, Bill Hasker, Jeff Jordan, Lorraine Juliano, Brian Leiter, David Lewis, Laurie Paul, Alvin Plantinga, Bill Ramsey, Juliane Rea, Ted Sider, Jim Stone, David vanderLaan, and Brian Weatherson, for helpful conversations and comments on various portions of the manuscript. Jeremy Cushing, Dan Nairn, and Marty Strachan served as my research assistants during the summers of 1998, 2000, and 2001, and provided valuable information on the topics of pragmatism and antirealism. Lauren Hess helped in proofreading a substantial portion of the manuscript. I am also very grateful to Jody, Corrie, Lacey, and Judy Maxwell, Katie and Amy Weber, and my parents, Bob and Georgiana Rea, for generously helping our family with childcare during the summers of 1999 and 2000. Without their assistance it surely would have been at least another year before the book was finished. Finally, and most importantly, I thank my wife, Juliane, for her love, patience, support, and encouragement—always, but especially during the time I spent working on this project.

This book is dedicated to Alvin Plantinga and Paul Viggiano. They, more than anyone else, have affected my thinking about the issues discussed herein (though perhaps neither will agree with everything I have to say on those issues). Plantinga's influence will be evident in almost every chapter, and those who know Viggiano will probably observe his influence most in the first and last chapters. I am immensely grateful for their friendship and for the impact they have had on my intellectual life.

Contents

Contents

1

Introduction

PHILOSOPHICAL naturalism has dominated the Western academy for well over a century. It is not just fashionable nowadays; it enjoys the lofty status of academic orthodoxy. However, there is an important sense in which naturalism's status as orthodoxy is without rational foundation. Furthermore, the costs of embracing it are surprisingly high. The goal of this book is to defend these two claims.

In the present chapter I will introduce several of the concepts and assumptions that will occupy center stage in the book's main argument. In Section 1, I will introduce the notion of a *research program*. I will also defend the conclusion that it is impossible to adopt a research program on the basis of evidence. This will constitute my argument for the conditional claim that *if* naturalism is a research program, its status as orthodoxy is without rational foundation. In later chapters I will argue that naturalism is indeed a research program. In Section 2, I will introduce the central thesis of the book and explain in some detail the concepts involved in that thesis. Finally, in Section 3, I will provide a brief outline of what is to come.

1. Research Programs

Inquiry is a process in which we try to revise our beliefs in some way—by acquiring new ones, discarding old ones, or both. This is so whether we are trying to answer scientific questions like 'What causes thunder?', philosophical questions like 'Is capital punishment immoral?', or more mundane questions like 'Where are my keys?', 'Why does my stomach hurt?', or 'What's in that dark room?' But not just any attempt at belief revision counts as a process of inquiry. A severe blow to the head might bring about revisions in your belief structure; but hitting yourself on the head with a baseball bat is not, all by itself, an investigative process. True inquiry is a process in which we try to revise our beliefs on the basis of what we take to be evidence.

But this means that, in order to inquire into anything, we must *already* be disposed to take some things as evidence. In order even to begin an inquiry, we must already have various dispositions to trust at least some of our cognitive faculties as sources of evidence and to take certain kinds of experiences and arguments to be evidence. Such dispositions (let's call them *methodological dispositions*) may be reflectively and deliberately acquired. But for most people most of the time, they are probably acquired unreflectively and even unconsciously. We tend automatically to trust our senses, our reasoning abilities, and our memories. The fact that mathematical and logical propositions seem obviously to be true we readily and unreflectively take as strong and sufficient evidence in their favor. But we cast a cool eye of skepticism upon our untested beliefs on other topics. In matters of health, auto mechanics, gardening, and the like, we demand empirical evidence or testimony from an expert. Hunches about the stock market we might trust if we are expert investors (perhaps assuming that good reasoning lurks tacitly behind them). But, in our sober moments, hunches about lottery tickets and games of Russian roulette are steadfastly ignored. We find deductive arguments compelling, inductive arguments less so, and many other sorts of arguments laughable. In short, we are disposed to trust certain ways of acquiring information with respect to various topics and to distrust others; and, though sometimes our being so disposed is a result of conscious and reflective activity on our part, quite often it is not.

We may also note that methodological dispositions differ from person to person. Some take hunches of various sorts or burnings in the breast very seriously as sources of evidence; others regard all such episodes as epistemically worthless. Some are inclined to trust just about anyone's testimony; others are recalcitrant skeptics. Furthermore, people differ with respect to what they take to be *basic* sources of evidence—sources that are to be trusted even in the absence of positive evidence in favor of their reliability. For some (maybe most), sense perception, reason, memory, rational intuition, and religious experience *all* count as basic sources. For others, at least some of these sources are derivative—they are to be trusted only after their reliability has been verified by evidence from the basic sources.

For purposes here, a *research program* is a set of methodological dispositions. *Individual* research programs are maximal sets of methodological dispositions, where a set of dispositions is maximal just in case it is possible to have all of the dispositions in the set but it is not possible to have all of them *and* to have other methodological dispositions as well. *Shared* research programs, on the other hand, are relevantly distinctive subsets of individual research programs. An example will help to clarify this. Consider the disposition to treat sense perception as a source of evidence under specific conditions $C_1 \ldots C_n$. All by itself, this disposition does not count as an individual research program since one could have it while at the same time having a disposition to trust (say) religious experience under various circumstances. But that disposition in conjunction with a disposition to treat as evidence nothing other than sense perception as exercised in circumstances $C_1 \ldots C_n$ would constitute an individual research program. Furthermore, the more general disposition to trust nothing other than sense perception, though compatible with a variety of different and more specific methodological dispositions, might nonetheless be characterized as a shared research program because (in some context of discussion) it might be seen as the relevantly distinctive core of a variety of different but closely related individual research programs.

I should mention in passing that the way in which I use the term 'research program' differs from, but is nevertheless related to, the way in which Imre Lakatos has famously used the term. For Lakatos, a (scientific) research program has three elements: a distinctive 'hard core' of theses that are, for all practical purposes, treated as immune to revision; a 'protective belt' of auxiliary theses that may be revised as needed to accommodate observations that would otherwise seem to threaten the hard core; and a set of problem-solving strategies.[1] The most obvious difference here is that, unlike research programs in my sense of the term, Lakatosian (scientific) research programs include theses, as well as methodological rules specifying which theses are potential candidates for rejection. Interestingly enough, however, Lakatos does say that the whole of science itself can be regarded as a kind of research program; and what constitutes it as such is not any particular set of hypotheses or rules aimed at protecting particular hypotheses but *simply* those problem-solving strategies that are

---

[1] See esp. Lakatos (1970: 4, 47 ff.).

distinctive of science in general (1970: 47). Thus, Lakatos seems to have, in addition to his more narrow notion of a scientific research program, a somewhat broader notion according to which some research programs may be nothing more than sets of problem-solving strategies. This broader notion is not far off from the notion I aim to characterize.

Despite the academic connotations normally associated with the term, I take it that every inquirer has a research program, and this regardless of whether the inquiry is conducted in a university research lab, an auto shop, or the person's own backyard. This is because I think that every inquirer must have some methodological dispositions, and that anyone who has methodological dispositions must have a maximal set thereof. It seems just obvious that, for any kind of experience or argument, anyone who is disposed to treat *some* experiences or arguments as evidence will either be disposed to treat *that* kind of experience or argument as evidence or be disposed not to treat it as evidence. But if that is right, then the person's total set of methodological dispositions will preclude all others. (For example, if such a person lacked a disposition to trust tabloids, she would not be able to acquire that disposition without losing a disposition not to trust them. Hence, she could not *retain* her original set of methodological dispositions while adding the new one.) But, of course, to say this is just to say that every such person has a maximal set of methodological dispositions. Thus, every inquirer has a research program.

Like methodological dispositions generally, our research program is something we *bring* to the table of inquiry. Method is therefore prior to theory; and so, at least in the first instance, our research program is not something that we intentionally adopt as a result of inquiry. Thus, in the first instance, a research program is not adopted on the basis of evidence. But must it always be this way? Can't we discard a research program and adopt a new one as a result of inquiry? Can't we theorize about our methods and acquire evidence that some methodological dispositions ought to be cultivated and others put aside? And then can't we respond to that evidence, and so embrace a research program for *reasons* rather than by happenstance, habit, or arbitrary preference? Initially, it might seem that we can. For example, we can acquire evidence that our vision is unreliable, that our memory is untrustworthy, or that we are unusually gullible; and so we can make a conscious effort to put aside our dispositions to trust our faculties in these domains. If we succeed, we will have acquired a new research program. And it appears that we will have done so on the basis of evidence.

But the appearances are misleading. Research programs can be discarded on the basis of evidence, but they cannot be adopted on that basis. To see why, let us consider a concrete example. Suppose you start with a research program that includes a disposition to distrust sources of information that you take to be unreliable *and* a disposition to treat all testimony as evidence. (Very small children sometimes seem to have this sort of research program.) But suppose that, over time, you acquire what you take to be good evidence that the testimony of slick Uncle Bill is terribly unreliable. Then one of three things might happen. (*a*) You might acquire a disposition to distrust Uncle Bill, thereby losing your disposition toward universal gullibility. (*b*) You might discount the evidence in favor of Uncle Bill's unreliability, thereby losing some of the dispositions that initially led you to take that evidence seriously. Or (*c*) you might lose your disposition to distrust sources that you believe are unreliable. Given that at least *one* of these three things must happen, we have here a situation where evidence forces you to discard your research program. But evidence does *not* determine which of these three responses is the correct one. And so your adoption (say) of a research program that retains the disposition to distrust sources that you believe to be unreliable is not something that is done on the basis of evidence.

In making this point, I assume that one cannot have contradictory dispositions (i.e., one cannot at the same time be disposed both to do A and not to do A). But one might object that this very assumption should lead one to believe that the scenario just described is impossible. After all, if one *really* has a general disposition to distrust apparently unreliable sources, doesn't that imply that one's disposition to trust testimony is really only a disposition to trust apparently reliable testimony? Or, alternatively, if one really has a disposition to trust all testimony, doesn't that imply that one's general disposition to distrust apparently unreliable sources does not apply to testimony? Perhaps; and if so, then it seems that the right conclusion to draw here is that (*a*) research programs cannot defeat themselves in the way described above, and so (*b*) just as research programs cannot be adopted on the basis of evidence, so too they cannot be discarded on that basis either. This is a consequence I could be content with. It would force some revisions in what I say later on. (Most importantly:

I will say later on that a certain shared research program—*intuition-ism*—is self-defeating under certain circumstances. But if I were to accept (*a*), I would recast the same argument as an argument for the conclusion that it is impossible for someone to be an intuitionist in those circumstances and so, for those who find themselves in those circumstances, intuitionism is not an alternative to naturalism.) But, as a matter of fact, I do not accept either the objection or its conse-quence. The reason is that, as I see it, the disposition toward universal gullibility and the disposition to distrust apparently unreliable sources do not come into conflict until the evidence of Uncle Bill's unreliability is uncovered. Thus, though the research program is ultimately self-defeating, it does not in fact defeat itself until the right sort of investigation has been undertaken. And I think that the same holds true for any other self-defeating research pro-gram.

In general, the reason why research programs cannot be adopted on the basis of evidence is that evidence can only be recognized as such from within a research program. As we have just illustrated, a research program might generate evidence that prescribes its own rejection. Furthermore, a research program might also generate evi-dence that some other research program is to be accepted. Still, it cannot be on the basis of this evidence that one accepts the favored program. For once the old program is rejected, the evidence arising out of the old program in favor of the new cannot be recognized as evidence. Or, at any rate, it cannot be recognized as evidence until a new program is in place which sanctions the sources that generated it. But even if this new program happens to be the program favored by the old, still it will not have been on the basis of the evidence generated by the old program that the new one was accepted. For the new program had to be accepted before that evidence could again be recognized as such. Thus, from an evidential point of view, the best we can say on behalf of a research program is that it is *self-supporting* (where a research program is self-supporting if and only if it does not prove self-defeating). We cannot say that it is supported by evidence that is somehow generated and recognizable as such independently of the program.

So when it comes to rejecting one program in favor of another, the decision to adopt the favored program must be made on pragmatic grounds, broadly speaking, rather than evidential grounds. In such cases, one chooses the program whose consequences are most attractive, or whose canons are most convenient to adopt, or whose adoption will most irritate one's enemies, or whatever.[2] Furthermore, even if it happens to be true that (say) one rationally ought to adopt the program whose consequences are more attractive rather than the program whose adoption will most irritate one's enemies, there are no discernible grounds for asserting this truth. For, again, one could discern the grounds for asserting it *as grounds* for asserting it only within the context of some research program.

Understanding all of this is crucial to understanding the proper place of philosophical naturalism on the methodological landscape. As I said earlier, philosophical naturalism now enjoys the status of orthodoxy (much like a certain religious program enjoyed the status of methodological orthodoxy during the medieval years). In light of the foregoing, however, it should be clear why, if naturalism is a research program, its status as orthodoxy is without rational foundation. As we have already seen, there is no method-neutral basis on which to assess the decision to adopt a particular research program. Hence, we can have no rational grounds for declaring any such decision to be either categorically rational or categorically irrational. Thus, if naturalism is indeed a research program, as I will later argue that it is, there is no basis at all for saying that it is the sort of program that everybody, or every intelligent or right-thinking person, ought to adopt. This, of course, is no special deficiency of naturalism. If it is a deficiency at all, it is one shared by every other research program. But the point is important nonetheless, for it goes some distance toward disarming the current presumption in favor of naturalism. It also suggests that, on the assumption that naturalism is not self-defeating, the most appropriate tactic for trying to persuade others to reject it is to provide pragmatic considerations against it—highlighting its unattractive consequences, showing that other research programs do not suffer from the same problems, and the like. Since I am not prepared to defend the conclusion that naturalism is self-defeating, I will adopt the latter strategy in my own attack on naturalism.[3]

---

[2] This is not to say that a research program can be adopted at will. Perhaps we have no direct voluntary control over what research program we adopt. Still, this is no reason to doubt that our adopting a particular research program is ultimately guided by pragmatic considerations.

[3] But see Ch. 8 for a limited defense of Alvin Plantinga's widely discussed 'evolutionary argument against naturalism'. Strictly speaking, Plantinga's argument is not directed at naturalism as I understand it; however, as I will note in Ch. 8, there is good reason to think that the argument nevertheless has some bearing on naturalism.

2. The Central Thesis

The central thesis of this book is that naturalists cannot, by their own lights, be justified in accepting two metaphysical views that many philosophers—naturalists in particular—very much want to accept. Those views are *realism about material objects* (RMO) and *materialism*. I will also argue that, on the assumption that standard naturalistic arguments against mind–body dualism are successful, naturalists must give up a third thesis: *realism about other minds* (ROM). Realism about other minds is, strictly speaking, a different thesis for every person. For me, it is the thesis that minds other than my own exist; for you it is the thesis that minds other than your own exist; and so on. Materialism and realism about material objects deserve more extended comment.

I will define materialism as the view that nothing exists except for spacetime, material objects and events in spacetime, and the properties exemplified by spacetime and the objects and events therein. The categories of material object and event are meant to be collectively broad enough to include things like electrons and fields; and they are meant to exclude such things as God (as traditionally conceived), Cartesian souls, angels, and the like. I admit that this definition is imprecise; but I am not aware of any definition in the literature that manages to be more precise while at the same time expressing a view that all materialists are plausibly thought to hold in common. Some, of course, will think that my definition is overly broad. For example, David Chalmers (1996) would surely admit that all mental properties are properties of material objects in spacetime; but he explicitly denies being a materialist. But that is no problem for present purposes. Materialism as I characterize it here is entailed by most of the theses standardly identified with materialism (and also physicalism). So in showing that naturalists must give up materialism as I have defined it, I will thereby also have shown that naturalists must give up those other doctrines as well.

Realism about material objects is, very roughly, the thesis that material objects exist independently of minds or mental activity. Notoriously, however, this very rough expression is not at all satisfactory. For one thing, many philosophers who count themselves realists about material objects are not at all opposed to the view that no material thing could possibly exist apart from God's mental activity; and those realists who do oppose this view do not usually take it as part of their realism to oppose it. The role, if any, that God's mental activity plays in the world is not what is at issue in the realism/antirealism debate. Thus, realism about material objects should be understood not just as the view that mind-independent material objects exist, but as the view that material objects exist independently of human or other creaturely minds.

A more significant problem with the rough-and-ready formulation lies in the fact that the bare thesis that mind-independent material objects exist is ambiguous between the weak thesis that *some* material thing exists independently of the mental and the stronger thesis that *familiar* material things, or tokens of most current common-sense and scientific types, exist independently of the mental. For convenience, let's call these versions of realism *weak realism* about material objects and *strong realism* about material objects, respectively. (We will also do well to note that one can be a realist about the *external world* without being a realist about material objects. That is, one might hold that *something* exists independently of the mental without holding that some *material object* exists independently of the mental.[4]) I suspect that most people who profess to be realists about material objects take the word 'realism' to refer only to weak realism, even if they happen in fact to embrace strong realism about material objects. The reason I say this is that philosophers like Peter Unger (1979) and Peter van Inwagen (1990), who reject strong realism about material objects because of familiar puzzles about composition, are never numbered among the 'antirealist' crowd. Accordingly, for present purposes, I will take RMO to be equivalent to weak realism about material objects.

Still, we do not yet have a fully satisfactory expression of RMO. There is the further problem of figuring out what it means for some material thing to exist independently of the mental. What sort of dependence is being denied? Most realists will want to say that the dependence relation must be understood in such a way that minds themselves exist independently of the mental.[5] Thus, we cannot say that the relevant dependence relation is bare logical dependence upon minds or mental activity; for minds are logically dependent upon the existence of minds and mental activity. Furthermore, realists also typically want to say that the dependence relation must be under-

---

[4] Cf. the distinctions drawn between various kinds of realism in Devitt (1991).

[5] A notable exception, however, is Michael Devitt. See Devitt (1991: 16).

stood in such a way that (for example) artifacts do not turn out to be mind-dependent simply by virtue of the fact that their existence is caused in part by the activity of a mind. If my house is mind-dependent, it is not because the builder's mental activity is among the causes of its existence. Some sort of mental activity is among the causes of the existence of most human beings; but, again, we do not think that that suffices to make *us* mind-dependent. Thus, the relevant dependence relation is not causal dependence either. But what other kinds of dependence are there?

One kind is the sort of dependence that thoughts bear to minds. Thoughts are essentially such as to be in a mind. Not only can they not exist in worlds without minds or mental activity, but they cannot exist in worlds with minds or mental activity unless they are among the contents of one of the minds. Clearly realists will want to say that neither minds nor material objects depend in this way upon the existence of minds. To say otherwise is to embrace idealism, the most extreme version of antirealism about material objects. But most participants in the realism/antirealism debate do not seem to think that idealism is the only version of antirealism about material objects. As most have it, antirealism about material objects comes in a variety that is compatible with realism about the external world. But if that is right, then there must be yet another kind of dependence relation that objects might bear to minds.

Often one hears antirealism about material objects characterized as the view that material objects are 'conceptual constructs', or as the view that we somehow 'carve up reality' according to our 'conceptual schemes', or as the view that by virtue of being concept users, we are in some sense 'worldmakers'. Making sense out of this sort of talk without construing antirealism about material objects as equivalent to idealism is extraordinarily difficult. After all, there is no obvious sense at all in which our minds or conceptual schemes function like carving knives upon a cosmic turkey. If the carving metaphor is not vacuous, at the very least it is obscure. And describing material objects as conceptual constructs, or talking about ourselves as if we make worlds by using our concepts, seems to do no better. Mythical creatures are, perhaps, conceptual constructs in some meaningful sense. After all, they exist only in our minds, and our ideas of them do indeed seem to be constructed out of other ideas or concepts. And mythical worlds (like Tolkien's Middle Earth) may in some sense be made by us. But understanding antirealism along these lines—i.e.

taking ourselves to make our world and its inhabitants in the same way that Tolkien made hobbits, orcs, and the rest of Middle Earth—takes us back to understanding antirealism as equivalent to idealism.

Nevertheless, I think that *some* sense can be made out of these metaphors. The way to do it is to understand the non-idealist variety of antirealism (let's call it 'constructivism') as nothing more than the thesis that none of the properties that appear to be sortal properties of nonabstract, nonmental objects are intrinsic to anything. Apparent sortal properties are properties that appear to correspond to sorts, or kinds, of objects. Examples include properties like *being an electron, being a horse, being a lump of cells, being a statue,* and so on. Intrinsic properties are properties that can be had by something regardless of whether it is accompanied or unaccompanied by any other contingent being.[6] Intrinsic properties are opposed to extrinsic properties—properties that are exemplified by a thing only by virtue of relations that the thing bears to other contingently existing objects.

If sortal properties are in fact extrinsic properties, it is a bit difficult to say exactly what relations they might involve. Though other options are available, everyone who in fact believes that sortal properties are extrinsic believes that all apparent sortal properties, and thus all apparent essential properties, involve relations between minds and something else. What is difficult is specifying the something else.

It is tempting to say that, on this view, sortal properties involve relations between minds and the objects the properties sort. So, for example, an object counts as a horse (on this way of understanding the view) by virtue of the fact that we conceive of it as a horse. The sortal property *being a horse* thus involves relations between our minds and the horse itself. The trouble with this view, however, is that saying this makes it sound like the object's existence is somehow prior to its having any sortal properties. And this is something that just about everybody (whether realist or antirealist) wants to deny.

Another alternative is to say that sortal properties involve relations between objects and the *stuff* that composes them. On this view, the

[6] This is a rough approximation of the definition defended in Langton and Lewis (1998). One untoward consequence of the definition is that the property *having been created by God* turns out to be intrinsic if God is a necessary being. I suspect the definition could be modified so as to avoid this consequence without substantially affecting the discussion that follows. But since the consequence does not matter for present purposes, I will not attempt to make such modifications.

word 'stuff' is supposed to refer to whatever it is that exists independently of our minds and is such that our conceiving of it in various ways is what makes it the case that the world contains the various material objects that we think it contains. A pure stuff ontology says that no objects exist independently of human mental activity, but only stuff. Unfortunately, however, it is not at all clear that a pure stuff ontology is coherent.[7] Furthermore, even if it were coherent, it seems that the only plausible explanation for why we conceive of some stuff as a horse and other stuff as a table is that the equine stuff is intrinsically propertied differently than the tabular stuff. But it is not clear how pure stuff can have any properties. Properties seem to be the sorts of things that have to be had by an *object.*

For this reason, my preference is to say that, if sortal properties are extrinsic, they involve relations between human minds and a mind-independent world which consists of one or more mind-independent objects of an unidentifiable sort. The objects must be of an *unidentifiable* sort because the constructivist thesis is that all of the sortal properties we are familiar with are extrinsic. If we can identify an object's sort, its sort is not intrinsic, and so the object is not mind-independent. Furthermore, constructivism also implies that we cannot know how many mind-independent objects there are. For, obviously enough, if we don't know *what* mind-independent objects exist, we can't count them. On this view, then, apart from the mind-independent world, whose ultimate composition is inscrutable, everything that exists does so only by virtue of our conceiving of the world in the ways that we do. (Whose concepts count? That is a difficult question with no clear answer, so we'll leave it aside.) Note too that there is still room for talk of stuff on this view. We can use the word 'stuff' to refer to whatever mind-independent reality makes up the material objects of everyday discourse. We *should* use this word because, if constructivism is true, we have absolutely no idea whether it is one mind-independent object or many that makes up the world of material objects. Thus, we have no guarantee that individual material objects will be made up of any mind-independent objects at all. (They all might be made of nonobjectual portions of a single mind-independent thing.) But using the word 'stuff' this way, we do not encounter the problems associated with a pure stuff ontology; for, on the present interpretation of constructivism, we have mind-

---

[7] On this, see Blackson (1992) and Carter and Bahde (1998).

independent objects in our ontology to serve as property bearers. This interpretation of constructivism therefore seems to be coherent. However, I should note that nothing in what follows depends on taking this interpretation rather than the one that presupposes a pure stuff ontology. My aim in offering it is just to show that even if, as I think, a pure stuff ontology is incoherent, still the view that sortal properties involve relations between minds and something else can be interpreted coherently.

A point worth highlighting is that, insofar as constructivism is distinct from idealism, it involves the view that some relationship to human minds is a necessary condition for an object's exemplifying any of the sortal properties that are apparently exemplified by material objects. It is perhaps also important to note that the view is not quite as crazy as it initially appears. Even realists will acknowledge that *some* apparent sortal properties are extrinsic. For example, many philosophers think that something can be a statue only if it is a work of art, and that something counts as a work of art only if it is the product of intelligent design. But if this is right, then the property *being a statue* is not intrinsic to anything. Constructivism just goes a (big) step further and says that *all* apparent sortal properties are this way. But this obviously does not imply that we 'make the world' by using our concepts in any radical sense. Indeed, on my interpretation, the view presupposes that the world exists and has intrinsic properties wholly independently of human beings and their mental activity. It's just that, according to constructivists, what makes it the case that (say) stuff in the world arranged horse-wise constitutes a horse rather than some other kind of object with a wholly different set of persistence conditions is the fact that the world which includes that stuff stands in a certain relation to us and our mental activity. Had we conceived of the world differently, different sortal properties would have been exemplified throughout, and thus different objects would have existed. Hence the carving metaphor; hence the metaphor of conceptual constructing; and hence the world-making metaphor.

I have made a point of distinguishing constructivism from idealism. But the two views are related. Though constructivism does not entail idealism, idealism does entail constructivism. The reason is that if apparent sortal properties are intrinsic to anything, they are intrinsic to the objects that they appear to sort; but, on idealism, those objects do not exist. So idealism trivially entails the thesis that apparent sortal properties are not intrinsic to anything, but not the

other way around. Furthermore, as we have already seen, constructivism is compatible with what I have called realism about the external
world. What it rules out is simply the claim that *apparent* sortal
properties—i.e. the properties that appear to us to be sortal properties—are intrinsic. It therefore also rules out the claim that the
property *being a material object* is intrinsic, since that is an apparent
sortal property. (Does it rule out the claim that the property *being an
object* is intrinsic? I say no. 'Object' is not a sortal term; rather, objects
are just the things that sortal terms sort. 'Material object', on the other
hand, is a sortal term—at least if the term 'material' is not devoid of
content, as I will assume it is not.)

I suspect that some will be inclined to think that if constructivism
is true, then strictly speaking there are no material objects at all.
On this view, then, constructivism does not really deny mind-
independence. Rather, it denies the existence of material objects
altogether.[8] One reason for taking constructivism this way is that it
might seem to be part of the very concept of a material object that
material objects have their sortal properties intrinsically. Thus, the
thesis that apparent sortal properties are not intrinsic to anything
might seem to be logically equivalent to the thesis that there are no
material objects. I am very sympathetic with this view about constructivism; but for present purposes I will presuppose that it is false.
Thus, I will continue to assume that the dispute between constructivists and their opponents is over the question whether material objects
(e.g. trees, human bodies, rocks, etc.) are mind-dependent rather
than over the question whether material objects exist. Nothing substantial depends on this presupposition; but making it will help the
discussion that follows to move along more smoothly.

Many readers will by now realize that the brand of antirealism I
have just been attempting to characterize is the sort commonly
attributed to philosophers like Immanuel Kant, John Dewey, Michael
Dummett, Richard Rorty, Nelson Goodman, and Hilary Putnam. No
doubt such readers also know that the view that I have just described
(as well as, perhaps, any other reasonably well-defined view that
might appear to be worthy of the label antirealism) cannot *uncontroversially* be attributed to any of these philosophers. So let me emphasize that, though I do claim to have made *some* sense out of the typical
antirealist metaphors, I make no pretense to having made complete

---

[8] Cf. the understanding of global anti-realism recommended in Cortens (1999).

sense out of them, or to having characterized antirealism in a way that most antirealists would accept, or even to having established that any nonidealist variety of antirealism really is coherent. However, I do believe that most contemporary philosophers who are typically seen as falling into the antirealist camp take themselves to be defending something *other* than realism or idealism; and I also believe that if there is any coherent characterization of their views that does not present them either as realists or idealists, that characterization must lie somewhat in the direction of the view described above.

Summing up, I see two ways of rejecting RMO (which, again, is equivalent to what I called *weak* realism about material objects). One way is to hold that everything that exists either is a mind or is among the contents of a mind. The other way is to endorse constructivism, the view that none of the properties that appear to be sortal properties of nonmental, nonabstract objects are intrinsic. Constructivism is compatible with realism about the external world; idealism is not. My main thesis, again, is that naturalists are committed to *rejecting* RMO and materialism (and, given certain assumptions, ROM as well). I will also argue that naturalists are committed to accepting constructivism, but not necessarily to accepting idealism.

3. What is to Come

Toward establishing the central thesis of the book, I will begin in Part I by defending my characterization of naturalism as a research program. One striking point of contrast between the naturalistic orthodoxy of the present century and the religious orthodoxy of earlier centuries is that the canons and consequences of the current orthodoxy—the doctrines that one is committed to by virtue of being orthodox—are not at all well defined. Much is done in the name of naturalism, but few have bothered to spell out in clear and precise terms what exactly it means to *be* a naturalist. For this reason, it is less than clear what (if any) philosophical costs or benefits attach to embracing naturalism. In Chapters 2 and 3, I argue that the characterization of naturalism that is most faithful to the tradition, and the one that best explains both the similarities and the differences one finds among contemporary naturalists, is one which takes naturalism to be not a view but a research program—strictly, a *shared* research program; but in what follows I will omit the qualifier. Chapter 2 provides a brief discussion of the prehistory of naturalism, together with a more extended discussion of the relevant views of naturalism's two main spokesmen in the twentieth century, John Dewey and W. V. Quine. The purpose of this chapter is to give the reader a clear perspective on the core dispositions underlying the naturalistic tradition. Chapter 3 then argues that characterizing naturalism as a view rather than a research program inevitably portrays naturalism either as a self-defeating thesis or as a view commitment to which would be inconsistent with the core dispositions of the tradition. Thus, I argue, the fairest and most plausible characterization of naturalism treats it as a research program—in particular, a research program wherein one treats the methods of science and those methods alone as basic sources of evidence.

In Part II, I argue that commitment to the naturalistic research program precludes one from accepting RMO and materialism. The argument turns on the prospects (or lack thereof) that naturalists have for solving what I call the Discovery Problem. Very roughly, the Discovery Problem is just the fact that intrinsic modal properties seem not to be discoverable by the methods of science. I describe this problem in Chapter 4, and I argue that *if* there is good reason to think that the problem cannot be solved, then naturalists cannot be justified in accepting RMO. In Chapters 5 and 6, I go on to argue that, indeed, there is good reason for thinking that the problem cannot be solved. In Chapter 7, I argue that, having been forced to give up RMO, naturalists are committed to accepting constructivism (but not necessarily idealism). I also argue that, in accepting constructivism, naturalists must give up materialism. Finally, I show that, once materialism has been given up, standard arguments against mind–body dualism turn their teeth toward ROM.

Finally, in Part III, I consider alternatives to naturalism. The alternatives that I consider are what I call *intuitionism*, a (shared) research program which takes the methods of natural science and rational intuition, but nothing else, as basic sources of evidence, and *supernaturalism*, a (shared) research program wherein one takes at least the methods of the natural sciences and religious experience as basic sources.[9] Though I think that the consequences of naturalism described in Part II are sufficiently unattractive to motivate one to

---

[9] I thus leave open the question whether supernaturalists will treat rational intuition, or anything else, as basic. As will become clear in Ch. 8, some versions of supernaturalism which treat rational intuition as a basic source will be viable, others will not be.

look for an alternative, not just any alternative will do. I argue in Chapter 8 that, unless one has intuitions that support the view that our world is the product of intelligent design (or unless one has very unusual beliefs or intuitions), intuitionism is self-defeating. I also argue that, though there might be empirical reason for thinking that intuition is reliable in some domains, this fact does not save intuitionism from self-defeat, nor is it of any use to a naturalist in trying to avoid the ontological consequences described in Part II. In Chapter 9, I argue that embracing supernaturalism offers our best hope of avoiding those consequences. However, I also argue that not just any version of supernaturalism will do the job, but only those that give rise to evidence for the conclusion that our world and, in particular, our cognitive faculties are the products of intelligent design.

The upshot, then, is that the most viable research programs that provide no evidence against the conclusion that our world is a world without design fare worse by certain widely accepted pragmatic standards than those that do. By the lights of any of the research programs discussed in this book, unless they somehow support the conclusion that our world is the product of design, both naturalism and intuitionism give rise to an ontology radically at odds with common belief and, surprisingly enough, also at odds with philosophical theses that many proponents of these research programs are most interested in accepting. Again, showing this is not sufficient to show that every right-thinking person *ought* to embrace supernaturalism or a design-friendly version of intuitionism (though, for all I know, this stronger claim may in fact be true). But the conclusion is significant nonetheless. For as a matter of fact the most effective way of persuading reflective people to reject one research program in favor of another is to make the rejected alternative appear less attractive than the former. I hope that I will be successful in persuading some naturalists to jump ship; but I make no pretense to having shown that it is irrational for them to do otherwise.

Part I
NATURALISM

2

Pillars of the Tradition

> ...there is now an almost general consensus of opinions that
> natural science must be the basis of every philosophy that lays
> claim to exactitude.
>
> (Ludwig Büchner, *Force and Matter*, 1891)

RECENT decades have witnessed a flurry of philosophical activity in
the name of naturalism. Most contemporary philosophers identify
themselves as naturalists, and much recent work in philosophy can be
seen as part of a general trend toward conducting philosophical
inquiry under the umbrella of naturalistic assumptions. Thus, we
find many philosophers engaged in such projects as naturalizing
epistemology, naturalizing rationality, naturalizing jurisprudence,
naturalizing the mind, naturalizing the a priori, naturalizing ontology, naturalizing morality, and so on.

But what is naturalism? Oddly enough, the question is not easy to
answer. By all accounts, naturalism involves a very high regard for the
natural sciences and a very low regard for nonscientific forms of
inquiry. One who believes with Parmenides and Plato that a priori
reflection is a more secure way of knowing than empirical investigation can be well assured of a cold reception in the house of
naturalism. But beyond this there is not much of substance that can
be said without controversy. Naturalism is identified sometimes with
materialism, sometimes with empiricism, and sometimes with scientism; but all of these positions are equally difficult to characterize and,
in any case, the identifications are controversial. It certainly carries a
commitment to the thesis that there is nothing but nature, or nothing
supernatural, but there is widespread disagreement among naturalists
about what it is for something to count as natural or supernatural.
Furthermore, there is even controversy over what *sort* of position

naturalism is. Some characterize it as a metaphysical thesis, others as an epistemological or methodological thesis, and still others as some combination of the three. Precise and relatively uncontroversial formulations are simply not available.

I will argue in Chapter 3 that we find such controversy because the methodological dispositions that unite naturalists under a common banner preclude the formulation of naturalism as a coherent, substantive philosophical thesis. It may be tempting to conclude from this that naturalism itself is incoherent; however, I will urge the more charitable conclusion that naturalism is best construed as something other than a philosophical position. As I have already indicated, I think that naturalism is not a view but a research program.[1] What unifies those who call themselves naturalists is not a particular philosophical thesis but rather a set of methodological dispositions, a commonly shared approach to philosophical inquiry.

Toward justifying these claims, I will present in this chapter a brief historical survey of the twentieth century naturalistic tradition, focusing on two of the most prominent pillars of that tradition, John Dewey and Willard van Orman Quine. In the end, we will have a clearer picture of the dispositions that unify naturalists and we will be in a better position to understand why various historical figures like Aristotle, Hobbes, and Hume are commonly characterized as naturalists or, at any rate, as allies of naturalism. In the next chapter I will explain why naturalistic dispositions preclude the formulation of naturalism as a substantive philosophical thesis and I will defend my claim that naturalism is best characterized as a certain kind of research program. Since this is a book about the consequences of naturalism, I will conclude Chapter 3 by explaining in what sense it is possible for a research program to have consequences.

1. Roots of the Tradition

Naturalism has always been associated with two related projects, both of which have roots in antiquity. The first project is that of trying to conduct all of one's philosophical theorizing in accord with the

[1] Something like this view of naturalism seems to have been rather widely held in the later part of the first half of the 20th century. See e.g. Dewey *et al.* (1945), Edel (1946), the essays in Krikorian (1944), Murphy (1945), and Sellars (1922, 1944*a,b*). Among contemporary writers, both Peter Forrest (1996) and Ronald Giere (1999) take a similar view.

methods and results of the natural sciences. The second is that of trying to understand the world as much as possible in terms compatible with materialist assumptions. The projects are related insofar as empirical methods are most obviously and straightforwardly useful for the investigation of material rather than nonmaterial phenomena. But the two projects can come apart. As many naturalists have agreed, science *could* discover that materialism is false. If it did, then those pursuing the first project would be unable to pursue the second. But in such an event, whither naturalism? Would naturalism follow science and reject materialism? Or would it follow materialism in being rejected by science?

My own view is that the methodological dispositions shared by naturalists are more central to their naturalism than the ontological commitments. Thus, if materialism were not supported by science (as I will later argue), naturalism would follow science and give up materialism rather than the other way around. This view is controversial. My reasons for holding it will become clear in the course of this chapter and the next; but I mention it up front because it influences much of what I will say in the present section about the historical roots of naturalism. Those who reject my view of what naturalism is may be inclined to say different things about how it developed.

It is difficult to say exactly when naturalism as a full-blown movement came into being. But I think that for those who agree that methodology rather than ontology lies at the heart of naturalism, the origin of naturalism is most plausibly located in the nineteenth century in the writings of such philosophers as Comte, Mill, and the German materialists. I will not attempt to trace out the origin and prehistory of naturalism in any kind of intricate detail. However, I do want to make a few very general remarks about the roots of the tradition. This is both to support my view that naturalism was born in the nineteenth century and also to explain why I think it is perfectly reasonable to identify earlier historical figures as allies of naturalism even if it is incorrect to identify them as naturalists.

Historians typically locate the origin of Western science and philosophy in ancient Greece, with the cosmological inquiries of Thales and Anaximander. So the common story goes, the Milesian cosmologists, unlike their predecessors, sought to explain natural phenomena in terms of natural causes rather than in terms of the interventions of gods and demigods. They sought to learn about the natural world not from established religious texts and traditions but rather through empirical investigation and the light of pure reason. This turn from the supernatural to the natural, from mythology and the authority of tradition to the hard labor of experimental investigation and rational deduction, constituted the first clear step toward modern scientific method. Insofar as the methodological shift spilled over in the work of later thinkers into the domain of psychology, moral philosophy, and social philosophy—that is, insofar as the 'new' methods came to be applied in all domains of inquiry rather than just a few—we find here also the first seeds of naturalism.

Of course, no one in ancient Greece from the time of the first cosmologists onward had even an inkling of the idea that all inquiry (or even any inquiry) ought to be conducted in accord with exactly those methods that we call scientific. Thus, it is at best anachronistic to characterize any of those thinkers as naturalists in our sense of the term. Nevertheless, we may retrospectively identify various thinkers among them as allies in varying respects of the contemporary naturalistic movement. For example, all of them count as allies to the extent that they were inclined to reject appeals to tradition, authority, or deity as explanations for natural phenomena. Despite this, however, Parmenides and Plato in particular are more commonly seen as enemies of naturalism owing to their tendency to discount sense perception as a source of true knowledge.

Parmenides threatened to bring natural science to a standstill with his powerful arguments for the conclusion that the world is unchanging, unmoving, ungenerated, and indestructible. Because this conclusion is radically at odds with what our senses appear to tell us about the world, Parmenides' argument carried the implication that the senses are not a source of knowledge but of error.[2] Hence, those who wanted to investigate the world empirically were forced to grapple first with Parmenides' arguments in order to show that they were not engaged in a pointless enterprise.

Plato did not share Parmenides' view that our senses provide us with mostly false beliefs about the world. Thus, on his view, scientific investigation would not be pointless. However, he did share the Parmenidean view that the most fundamentally real things in the world are unchanging, and that one can have knowledge only of

---

[2] I say it *seems* to be radically at odds with what our senses tell us because our beliefs about change, motion, and so on presuppose various beliefs about metaphysics, and one might wonder whether the relevant facts about metaphysics are revealed by our senses.

things that do not change. Thus, he rejected the idea that empirical investigation could produce knowledge, and he embraced the view that knowledge could be acquired only through philosophical reflection. On his view, the objects of genuine knowledge were not physical objects or natural phenomena, but supernatural Ideas, or Forms, which could be 'perceived' only by the intellect. He thought that, by contemplating the Forms, we could come to know the timeless, unchanging truths about the nature of such things as virtue, wisdom, and beauty. (Indeed, contemplating the Forms was, for him, nothing other than contemplating the natures of such things.) About mundane things like the positions of planets and the diets of dogs, we can have, at best, true opinions. According to Plato, truths about the Forms can be grasped by the intellect with a kind of clarity, certainty, and depth of understanding that cannot attend our grasp of mundane truths; and, on his view, it is precisely this difference in depth, clarity, and certainty that separates knowledge from mere true opinion.

But such views as those just attributed to Plato and Parmenides are anathema to the modern naturalist, who respects the empirical methods of modern science above any other form of investigation as a way of learning about the world. Hence, contemporary naturalists are more likely to align themselves with other ancient thinkers, such as Lucretius, Epicurus, Empedocles, Leucippus, Anaxagoras, and the Sophists. By contrast with Plato and Parmenides, all of these thinkers were materialists.[3] Furthermore, all opposed the rationalism of Parmenides and Plato, defending the view that sense perception is a source of knowledge and that empirical investigation is an important way of arriving at systematic explanations for at least some of the phenomena in the natural world. Of those just mentioned, Lucretius is a particularly significant ally of contemporary naturalism owing to the fact that, of the works that survive from the ancient world, his *Nature of Things* presents by far the most detailed and comprehensive attempt to provide a thoroughly materialistic and empirically grounded explanation of the phenomena of nature and the origin and development of human life, society, religion, and science.[4]

Conspicuously omitted from the list of ancient allies of naturalism is Aristotle. This is because his place on that list is controversial. On

---

[3] On ancient materialism, see Vitzthum (1995) and Lange (1879: i).
[4] Vitzthum (1995).

the one hand, Aristotle is an obvious ally in that he too emphasized the importance of empirical investigation, rejecting the Platonic and Parmenidean view that true reality is somehow inaccessible to the senses. Furthermore, Aristotle's ethics and political philosophy are much more naturalistic than Plato's. For Plato, the goodness of a thing is grounded in its resemblance to an other-worldly Form. Things are good, on his view, because they resemble the Form of the Good, which is the perfect embodiment of the very nature of goodness. For Aristotle, however, there is no such thing as the nature of *goodness*. The goodness of every particular thing is grounded in its nature; and the natures of individual things, according to Aristotle, are just complex biological, chemical, and physical properties that are knowable by way of ordinary empirical investigation. Thus, given the contrast between Plato and Aristotle on this point and others, it is easy to see why ethicists often number Aristotle among the naturalists rather than the nonnaturalists.[5] On the other hand, there are reasons for seeing Aristotle as an opponent of naturalism. After all, modern scientific method was developed partly in *contrast* with Aristotelian science; and his essentialism and teleology have been favorite targets of criticism among the scientifically minded ever since the seventeenth century. There is truth in both positions. Aristotle was an ally in some respects, but not in others.

Moving ahead nearly twenty centuries, we find the next event in the prehistory of naturalism that commands our attention: the scientific revolution of the seventeenth century.[6] The scientific revolution brought about two relevant changes in the way that scientific inquiry was conducted. The first was an increased emphasis on the use of experimental methods. The second was more extensive employment of mathematics in theory construction. The theories of Copernicus, Galileo, Kepler, and others were novel in large part because they were the products of this methodological shift. They were revolutionary largely because they were much more successful than the theories they overturned.

As in Greece, application of novel methods in the study of nature was followed shortly by an attempt to apply those same methods in

[5] See e.g. McDowell (1995) and Annas (1988). But note that McDowell, at any rate, sees Aristotle as a naturalist of a markedly different sort from more 'scientistic' naturalists like Quine and Dewey.

[6] The following remarks about 17th century philosophy and science have been influenced by Ayers (1998), Butterfield (1959), Curley (1992), and Menn (1998).

the study of mind, morals, and politics. Striving for methodological continuity between the study of nature and the study of traditional topics in philosophy, however, meant different things to different philosophers. Thus, for example, Descartes sought methodological continuity by attempting to model philosophical inquiry on geometrical reasoning—deducing conclusions from self-evident first principles known a priori. Hobbes also sought to apply the methods of geometry in philosophy; but for him this was not so much a matter of deducing conclusions from self-evident axioms as of synthesizing and analyzing the ideas that we obtain through sense experience.[7] Hume, on the other hand, focused on experimental methods, as is evident from the subtitle of his *Treatise of Human Nature: Being an Attempt to Introduce the Experimental Method of Reasoning into Moral Subjects.* According to Hume, the foundation for all sciences is experience and observation—no less for the sciences of 'logic, morals, criticism and politics' than for the sciences of 'mathematics, natural philosophy, and natural religion'.[8]

Insofar as these thinkers, and others in the Modern period, shared the vision of methodological continuity between the natural sciences and philosophy, they count clearly as allies of contemporary naturalism. It is for this reason, I think, that Philip Kitcher simply *identifies* Descartes, Locke, Leibniz, Hume, Kant, and Mill as naturalists. He writes:

Frege is the emblem of a revolution which overthrew philosophical naturalism, both in the hyperextended forms apparent in Haeckel, and in the more restrained versions of the early modern heroes, Descartes, Locke, Leibniz, Hume, Kant, and Mill. . . . Pre-Fregean modern philosophy was distinguished not only by its emphasis on problems of knowledge, but also by its willingness to draw on the ideas of the emerging sciences, to cull concepts from ventures in psychology and physics, later still to find inspiration in Darwin. (Kitcher 1992: 54)

I will comment later on the fact that these remarks take a completely different view of the development of naturalism from the one I am taking in this chapter; but for now what I want to point out is that the blanket identification of Descartes *et al.* as naturalists is one that many contemporary naturalists will find disconcerting. To take just one example: Descartes was a theist; he was engaged in the project of

---

[7] Hobbes (1989: 5–15).   [8] Hume (1978, pp. xv–xvi).

refuting skepticism, trying to provide a foundation for science in pure reason; and he relied heavily on a priori intuition in his theorizing. In short, he stands as the Modern paradigm of an approach to philosophy by *contrast* with which contemporary naturalism is typically characterized. Of course, Kitcher does not mean to suggest that Descartes was a naturalist in precisely the same sense in which Quine is a naturalist. On the contrary, he notes that the naturalism of the modern period was 'more restrained' than the naturalism of more recent thinkers (like Ernst Haeckel). Still, if Descartes counts as a naturalist, one must wonder where the battle lines between naturalism and antinaturalism are really to be drawn. If modeling philosophy on geometry counts as striving enough for methodological continuity—no matter how much one is inclined to trust a priori intuition, no matter whether one is inclined to believe in God apart from scientific evidence, and no matter how much one is inclined to think that science stands in need of justification at the bar of pure reason—then who would *fail* to be a naturalist? Even Plato would seem to get in the door. But contemporary naturalism is not nearly so malleable. Closely allied with empiricism, contemporary naturalism is characterized in part by a tendency to be skeptical of a priori theorizing and by a corresponding emphasis on seeking empirical justification as much as possible for philosophical claims. (As is well known, the degree of skepticism about a priori reasoning and the degree of emphasis on empirical justification vary among contemporary naturalists; but we'll leave that issue aside for now.) Hume might well have counted as a naturalist by today's standards; but I doubt that the same is true of anyone else on Kitcher's list of 'restrained' naturalists. Descartes certainly would not have counted, though he might have been numbered among the friends of naturalism by way of contrast with some of his peers more ensconced in medieval scholasticism.

Hume so much resembles contemporary naturalists that it is quite tempting to say that the naturalist movement began in the eighteenth century with the publication of Hume's *Treatise*. It is probably pointless to insist dogmatically that we should not yield to the temptation. But three developments in the nineteenth century seem so significant with respect to giving impetus to the naturalist movement that I am inclined to resist the temptation and to regard Hume as standing alone in the eighteenth century as a man ahead of his time.

One important development was the publication of several books specifically aimed at analyzing and understanding the nature of scientific method. John Herschel's *Preliminary Discourse on the Study of Natural Philosophy* (published in 1830), William Whewell's *History of the Inductive Sciences* (published in 1837) and *The Philosophy of the Inductive Sciences, Founded upon their History* (published in 1840), and John Stuart Mill's *System of Logic* (published in 1843) were significant with respect to the naturalistic movement in at least two ways. Prior to their publication there was little in the way of explicit, detailed analysis of modern scientific method. Bacon's work articulated the method; Newton's work exemplified it. But not much existed beyond that.[9] The work of Herschel, Mill, and Whewell rectified this, thereby helping the vision of applying the methods of science in the philosophical domain to come into sharper focus and to receive clearer articulation and application. Furthermore, their work contributed to the growth and development of that vision by supporting the view that supernatural explanations have no place in properly scientific work and by furthering the growing interest in expanding the range of phenomena for which scientific explanation would seem appropriate.[10]

A second important development (second in order of discussion, but not exactly in order of history) was the rise of materialism in Germany and the birth of positivism in France. The eighteenth century witnessed the pseudonymous publication in France of German philosopher Baron D'Holbach's materialist manifesto *The System of Nature*; but materialism did not take firm hold on Germany until the nineteenth century. Frederick Gregory (1977) credits Ludwig Feuerbach as the founder of German materialism, and Karl Vogt, Jacob Moleschott, Ludwig Büchner, and Heinrich Czolbe as its most significant proponents. Importantly, the work of all of these philosophers seemed both to be motivated by and to encourage the goal of applying scientific methods in as many domains of inquiry as possible. Feuerbach described himself as nothing more than a natural philosopher of the mind; Czolbe lauded the work of Comte and Mill as attempts to bring the ideas of Francis Bacon to bear on disciplines other than the natural sciences; Moleschott held that physics provided the method for all science, *including* metaphysics; and, as the epigraph at the beginning of this chapter indicates,

---

[9] Hull (1973: 115–16).   [10] Hull (1973: 124–5).

Büchner believed that scientific method should be the basis for all philosophy.[11] Though not a materialist, Nietzsche too advocated an application of the methods of science in all domains.[12] In short, naturalistic methodological dispositions became increasingly popular in nineteenth century Germany.

Naturalistic sentiments were also being given vocal expression in France in the work of positivist philosopher Auguste Comte. Comte's *Cours de philosophie positive* was published in the mid-1830s, around the time of Feuerbach's rise to fame in Germany. In that work Comte articulates in clear detail the methodological vision of a unified empirical method applied in all fields of human inquiry that is commonly taken to be distinctive of naturalism. Furthermore, like later naturalists, he expresses skepticism about a priori theorizing; he rejects the quest for certainty, essences, and teleology in nature; and he goes on to lay out a plan for the empirical study of human social behavior (thus giving birth to the discipline of sociology). The resemblance between the ideas of Comte and Büchner on the one hand and the ideas of paradigmatic naturalists like Dewey and Quine on the other is striking, even more so than the resemblance the ideas of the latter philosophers bear to those of Hume.

Finally, a third significant development was the publication of Darwin's *Origin of Species* in 1859. Some go so far as to say that the naturalistic vision was not even viable prior to the publication of Darwin's *Origin*. Perhaps that is true; but even if it is not, there can be no doubt that Darwin's work lent tremendous force to the naturalistic movement. Prior to the publication of Darwin's opus, at least some domains of inquiry plausibly seemed immune to anything like empirical, materialistic treatment. Most notably, questions about the origin of species were an embarrassment to those who wished to explain as much as possible in terms of the experimentally discovered laws of nature. As David Hull notes: 'Regardless of what they might have thought on the subject, one thing is certain—most serious British scientists in Darwin's day studiously avoided the question of the origin of species. . . . Certain questions were beyond the reach of science' (Hull 1973: 124). Thus, there was still room for the idea that some domains of inquiry were better explored by other methods. But the publication of Darwin's *Origin* lent encouragement to those who thought otherwise. In a well-known passage Richard Dawkins

[11] Gregory (1977, *passim*).   [12] Leiter (2002).

points out that, 'although atheism might have been *logically tenable* before Darwin, Darwin made it possible to be an intellectually ful- filled atheist' (Dawkins 1996: 6). But more than just atheism came into its own with the publication of Darwin's *Origin*. The theory advanced in the *Origin* represented a victory for empirical science generally, for materialism, and for a mechanistic understanding of the universe. Darwinism was fertile. It suggested ways of empirically investigating not only the origin of life but many other phenomena as well.

John Dewey sums up the revolutionary impact of the *Origin* as follows:

Without the methods of Copernicus, Kepler, Galileo and their successors in astronomy, physics and chemistry, Darwin would have been helpless in the organic sciences. But prior to Darwin the impact of the new scientific method upon life, mind and politics had been arrested, because between these ideal or moral interests and the inorganic world intervened the king- dom of plants and animals. The gates of the garden of life were barred to the new ideas; and only through this garden was there access to mind and politics. The influence of Darwin upon philosophy resides in his having conquered the phenomena of life for the principle of transition, and there- by freed the new logic [i.e. the new scientific methods of Copernicus, Galileo, Kepler, and their successors] for application to mind and morals and life. When he said of species what Galileo said of the earth, *e pur si muove*, he emancipated, once for all, genetic and experimental ideas as an organon of asking questions and looking for explanations. (Dewey 1909: 41)

Perhaps this is a bit overstated. For example, contrary to what Dewey suggests, there seems to be no reason to think that the publication of Darwin's *Origin* removed otherwise insurmountable obstacles to the growth and development of empirical psychology. Though Dar- win's work had a significant impact on the history of psychology, the impact seems not to have been quite so monumental as Dewey would have us believe. Still, Darwin provided reason to be optimistic about the prospects for applying a single methodology, the method- ology of the natural sciences, in all domains of inquiry. He also gave reason to be optimistic about the prospects of a completely materialistic explanation of all phenomena and for a complete aban- donment of the need to posit supernatural entities to explain features of the natural world. As the optimism grew, naturalism flourished.

2. Dewey

The naturalistic movement was already well under way before John Dewey signed on; but he, more than anyone else, stands out as its primary spokesman in the early part of the twentieth century. This, of course, does not automatically make Dewey the final authority on what naturalism is. But surely it makes him some kind of authority—certainly as good as any other apart from Quine, who has done a great deal both to define and to promote naturalism in the latter half of the twentieth century. Thus, Dewey's work is a natural starting place for our attempt to gain some insight into the naturalist tradition. I will begin by describing Dewey's own characterization of naturalism.[13] I will conclude by exploring the relations between naturalism as Dewey understands it and empiricism, materialism, and pragmatism.

Dewey's clearest and most detailed description of his own naturalism comes in the first chapter of *Experience and Nature*. There he makes it clear that, on his view, to be a naturalist is just to be one who strives as much as possible to conduct one's philosophical theorizing in a manner continuous with natural science.[14] As I have already noted, however, continuity between natural science and philosophy means different things to different people. One might seek continuity of results, or continuity of method, or both.[15] Furthermore, as we have already seen, even those who agree that we should seek methodological continuity between philosophy and science nevertheless seek it in different ways. Like Comte and Hume, Dewey sought continuity of both methods and results; and continuity of method was understood primarily as involving the application of empirical methods (rather than mathematical methods) to philosophical questions.

On Dewey's view, the goal of philosophy is to produce a kind of harmony between philosophical and scientific theories. Together, philosophy and science aim to provide, as much as possible, a total comprehensive explanation of the phenomena of experience so that we might better be able to live our lives. But, he thinks, we are better able to live our lives—better able to survive and achieve our goals—only to the extent that we are able to predict, control, understand, and

---

[13] Much of what I say on this topic has been influenced by R. Dewey (1977).

[14] Dewey (1929a, esp. 3–20).

[15] Cf. Leiter (1998: 82–3).

appropriately respond to what we experience. The methods of science have proven effective at prediction and control; the goal of philosophy is to facilitate understanding and response. Thus, if philosophical theorizing fails to take account of relevant results of scientific research, it will also fail at its goal of helping us to live our lives better. Furthermore, if philosophy departs from the methods of science, it will be departing from the method that, on Dewey's view, is most effective for accomplishing the tasks of scientific and philosophical theorizing. Accordingly, he recommends that questions, traditional or otherwise, that cannot be resolved by empirical methods be abandoned in favor of ones that can.[16] Much of his work was devoted either to urging the philosophical community to strive for continuity of methods and results with the sciences, or to displaying how such continuity might be achieved in various domains. *Experience and Nature*, for example, begins with a description of the empirical method in philosophy and then embarks upon a sustained attempt to apply it to various topics. *Reconstruction in Philosophy* unfolds in a similar way. Indeed, at least one commentator has gone so far as to characterize Dewey as primarily a philosopher of method.[17]

Philosophical theorizing, then, is a kind of practical extension of science. Dewey (unlike Quine) thought that there was a sharp distinction between the subject matter of science and the subject matter of philosophy. As he saw it, the distinctive business of philosophy is to study values, ends, and purposes.[18] But, again, the point of philosophy is to produce theories on this topic that are in harmony with the rest of what we know by way of scientific inquiry. As Dewey puts it in *The Quest for Certainty*, the role of philosophy is 'to facilitate the fruitful interaction of our cognitive beliefs, our beliefs resting upon the most dependable methods of inquiry [i.e., the methods of the natural sciences], with our practical beliefs about the values, the ends and purposes, that should control human action in the things of large and liberal human import' (Dewey 1929b: 29). In other words, the task of the philosopher *qua* philosopher is to take seriously what we learn about ourselves and the world by way of science and apply those truths to questions about how we should live, how we should conduct our theorizing, how we should solve our social and political

---

[16] Dewey (1929a, ch. 1); Ratner (1951).
[17] R. Dewey (1977, ch. 1).
[18] Cf. Ratner (1951: 59–60); Dewey (1929b, ch. 2).

problems, and so on. This, together with a stern refusal to go beyond the ontology of science in the construction of philosophical theories, is what is involved in striving for continuity of *results*.

The way in which Dewey thinks that philosophical views might be shaped by the results of science is nicely illustrated by Dewey's views about how we ought to approach ethics. According to Dewey, the theory of evolution portrays human beings as organisms equipped with cognitive faculties whose main purpose is *not* to acquire knowledge but rather to ensure survival.[19] Our brain is a practical organ designed to serve practical ends; and the strongest suggestion from biology is that our brains evolved to serve a variety of specific ends rather than a single very general end. Taking all of this seriously, Dewey rejects out of hand the traditional search for a chief or final end of humankind. Furthermore, he rejects on evolutionary grounds the idea that we have a faculty of moral intuition by which to discover eternal and necessary truths about morality; and he accordingly dismisses the traditional ethical project of trying to discover, through rational reflection, a supreme moral principle to guide all human behavior. Instead, he urges a thoroughly empirical study of ethics— one focused on discovering the most reliable means for human beings to formulate and to meet their specific goals in the specific situations in which they find themselves.[20]

It is clear enough, then, what is involved in striving for continuity of results between philosophy and science. But how does one go about applying empirical methods in philosophy? This is a difficult question, especially in light of Dewey's view that philosophy and science are disciplines with separate subject matter. Traditional questions like 'What makes an action right or wrong?' are not obviously amenable to investigation by empirical methods.[21] Granted, as we have seen, Dewey thinks that some traditional questions (e.g. 'What is the chief end of man?') should fall by the wayside. But the danger lurking here is that *all* of the traditional questions will be supplanted by empirical questions, and nothing distinctively *philosophical* will remain. It is telling that Comte, in making a concerted attempt to bring empirical methods to bear on the study of human social

---

[19] Dewey (1948: 84–7). For other references and quotations plus further discussion of this topic, see R. Dewey (1977: 54–60).

[20] See e.g. Dewey (1902*a,b*; 1948, ch. 7).

[21] At any rate, it is not likely to be obvious to one not already steeped in the naturalist tradition.

behavior, saw himself as the founder of a new discipline—namely, sociology.

Dewey's clearest explanation of what he thinks it means to apply the empirical method in philosophy is laid out in the first chapter of *Experience and Nature*. In that chapter Dewey begins by offering a rough characterization of the empirical method as it is applied in the natural sciences:

The investigator assumes as a matter of course that experience, controlled in specifiable ways, is the avenue that leads to the facts and laws of nature. He uses reason and calculation freely; he could not get along without them. But he sees to it that ventures of this theoretical sort start from and terminate in directly experienced subject-matter. Theory may intervene in a long course of reasoning, many portions of which are remote from what is directly experienced. But the vine of pendant theory is attached at both ends to the pillars of observed subject-matter. And this experienced material is the same for the scientific man and the man in the street. The latter cannot follow the intervening reasoning without special preparation. But stars, rocks, trees, and creeping things are the same material of experience for both. (Dewey 1929*a*: 11)

This is a now familiar picture of how science works: direct experience is the starting place for the scientific enterprise in that it provides us with the first set of data from which we begin to construct our theories; it is also the terminus in that theories are always eventually linked back to direct experience by way of their testable implications. Significant portions of a scientific theory may involve claims that, taken in isolation, have no immediate consequences at all for direct experience; but this is perfectly acceptable so long as the theoretical claims are ultimately linked back to direct experience by way of bridge principles which describe connections between the behavior of theoretical entities and observable phenomena. Dewey develops the sketch further by distinguishing between two different kinds of experience—what he calls *primary* and *secondary* experience. Primary experience is direct experience of observable macrophenomena (e.g. experience of stars, rocks, trees, and creeping things). Secondary experience encompasses our knowledge or awareness of 'the refined, derived objects of reflection' (1929*a*: 15).[22] According to Dewey, the objects talked about in both philosophical and scientific theories are

[22] According to Robert Dewey, John Dewey actually has *two* conceptions of primary experience. He writes:

objects of secondary experience: in more familiar terminology, they are theoretical objects. But, whereas scientists impose upon themselves the burden of tethering their claims about theoretical objects, the objects of secondary experience, to claims about objects of primary experience by way of bridge principles that allow scientific theories to be tested, traditional philosophers (according to Dewey) have imposed no such burden upon themselves. On Dewey's view, to employ the empirical method in philosophy is just to remedy this defect: it is to make a point of providing bridge principles between philosophical theories and primary experience so that philosophical theories can be tested.

But how does all of this work itself out in practice? How does one actually go about producing theories that are, on the one hand, distinctively *philosophical* and, on the other hand, tethered to experience in the way Dewey describes? Consider again Dewey's views about ethics. As we have seen, Dewey thinks that the *results* of science tell us that we can know nothing of supreme moral principles or universal goods. Accordingly, in various places he recommends that we stop looking for such principles and goods in our moral theorizing and

On the one hand, the objects of primary experience are identified with the common-sense world of objects observed by ordinary men, whom we may presume are not influenced by the sophistications of theory. On the other hand, primary experience is technically conceived...as an integrated and undifferentiated unity of activity which includes both the organism and the environment. (1977: 37)

(Robert) Dewey then goes on to point out that these two conceptions of primary experience are incompatible with one another. The point in short is that insofar as rocks and trees and so on are not objectively differentiated as such prior to experience (as is implied by the second conception), they cannot be objects of direct experience (as is implied by the first conception). Or, to put the point another way: Familiar objects cannot *both* be theoretical entities and objects of direct sensation.

Putting the point in this latter way reveals what might be the source of the problem: the fact that familiar objects are as much theoretical posits as electrons and quarks is often ignored in discussions of the status of theoretical entities. Thus, in formulating the first conception of primary experience, perhaps Dewey followed the familiar practice of taking it for granted that rocks and such are not theoretical entities but later on saw fit to make the point that, strictly speaking, they *are* theoretical entities and primary experience really includes only the manifold of sense data.

This interpretation seems plausible to me, but I will not try to defend its correctness. I raise the issues here simply to note that there is an apparent problem in Dewey's conception of experience and to make it clear that my own remarks about primary experience are in accord with the first conception. I see no reason to think that our understanding of Dewey's naturalism will be enhanced either by pursuing the problem further or by understanding 'primary experience' in accord with the second conception rather than the first.

focus instead on trying to discover what is practically reasonable to do given one's contingent goals, particular circumstances, and prior understanding of the canons of practical rationality. (Cf. Dewey 1902 and 1948: 116.) But, of course, this latter kind of inquiry will be straightforwardly empirical.

One might object that, despite what Dewey calls it, theorizing about what is practically reasonable to do while *taking for granted* our goals and canons of rationality and the like is not so much moral theorizing as simple means–ends reasoning. The business of ethics (or, at any rate, the distinctively philosophical side of ethics), one might think, is to explore precisely those things that Dewey proposes we take as given: the rationality and moral worth of our contingent goals, the validity of our presupposed canons of practical rationality, and so on. And, of course, these latter topics seem not at all to be suitable for scientific investigation. But I take it that Dewey's response would be that it is precisely for this reason that the latter topics are not suitable topics for *any* sort of investigation. We have no access to information about what goals we absolutely ought to have, or about what principles of rationality we absolutely ought to adopt. The best we can do is to take for granted certain goals and canons of rationality and then derive hypothetical imperatives. Thus, as I see it, on Dewey's view there is nothing more to morality than a certain kind of means–ends reasoning; and he thinks that this view of the nature of morality is precisely what one will arrive at if one takes the results of science seriously and does not aim to go beyond them. Once this view is adopted, it is very easy to see how moral theorizing can be done by employing the methods of natural science. But it still counts as philosophical theorizing, if for no other reason than that the topic of morality falls within the purview of philosophy.

Dewey's recommendation that scientific methods be applied in philosophy is grounded, ultimately, in a view about human nature that is itself arrived at by scientific methods. Taking his cue from the biological, psychological, sociological, and anthropological theories available to him, Dewey arrived at a view of human beings which Robert Dewey (1977) calls 'the instrumentalist view of man'. On that view, human beings are primarily problem-solvers and human cognitive capacities primarily instruments for problem-solving. Human reason supplies means to ends, but nothing else; and human methods for problem-solving are, effectively, the same as the methods employed in the natural sciences. Reason does not provide access to first principles, absolute values, or eternal truths about some supernatural realm. Given this view of human beings, it is easy to see why Dewey recommends the application of empirical methods in all domains of inquiry: those methods are precisely the methods that have been refined by the evolutionary process to ensure our survival, and there is no scientific reason for thinking that any other method will be successful.[23]

The naturalistic philosopher, then, is first and foremost one who aims as much as possible to produce empirically grounded theories about philosophical matters, and who allows the results of the natural sciences to provide both the boundaries and the input for the construction of his or her theories. Allowing the results of natural science to constrain and shape philosophical theories is important mainly because it prevents those theories from straying in their ontology too far away from what our best methods of inquiry tell us about reality. Testability is important for a variety of reasons. It allows philosophical theories to enjoy the sort of confirmation that scientific theories enjoy. It also permits philosophers to make genuine progress toward consensus in the way that scientists do. Furthermore, and perhaps most importantly, it protects us from creating and chasing after pseudo-problems, allowing us to focus our attention on problems that are of real importance.[24] Adoption of the empirical method is a way of preventing philosophical theories from becoming irrelevant 'curiosities to be deposited, with appropriate labels, in a metaphysical museum' (Dewey 1929a: 26). It helps to ensure that the problems focused on by philosophers will have some tangible impact on our lives.

To the extent that Dewey's naturalism is representative of naturalism generally, we may now gain some insight into the relations between naturalism and various philosophical positions that are sometimes mistaken for it and, in any case, are widely recognized to be closely allied with it. The positions I have in mind are empiricism, materialism, and pragmatism.

Empiricism is standardly defined as the view that, at most, only analytic truths can be justified a priori.[25] Analytic truths are so called

---

[23] The claim that Dewey's recommendation of the empirical method is grounded in his view of human beings is both developed and defended in detail in R. Dewey (1977, esp. ch. 2 and 3).

[24] Dewey (1929a: 26–34).

[25] Cf. e.g. Bonjour (1998: 18–19). Note that this definition does not commit empiricists to believing that there are analytic truths. One might count as an empiricist by this definition if one rejected analytic truths altogether but, furthermore, also rejected a priori justification.

because they are taken to be discoverable via conceptual analysis—the rational process of breaking a concept down into its component parts. They are commonly distinguished from truths about matters of fact—the latter being 'about the world' in a way in which the former are not.[26] Thus, the (admittedly very imprecise) idea underlying empiricism is that beliefs about the world cannot be justified independently of sense perception; they must be justified empirically, if at all. Most naturalists, including Dewey, seem to endorse some brand of empiricism. But we must be careful about identifying naturalism with empiricism. Consider what would happen if a well-confirmed scientific theory lent strong support to the view that substantive (nonanalytic) truths can be known a priori. To suppose a priori that there could be no such theory is surely unacceptable from a naturalistic point of view. After all, from that point of view, the role of philosophy is to *follow* science, not to impose a priori constraints upon its results. So it looks like we must admit that science could, in principle, discover empiricism to be false. If it did, the proper naturalistic response would be to reject empiricism. (On these points, Quine is in full agreement, as we'll see below.) But clearly such a response would not amount to a rejection of *naturalism* as Dewey understands it.[27]

Just as many assume that naturalism implies or is identical with empiricism, so too many assume that naturalism entails or is identical with materialism. According to Dewey, naturalism does not entail *reductive* materialism—the view that all phenomena of experience are reducible to facts about physical objects and their physical properties.[28] But it does (on his view) imply that all the phenomena of human experience causally depend on facts about physical objects and their physical properties. Particular tokens or types of mental states, for example, are not to be *identified* with particular tokens or types of physical states on his view; but the former are causally

---

[26] The view that so-called analytic truths are not about the world is controversial. For example, the proposition that all bachelors are unmarried *seems* to be about the world by virtue of being about bachelors. However, one might argue that in fact it is not about bachelors in any deep sense, as evidenced by the fact that its truth is wholly independent of whether or not there are (or even could be) any bachelors.

[27] One might observe here that if naturalists think that empiricism is at the mercy of science, then they are committed to thinking that the only justification empiricism can receive is *empirical* justification, and this raises the threat of epistemic circularity. I address this worry in Sect. 1.2 of Ch. 3.

[28] Dewey *et al.* (1945: 105–7).

determined by the latter.[29] What is important to note, however, is that adherence to materialism (reductive or not) is not an article of faith for the naturalist. Rather, it is an empirical matter. Thus, materialism is not to be identified with naturalism.[30] Materialism is a definite ontological thesis—a particular view about what there is. Naturalism is not that; and being a naturalist carries commitment to materialism *only* insofar as science itself carries such a commitment. (And I will be arguing that science *does not* carry any such commitment.) On Dewey's view, neither science nor philosophy is in the business of dogmatically defending any particular conception of the nature of reality.[31] Naturalism (like science) might tentatively commit one to a particular ontological view, like materialism; but where science goes, there go the naturalists.[32]

Finally, pragmatism. Pragmatism is sometimes formulated as a philosophical method, sometimes as a theory of meaning, and sometimes as a theory of truth. As method, pragmatism is virtually indistinguishable from naturalism. In 'The Development of American Pragmatism' Dewey expresses agreement with William James that pragmatism 'is merely empiricism pushed to its legitimate conclusions' (Dewey 1952: 7). He then goes on to describe the 'pragmatic attitude': 'From a general point of view, the pragmatic attitude consists in "looking away from first things, principles, 'categories,' supposed necessities; and of looking towards last things, fruits, consequences, facts"' (Dewey 1952: 7). The idea, roughly, is that instead of taking derivability from a priori necessary principles as the distinguishing mark of a good philosophical theory, and instead of looking toward such principles as the foundations for our theories, what we ought to do is to build theories that have practical (empirically detectable) consequences and to evaluate our theories on the basis of their consequences. This sounds very much like the naturalistic

---

[29] Dewey *et al.* (1945: 107).

[30] This point, in fact, was made repeatedly in the literature on naturalism in the 1940s. In addition to Dewey *et al.* (1945), see e.g. Dennes (1944), Edel (1946), and Sellars (1944*a,b*).

[31] Ratner (1951: 59).

[32] Perhaps I should note here that in saying that naturalists as such will follow science wherever it leads, I do not mean to suggest that they will or should (*qua* naturalists) blindly endorse every theory, however tentative, put forth by working scientists. Nor do I mean to suggest that naturalists as such can never challenge a well-confirmed theory. Surely they can, just as working scientists can. But part of what sets naturalists apart from their rivals is the fact that they will take seriously only those challenges that arise from within science itself, and they will look to the methods of science and those methods alone to adjudicate between rival theories.

approach described above—an approach wherein one abandons the quest for answers to foundational questions and strives to develop theories that will in some way impinge upon primary experience. Elsewhere Dewey writes that in matters of ontology, 'pragmatism is content to take its stand with science'.[33] This too has a decidedly naturalistic flavor. Nevertheless, pragmatism is often associated with verification theories of meaning according to which the meaning of a term is exhausted by its empirical content, or with theories of truth according to which what is true is what is useful in some respect, or verifiable, or fated to be agreed upon by all who investigate.[34] Pragmatism is also often associated with what I have called constructivism. Indeed, Dewey himself thought that constructivism and verificationism about meaning and truth were direct consequences of pragmatism.[35] But none of these views are commonly taken to be germane to naturalism; and constructivism in particular is often taken to be antithetical to naturalism, even though (as I will argue later) naturalists are committed to it. Thus, we should at least be wary about identifying pragmatism with naturalism, despite the fact that the pragmatic method as understood by Dewey and others is virtually indistinguishable from naturalism.[36]

3. Quine

Whereas Dewey was naturalism's chief spokesman in the early half of the twentieth century, there can be no question that W. V. Quine was its chief spokesman in the later half. If Dewey brought naturalism into its own as a philosophical movement, Quine, more than anyone else, helped to bring it to almost complete hegemony. The structure of this section will mirror that of the previous: I will begin by describing Quine's naturalism and by comparing and contrasting it with Dewey's. I will then explore the relationship between naturalism

---

[33] Dewey (1917: 64).

[34] Cf. Peirce (1878: 139) and James (1907: 142).

[35] Dewey (1952: 7–8).

[36] At least Peirce and James understood pragmatic method in such a way that it is virtually indistinguishable from naturalism. (Cf. Haack 1992.) Note that I say 'virtually' indistinguishable because there are different emphases. Pragmatists typically emphasize *usefulness* more than continuity with science; naturalists typically emphasize continuity with science. But, emphasis aside, pragmatists seem willing to endorse precisely the methodology that naturalists urge and vice versa.

as Quine understands it and empiricism, materialism, and pragmatism.

Naturalism, according to Quine, is one of the 'five milestones of empiricism'—one of the five ways in which empiricism has taken a turn for the better in the last two centuries. As he defines it, naturalism is 'the recognition that it is within science itself, and not in some prior philosophy, that reality is to be identified and described' (1981: 21), and it is 'the abandonment of the goal of a first philosophy prior to natural science' (1981: 66). But what exactly is included in 'science itself' or 'first philosophy'? In 'Naturalism; or, Living within One's Means' Quine asks this question himself and offers the following response:

In science itself I certainly want to include the farthest flights of physics and cosmology, as well as experimental psychology, history, and the social sciences. Also mathematics, insofar at least as it is applied, for it is indispensable to natural science. What then am I excluding as 'some prior philosophy,' and why? Descartes' dualism between mind and body is called metaphysics, but it could as well be reckoned as science, however false. He even had a causal theory of the interaction of mind and body through the pineal gland. If I saw indirect explanatory benefit in positing sensibilia, possibilia, spirits, a Creator, I would joyfully accord them scientific status too, on a par with such avowedly scientific posits as quarks and black holes. What then *have* I banned under the name of prior philosophy?

Demarcation is not my purpose. My point in the characterizations of naturalism [quoted above] is just that the *most* we can reasonably seek in support of an inventory and description of reality is testability of its observable consequences in the time-honored hypothetico-deductive way. . . . Naturalism need not cast aspersions on irresponsible metaphysics, however deserved, much less on soft sciences or on the speculative reaches of the hard ones, except insofar as a firmer basis is claimed for them than the experimental method itself. (Quine 1995*b*: 252)

At first blush it might appear that this response simply dodges the crucial questions. If naturalism is a well-defined view, why beg off the challenge to draw lines between naturalistic philosophy and nonnaturalistic philosophy? But if we take the view (which Quine seems here to agree with) that methodology is more central to naturalism than any thesis, ontological or otherwise, and if we keep in mind the fact that the nature of scientific method is not precisely defined, it becomes very easy to see why Quine says that 'demarcation is not his purpose'.

Testability via observable consequences is the hallmark of a scientific hypothesis; but Quine, like Dewey, is prepared to acknowledge that there are many scientifically respectable claims that are not empirically testable (1995*b*: 256). Such claims, Quine says, 'fill out interstices of theory and lead to further hypotheses that are testable' (1995*b*: 251). At any rate, the acceptable ones do this. But it is not always clear when an untestable claim is filling out interstices of theory in the way just described and when it is not. Thus, the boundary between science and first philosophy is unclear. But that does not matter for Quine. The positive side of naturalism is easy to characterize. It involves highest regard for the methods of science and an attempt to apply those methods in all domains of inquiry. The negative side of naturalism (the side that tells us what to avoid) is hard to characterize, but only because there is controversy over just how much abstract theorizing, a priori ratiocination, and so on are legitimate within the boundaries of natural science. Nevertheless, we have a rough idea of where the boundaries lie; and what Quine wants to say is that, as philosophers, we are permitted to approach those boundaries, wherever they are (indeed, much of our work will probably take place quite near the boundaries), but we should try not to go beyond. Our resources for acquiring new information about the world outside our own minds include only our senses. Our reasoning capabilities have no independent access on their own; they simply enable us to build theories to help us to understand and predict our sensory experience. Naturalism involves doing the best we can to live within our means—to rely on the resources we have without pretending that we have others. Thus, it prescribes keeping a tight rein on our speculations, leashing them to observable consequences as much as possible and allowing them to venture beyond the bounds of testability only with fear and trepidation.

Quine's naturalism strongly resembles Dewey's in most respects. Both prefer the methods of science above all others as methods for understanding the world; and both urge us to apply those methods alone in developing philosophical theories. Quine also thinks that it is important to incorporate the results of the natural sciences in philosophical theorizing. In his own work he consistently incorporates the results of psychology, linguistics, and the physical sciences; and he recommends that others do the same.[37] Furthermore, Quine also

---

[37] See e.g. Quine (1968*b*, 1976, 1980, 1981, 1992, 1995*a,b*).

shares Dewey's view that questions about the foundations of empirical knowledge (i.e. questions like 'Is empirical knowledge possible?'
or 'Am I justified in believing what I learn by way of scientific
methods?') are not to be pursued. On his view, science stands in no
need of justification from any higher authority. Naturalism 'sees
natural science as an inquiry into reality, fallible and corrigible but
not answerable to any supra-scientific tribunal, and not in need of any
justification beyond observation and the hypothetico-deductive
method' (Quine 1981: 72). On his view, the reason science need not
be justified by any higher authority is that there *is* no higher authority
than science.

But does this mean that science justifies itself, in circular fashion?
Apparently not. Quine says in several places that once we abandon the
quest for a foundation in prior philosophy for natural science, we
have 'free access to the resources of natural science, without fear of
circularity' (1995*b*: 256). Taking this at face value, it looks like
Quine's view is that, in abandoning the quest for foundations, we
not only give up the attempt to justify science at the bar of reason; we
give up the attempt to justify it at all. The proper answer to questions
like 'What justifies me in believing what I learn by way of scientific
method?' is simply 'Do not ask that question'.[38]

Despite the affinities between Dewey's naturalism and Quine's, one
difference is worthy of note. Quine, unlike Dewey, takes philosophy
to be continuous with science not only in methods and results but in
subject matter as well. He makes this point most clearly and forcefully
in his various discussions of epistemology. Thus:

Naturalism does not repudiate epistemology, but assimilates it to empirical
psychology. Science itself tells us that our information about the world is
limited to irritations of our surfaces, and then the epistemological question is
in turn a question within science: the question how we human animals can
have managed to arrive at science from such limited information. Our
scientific epistemologist pursues this inquiry and comes out with an account
that has a good deal to do with the learning of language and with the
neurology of perception. He talks of how men posit bodies and hypothetical
particles, but he does not mean to suggest that the things thus posited do not
exist. Evolution and natural selection will doubtless figure in this account,
and he will feel free to apply physics if he sees a way. (Quine 1981: 72)

---

[38] Robert Fogelin suggests and defends a similar view about Quine's attitude toward the
epistemic credentials of science (Fogelin 1997, esp. 546 ff.). Roger Gibson, on the other
hand, seems to think that Quine regards science as self-justifying (Gibson 1987, esp. 63–5).

Epistemology is part of psychology and, on Quine's view, philosophy in general is a part of science. It is not a separate discipline with a distinctive subject matter.

Perhaps, however, Quine and Dewey are not so far apart on this issue as they initially appear. Consider a different example. Currently there is some controversy over whether the interpretation of quantum mechanics is an exercise in physics or metaphysics. Quine, of course, will say that physics and (legitimate) metaphysics overlap, metaphysics being just the investigation of highly theoretical matters in various natural sciences such as physics, biology, chemistry, and so on. But note that even someone who disagrees with him about the claim that metaphysics overlaps with physics (and with other disciplines like biology and chemistry) might nonetheless agree that it is possible to approach the questions of metaphysics in a scientific way. In other words, one might, for example, hold that the interpretation of quantum mechanics is something that can and should be done in accord with the methods of science, but nevertheless also believe that it is the business of metaphysics and *not* physics or any other discipline within science to interpret quantum mechanics. One will then be in some disagreement with Quine; but the disagreement will not be strong. For the disagreement over whether philosophy (or a particular sub-discipline within philosophy) is a part of the sciences is not nearly so substantive as a disagreement over whether it is possible to investigate philosophical questions in a scientific way; and on the latter point there is no disagreement between Dewey and Quine.

Like Dewey, Quine characterizes himself as an empiricist and is characterized that way by others. But Quine makes it very clear that his naturalism is not to be identified with empiricism. For example, in *The Pursuit of Truth* he writes:

Even telepathy and clairvoyance are scientific options, however moribund. It would take some extraordinary evidence to enliven them, but if that were to happen, then empiricism itself—the crowning norm . . . of naturalized epistemology—would go by the board. For remember that that norm, and naturalized epistemology itself, are integral to science, and science is fallible and corrigible.

Science after such a convulsion would still be science, the same old language game, hinging still on checkpoints in sensory prediction. The collapse of empiricism would admit extra input by telepathy or revelation, but the test of the resulting science would still be predicted sensation. (Quine 1992: 20–1)

One might object that some of Quine's own formulations of naturalism seem roughly equivalent to empiricism as defined earlier. But in light of what has just been said, I think the most reasonable response to this objection is to say that those formulations of naturalism that seem to identify it with empiricism as defined above are simply imprecise mischaracterizations. That at least some of Quine's own formulations are defective is admitted by Quine himself, as we have already seen. Furthermore, even the language surrounding the 'cleaned up' formulation in 'Naturalism; or, Living within One's Means' suggests that Quine is not quite sure that it has been cleaned up enough to capture the idea precisely.[39]

Just as Quine's naturalism is not to be identified with empiricism (or any other epistemological thesis), so too his naturalism is not to be identified with materialism or any other ontological thesis. Here is yet another point of agreement with Dewey. The ontology of science is ever subject to change; hence, so too is the ontology of naturalism. Indeed, in 'Whither Physical Objects?' Quine acknowledges one such change. He suggests that science may now prescribe rejection of physicalism. But, contrary to what is implied by the common identification of naturalism with physicalism, it does not follow from this that science also prescribes rejection of naturalism. Likewise, then, for materialism.

Whether and to what extent Quine is (or was at one time) a pragmatist is the subject of some debate. Christopher Hookway, for example, remarks that, though Quine explicitly endorsed pragmatism in 'Two Dogmas of Empiricism' and various other essays, it is 'very misleading' to place him in the pragmatist tradition that includes Peirce, James, Dewey, and others. Doing so, he says, 'encourages a distorted reading of the work of the earlier pragmatists, who would have found many of Quine's views uncongenial' (Hookway 1988: 2). Perhaps so; but what I want to observe here is that Quine certainly embraced the 'pragmatic method' as it was understood by Dewey, even if he rejected many of the attending views about meaning and truth. More importantly, in several places he seems to affirm something like the sort of constructivism that Dewey thought went hand in hand with adoption of the pragmatic method. Thus, for example, in 'Two Dogmas of Empiricism', Quine writes:

---

[39] Quine (1995b: 257).

Consider the question whether to countenance classes as entities. This ... is the question whether to quantify with respect to variables which take classes as values. Now, Carnap ... has maintained that this is a question not of matters of fact but of choosing a convenient language form, a convenient conceptual scheme or framework for science. With this I agree, but only on the proviso that the same be conceded regarding scientific hypotheses generally. ... The issue over there being classes seems more a question of convenient conceptual scheme; the issue over there being centaurs, or brick houses on Elm Street, seems more a question of fact. But I have been urging that this difference is only one of degree, and that it turns upon our vaguely pragmatic inclination to adjust one strand of the fabric of science rather than another in accommodating some particular recalcitrant experience. Conservatism figures in such choices, and so does the quest for simplicity. (Quine 1951: 45–6)

This same basic idea—that the 'fact' that there are, or are not, physical objects like brick houses or centaurs, or abstract objects like classes or sets, depends upon our choice of conceptual scheme—reappears in various of Quine's writings.[40]

However, Quine does not want to abandon the realist view that science provides us with objective knowledge of the world. Granted, some of Quine's early work has a decidedly anti-objectivist ring to it. But Hookway plausibly speculates that one reason for this might simply be that in those places the full implications of Quine's methodological holism had not yet been worked out.[41] And Quine's later work makes a point of affirming at least a weak brand of realism. For example, in his review of Goodman's *Ways of Worldmaking*, Quine says that, although multiple physical theories may equally fit the data, the conceptual scheme(s) described by physics are privileged over any others as descriptions of the world.[42] The reason is that physical theory aims at 'full coverage' of the phenomena. Similarly, in 'Naturalism; or, Living within One's Means' Quine explains how our decision about whether to adopt an ontology of physical objects will depend in part on various pragmatic considerations. We might, for example, purge physical objects from our ontology by identifying them with portions of spacetime. Doing so, he says, confers economy but leaves all matters of evidence undisturbed.[43] Yet he resists the charge of skepticism and antirealism about the external world:

---

[40] See e.g. Quine (1968a, 1981, and 1995a, to name just a few).
[41] Hookway (1988: 54).
[42] Quine (1978: 97–8).
[43] Quine (1995b: 259).

In any event, we are now seeing ontology as more utterly a human option than we used to. We are drawn to Lauener's pragmatism. Must we then conclude that true reality is beyond our ken? No, that would be to forsake naturalism. Rather, the notion of reality is itself part of the apparatus; and sticks, stones, atoms, quarks, numbers, and classes all are utterly real denizens of an ultimate real world, except insofar as our present science may prove false on further testing. (Quine 1995*b*: 260)

The idea is that there is indeed a 'mind-independent' world to which science gives us access and, though that world may be described equally well by various different conceptual schemes, still not every conceptual scheme is as good as every other.

Emerging here is a picture according to which realism about the external world is true but realism about material objects is not. The world exists independently of our minds, but sortal properties are exemplified only by virtue of the relations obtaining between our minds and the world. This, again, is precisely the sort of picture that, so I will argue, naturalists are committed to accepting. It is telling that both Dewey and Quine seem to agree.

4. Conclusion

I would like to close this chapter by revisiting an objection that I considered much earlier: the objection that some philosophers take a very different view of the history of naturalism from what I have just presented. For example, Philip Kitcher's important survey of twentieth century naturalism 'The Naturalists Return' opens with the following remark:

Ernst Haeckel, intellectual star of late-nineteenth-century Jena, continued a philosophical tradition by drawing on science to address the great questions of epistemology and ethics. Haeckel would have been surprised to learn that one of his relatively obscure colleagues [Gottlob Frege] would help to overthrow that tradition. (Kitcher 1992: 53)

We have already seen above that, on Kitcher's view, the naturalistic movement was thriving in the sixteenth to eighteenth centuries in the work of Descartes, Leibniz, Hume, *et al.* As he sees it, naturalism was down for a time in the late nineteenth and early twentieth centuries, but toward the middle of the twentieth century it rose again from its ashes to take the place of prominence it currently occupies. But, of course, Kitcher's view stands in stark contrast with my own view that naturalism was born in the nineteenth century and that everything prior was prehistory.

I have already said that I do not mean to be dogmatic about locating the origin of naturalism in the nineteenth century. My main reason for revisiting the objection is to call attention to the fact that what I am here calling 'naturalism' is probably what Kitcher would call 'hyperextended' or, at the very least, 'not entirely restrained' naturalism. Where I see precursors to naturalism he sees restrained naturalism; where I see naturalism proper, he sees simply a less bridled form of naturalism. But now another objection arises: have I not just admitted that what I call naturalism is really what prominent contemporary naturalists would take to be an extreme (and thus perhaps controversial) version of their position? And, since part of my aim in this book is to criticize naturalism, am I not therefore appropriately accused of stacking the deck against the naturalist?

In my view, the answer to both of these questions is no. No one will deny that the methodological dispositions shared by Quine and Dewey—high regard for science and scientific method, a disposition to employ scientific methods and results in all domains of inquiry as much as possible to the exclusion of a priori speculative methods, opposition to theories, particularly religious ones, that are untestable and do not play any significant role in filling out interstices of scientific theory—are the crucial identifying dispositions of naturalism. And no one should deny that one counts as a full-blooded naturalist only if one fully shares these dispositions. Of course, we might quibble about whether people who share only some of the naturalist's dispositions, or people who share them only intermittently, should count as naturalists. On this matter, Kitcher seems rather liberal whereas I am not. No doubt my failure to be liberal will be controversial; but that, I think, is only because few nowadays want to find themselves ranked among the antinaturalists. But I believe my conservatism here is well motivated. In this book what I am mainly interested in are the ontological consequences of full-blown adherence to naturalism, not the consequences of partial or half-hearted adherence to naturalism. Thus, it seems most appropriate to characterize naturalism so that one counts as a naturalist only if one shares all of the methodological dispositions that are distinctive of it.

3

Naturalism Characterized

To define naturalism in a narrow and indefensible way and then to tear it to pieces may be a pleasant enough dialectical exercise, but surely it is not consonant with the serious aim of philosophy to discover the truth about nature and ourselves as children of nature.

(Roy Wood Sellars, *Evolutionary Naturalism*, 1922)

THERE are...at least three ways of frisking a philosophical theory. You may try to misunderstand it which in philosophy requires almost no effort at all.... This method is very popular, very chuckling, but also very exasperating.... Fortunately there are other ways. You may...try to refute the theory in question. In this case you settle upon some clear and plausible import of the theory, and then you discover some contradiction. The contradiction must be hidden, subtle, and for the best results should pop out like a jack-in-the-box. You show that the theory conceals a jack-in-the-theory, which the theory on its face denied. The theory said: 'No, no, there's no little jack,' and then you pressed a little word, and out popped jack. This method is ideal, absolutely ruinous, guaranteed to fluster.... There is a third method which is this. You may try to understand the theory in question. This is, of course, a very dangerous expedient.

(O. K. Bouwsma, 'Naturalism,' 1948)

IF naturalism is indeed a substantive philosophical position, it is certainly a peculiar one. Almost every substantive view in philosophy is such that there is *some* disagreement about how best to characterize it. But the degree of variance among characterizations of naturalism is striking and unexpected. To take just two examples: Michael Devitt characterizes naturalism as the view that 'there is only one way of knowing: the empirical way that is the basis of science (whatever that way may be)' (1998: 45), whereas David Armstrong characterizes it as the view that there exists a single all-embracing spatiotemporal system (1980: 35). If there is a common thread linking these two characterizations, it is not at all obvious what it is. Some might think that the variance, at least in the present case, is explained by the fact that the two philosophers are characterizing different views: Devitt is characterizing *epistemological* naturalism whereas Armstrong is characterizing *metaphysical* naturalism. But even this explanatory claim is controversial. According to some naturalists, there is no such thing as metaphysical naturalism, or *the* metaphysics of naturalism. For example, in his discussion of naturalism in the early part of the twentieth century William Dennes writes:

[Contemporary naturalism] leaves to ordinary scientific observation and inference all questions as to what the patterns of processes in the world probably are. Its spirit is in these respects very close to the spirit of traditional and more specifically materialistic naturalism.... But contemporary naturalism recognizes much more clearly than did the tradition from which it stems that its distinction from other philosophical positions lies in the postulates and procedures which it criticizes and rejects rather than in any positive tenets of its own about the cosmos. (Dennes 1944: 288–9)

Such fundamental disagreement—disagreement about what sort of thesis naturalism could be, never mind its content—is surprising. Whatever we might think about the variance in expressions of other substantive philosophical theses such as foundationalism, essentialism, spacetime substantivalism, and so on, we must at least admit that we have a clear view of what sort of thesis each one purports to be. But even this much is lacking in the case of naturalism.

Why all the controversy? As I see it, the problem lies in the fact that (*a*) those who call themselves naturalists are united at least in part by methodological dispositions that preclude allegiance to views that cannot be called into question by further developments in science, but (*b*) no one seems to think that developments in science could force someone to reject naturalism. So those who want to formulate naturalism as a thesis face a dilemma. On the one hand, if they formulate it as a thesis that cannot be overturned by scientific investigation, then naturalism turns out to be precisely the sort of thesis that naturalists are unwilling to accept. In the worst cases such formulations are either vacuous or self-defeating. On the other hand, if they formulate it as a thesis that could be overturned by scientific investigation, then (obviously enough) naturalism stands at the mercy of science.

One might think it odd that naturalists would resist this second horn of the dilemma. After all, if everything else is at the mercy of science, why not naturalism? But the question is confused. Naturalism is motivated by a high regard for scientific method. It would be completely absurd, therefore, to think that empirical investigation could overthrow naturalism without overthrowing scientific method itself in the process. So long as scientific method remains intact as a way of judging between two theses, naturalism will always prescribe taking sides with science and could therefore never find itself condemned by science. This much has been uncontroversial in the literature. But then the dilemma stands; and I think that the fact that there is such a dilemma, along with the fact that the dilemma seems to have gone largely unnoticed, helps to explain the widespread disagreement over how best to formulate naturalism.

Toward substantiating this diagnosis, I will survey in this chapter a variety of characterizations of naturalism, or of alleged versions of naturalism, and show that all fall prey to the dilemma presented above: all are either empirically refutable or else vacuous, self-defeating, or otherwise unacceptable from a naturalistic point of view. I will conclude that the alleged versions of naturalism are nonexistent and that naturalism itself cannot be formulated as a substantive philosophical thesis. Having shown what naturalism cannot be, I will then go on to explain what naturalism is. As I have said, I take naturalism to be a research program. I will explain what sort of research program it is, and then I will conclude the chapter by explaining what is involved in drawing out the ontological consequences of a research program.

1. Varieties of Naturalism?

Owing to the proliferation in the literature of different and conflicting formulations of naturalism, it is now common for people to say that naturalism comes in several different varieties, each expressible by a different philosophical thesis. Typically, the putative varieties are metaphysical, epistemological, and methodological; though once in a while someone identifies a fourth or a fifth variety.[1] Different philosophers are then labeled not simply as naturalists but as metaphysical, epistemological, or methodological naturalists, depending on which of the relevant theses they seem to endorse.

But, though it is certainly true that there are various doctrines in the literature all going under the label 'naturalism', we needn't infer from this that there are different versions of naturalism corresponding to the different doctrines. Another possibility is that there is just one version of naturalism but various mischaracterizations of it. Saying that many naturalists have mischaracterized their own naturalism might seem uncharitable. It might also seem implausible, particularly since I am *not* a naturalist and so (presumably) speak with less authority about what naturalism is than one who is. Nevertheless, I think that there are good reasons for saying this.

One reason is that identifying various metaphysical, epistemological, and methodological theses as different versions of naturalism simply skirts the question of what the distinctive naturalistic connection between the various theses is supposed to be. There must be some reason why the relevant doctrines are rightly identified as versions of *naturalism* rather than as disparate theses that bear no substantive relation to one another. Perhaps they presuppose a common view about nature, or a common view about how philosophical inquiry should be conducted. But if so, then it seems that naturalism itself ought to be characterized as whatever it is that the different 'versions' have in common. As it is, however, we are often left largely in the dark as to what the connection between the various putative versions of naturalism is supposed to be.

But there is a more important reason for saying that there is only one version of naturalism which has been persistently mischaracterized by its proponents. As I have already indicated, my plan in this chapter is to show that neither naturalism nor any alleged version thereof can be expressed as a substantive philosophical thesis that is neither at the mercy of science nor self-defeating, vacuous, or otherwise naturalistically unacceptable. If I am right, then we have only two options: either we reject naturalism and its alleged varieties as severely internally defective, or we draw the conclusion that naturalism is not a substantive philosophical position. Charity requires us to take the

---

[1] Jeffrey King, for example, talks about 'linguistic naturalism' (King 1994: 55–6).

latter option. But doing so provides no motivation for thinking that there are different versions of naturalism, and it commits us to thinking that those many philosophers (naturalists and nonnaturalists alike) who have identified naturalism or some version thereof with a philosophical thesis have unwittingly mischaracterized it. Antinaturalists might object to the charity, but hopefully naturalists will welcome it. In any case, I *must* follow the route of charity lest my criticisms of naturalism later on appear to be assaults upon a straw man. Thus, I will conclude that no substantive philosophical position is to be identified with naturalism or any version thereof.

Having said this, let me now add one qualification: I do not mean to suggest that the terms 'metaphysical naturalism', 'methodological naturalism', and so on ought to be banished from our vocabulary. Nor do I mean to suggest that naturalists are somehow precluded from endorsing any substantive metaphysical, methodological, or epistemological theses. Quite the contrary. The naturalistic research program may well commit one to a variety of substantive theses about metaphysics, epistemology, and the like; and the terms 'metaphysical naturalism', 'epistemological naturalism', and their relatives might well be appropriate (even if somewhat misleading) labels for those sorts of theses. In other words, I have no objection to someone describing herself as (for example) a metaphysical naturalist if in doing so she simply means to identify herself as someone who endorses the *metaphysics of naturalism* (i.e. the metaphysics to which one is presently committed by virtue of being a naturalist). All I am objecting to is the idea that by accepting some particular metaphysical, epistemological, or methodological thesis, one thereby counts as a naturalist, or as a particular *kind* of naturalist, or as a proponent of some particular *version* of naturalism.

1.1. Metaphysical Naturalism

Perhaps the only clearly formulated explicitly ontological thesis that *all* naturalists agree on is the terribly uninformative thesis that *there are no supernatural entities*. The reason this thesis is uninformative is that naturalists disagree about what it is for something to count as natural or supernatural. There are common paradigms: men, beasts, plants, atoms, and electrons are natural; God, angels, ghosts, and immaterial souls are supernatural. But even these paradigms are controversial; and, in any case, it is not clear what the items on each list have in common with their other list-mates that makes them examples of natural or supernatural entities. The claim that there are no supernatural entities, therefore, will not do as a characterization of naturalism or any version thereof. More must be said if a clear position is to be articulated. At the very least, the claim must be supplemented by some account of what nature and supernature are like.

The problem, however, is that no version of naturalism can include any such supplementary account. As we saw in the last chapter, naturalists respect the natural sciences as absolutely authoritative with respect to what there is and what the world is like. Naturalism demands that we follow science wherever it leads with respect to such issues. This much is uncontroversial. Indeed, it is affirmed most emphatically by those typically characterized as metaphysical naturalists. It is furthermore uncontroversial among naturalists that science *will* lead somewhere—that it will in fact tell us something about what the world is like.[2] But then naturalism, whatever it is, must be compatible with *anything* science might tell us about nature or supernature. Thus, no version of naturalism can include any substantive thesis about the nature of nature or supernature.

What has just been said disqualifies several familiar statements from being adequate characterizations of any version of naturalism. For example, it disqualifies the following:

(3.1) Naturalism [is] the doctrine that reality consists of nothing but a single, all-embracing spatio-temporal system. (Armstrong 1980: 35)

(3.2) ...on the naturalist view, the world contains nothing supernatural...at the bottom level there are microphysical phenomena governed by the laws of microphysics, and, at higher levels, phenomena that not only participate in causal interactions describable in scientific laws but also bear the same general ontic relationship to microphysical items as do the entities quantified over and referred to [in] such higher-level laws as those which obtain in, for example, geology and neurophysiology. (Tye 1994: 129)

(3.3) ...naturalism [is] the belief that the world is a single system of things or events every one of which is bound to every other in a network of relations and laws, and...outside this 'natural order' there is nothing. (Stace 1949: 22)

---

[2] But it may not tell us much. It is a serious question whether empiricism (with which naturalism is closely allied) admits justification for beliefs that are not strictly implied by our empirical data.

Insofar as these theses are substantive, they are at the mercy of scientific research and so not compatible with every possible development in science. On the other hand, to the extent that they are lacking in substance (as, for example, 3.2 or 3.3 might be), they are no better characterizations of naturalism than the claim that naturalism is the view that there is nothing supernatural.[3]

Of course, I do not mean to suggest (here) that naturalists cannot endorse such theses as 3.1–3.3. Moreover, it is conceivable that, contrary to what I argue later in this book, naturalism even implies one or more of these theses (taken as a substantive claim about what there is).[4] But I take it that the way in which naturalism implies one or more of these theses, if it does at all, is just this: to be a naturalist is, in part, to take the natural sciences as authoritative with respect to what there is; and, at present, the natural sciences tell us that 3.1–3.3 are true; therefore, naturalists *at present* are committed to 3.1–3.3. But to say this is not at all to say that any of those theses are adequate as definitive statements or characterizations of naturalism. They are not because, like any substantive thesis about what there is, they are not the sorts of theses that one could unconditionally endorse while at the same time following scientific investigation *wherever* it might lead. So no substantive ontological thesis will do as a characterization of any version of naturalism. It might do as a characterization of the metaphysics *of* naturalism (at a given time), but that is different.

Metaphysical naturalism—taken as a version of naturalism—is not always characterized as a specific or definite ontological thesis. Sometimes it is characterized as a quasi-ontological thesis as follows:

(3.4) Science is the measure of all things, of what is that it is and of what is not that it is not. (W. Sellars 1963: 173)

(3.5) Naturalism ... is a species of philosophical monism, according to which whatever exists or happens is *natural* in the sense of being susceptible to explanation through methods which, although paradigmatically exemplified in the natural sciences, are continuous from domain to domain of objects and events. (Danto 1967: 448)

(3.6) *Ontological* naturalism is the view ... that only *natural* objects, kinds, and properties are real. ... Since ontological naturalism is supported by the success of natural science, and success is success in recognizing what is real, it would do best to define 'natural' as 'what is recognized by natural science.' (Schmitt 1995: 343)

[3] On the possible vacuity of 3.2 and 3.3, see van Fraassen (1998) and Dennes (1944).
[4] Cf. Kornblith (1994) and Papineau (1993).

(3.7) Naturalism imposes a constraint on what there can be, stipulating that there are no nonnatural or unnatural, praeternatural or supernatural entities.... Nature comprises those entities and constructs made of those entities that the ideal physics, realistically interpreted, posits. (Pettit 1992: 245, 247)

It is not exactly clear what to make of these theses.[5] Consider first 3.4–3.6. Note that there are three ways to read them. First, they might be taken as definite ontological theses. That is, they might be read in such a way that they declare that what exists is whatever mid- to late twentieth century scientific theories (realistically interpreted) in fact report to exist. To take them this way is to take the terms 'science', 'microphysics', and so on as referring to particular bodies of theory that were accepted at the time at which the relevant author was writing. But, of course, if they are read in this way, then they may be immediately ruled out as characterizations of naturalism for reasons already cited. On the other hand, they might be read as conditional claims asserting that, for any time *t*, a particular ontological thesis is true at *t* if and only if it is implied by a scientific theory that is accepted at *t*. Taken this way, they imply a rather ridiculous version of the view that what exists depends importantly upon what human beings (or some small class of human beings) believe to exist. Though I will argue later that naturalists are committed to a more sophisticated version of this view (constructivism), I think that the present version can be dismissed without controversy. Thus, we are left with only the third reading of 3.4–3.6: we must take them as conditional claims suggesting, roughly, that the correct ontology is the ontology of *ideal* science, or the *best* science (where 'best' presumably means 'best possible, for human beings'). Taken this way, 3.4–3.6 are not substantially different from 3.7. But 3.7 is either an obviously false metaphysical thesis or else a disguised epistemological thesis. As we all know, there is in fact no such thing as the ideal physics or the best physics. The physics we now have is not the best (otherwise there would be no reason to continue trying to improve it) and it is less than ideal. But if there is no ideal physics, then there is no *ontology of the ideal physics*. Thus, taken at face value, 3.7 implies that *no* ontology is correct. But that is obviously false. Of course, the idea probably

---

[5] A similar problem plagues various formulations of physicalism. See e.g. Crane and Mellor (1990), Melnyk (1997), and Poland (1994: 118 ff). Melnyk's response to the problem is analogous to taking the first option mentioned below; Poland's seems to be analogous to taking a combination of the first and third.

is that the correct ontology is whatever ontology *would be* (or, more optimistically, *will be*) implied by an ideal physical theory if (or when) such a one were to exist. But if that is right, then 3.7 is not so much a metaphysical thesis as an affirmation of the ability of physics to tell us the whole truth about the world. In other words, it is a disguised epistemological thesis. It does not tell us what, specifically, exists. Rather, it just expresses the conviction that, *whatever* exists, an ideal physics will be able to detect it. But if it is a disguised epistemological thesis, then taken as a version of naturalism it will fall prey to the objections discussed in the next section.

As before, I do not mean to suggest that naturalists should not endorse 3.4–3.6 taken in the first way that I described. In fact, I think that they should. Mid- to late twentieth-century naturalists should definitely accept the ontology of mid- to late twentieth-century scientific theories (though there might be a lot of dispute about what exactly that ontology amounts to).[6] But that does not mean that naturalism in metaphysics is to be identified with the ontology of mid- to late twentieth-century scientific theories. A nineteenth-century Newtonian might have counted as a naturalist in metaphysics, despite believing in things (e.g. absolute space and time) that are not countenanced by mid- to late twentieth-century scientific theories. Similarly, I do not mean to suggest that naturalists should not accept 3.7. My point about 3.7 is simply that, whatever it might express, it does not express anything like a plausible, substantive ontological thesis, conditional or otherwise. It might reasonably be taken to express an epistemological or methodological thesis, such as 3.8:

> (3.8) In deciding what ontology to adopt, science (or an idealized version of science) should be our final authoritative guide.

---

[6] But let us note a complication: in Ch. 6, I will argue that pragmatic arguments are not a source of epistemic justification unless a pragmatic theory of truth is presupposed. I will also argue that naturalists should not accept a pragmatic theory of truth. But I qualify this by saying that *if* pragmatic arguments enter significantly into the development and assessment of scientific theories, naturalists will be able to treat pragmatic arguments as a source of epistemic justification (perhaps even independently of a pragmatic theory of truth), but they will also be straightforwardly committed to constructivism. Thus, I think that regardless of whether pragmatic arguments enter significantly into the construction and assessment of scientific theories, naturalists can accept the ontology of science. But I do not *assume* that pragmatic arguments play such a role because, though I think the assumption is true, I am not prepared to defend it, and making it gives my argument too much of a running start.

But, though 3.8 is indeed a candidate for being a statement of some version of naturalism, it is clearly not a version of metaphysical naturalism. Rather, if anything, it is a version of epistemological or methodological naturalism, and so will fall prey to objections raised in later sections.

It seems to me that any putatively ontological thesis that might be put forth as a version of naturalism will suffer from one of the defects mentioned above: it will be vacuous, obviously false, or incompatible with possible developments in the natural sciences. Thus, I conclude that no ontological thesis can characterize a version of naturalism and, therefore, there is no such thing as 'metaphysical naturalism' as that term is ordinarily understood.

1.2. Epistemological Naturalism

There are two sorts of theses that can be and often are referred to by the label 'epistemological naturalism': theses about the discipline of epistemology, and theses about knowledge or justified belief. An example of the former might be:

> (3.9) Epistemology is a branch of science. The statements of epistemology are a subset of the statements of science, and the proper method of doing epistemology is the empirical method of science. (Goldman 1999: 2)[7]

Examples of the latter might be:

> (3.10) It is within science itself, and not in some prior philosophy, that reality is to be identified and described. (Quine 1981: 21)
> (3.11) In our pursuit of truth about the world we cannot do better than our traditional scientific procedure, the hypothetico-deductive method. (Quine 1995*b*: 257)
> (3.12) There is only one way of knowing: the empirical way that is the basis of science (whatever that way may be). (Devitt 1998: 45)

I will discuss the two sorts of thesis in turn.

Theses like 3.9 about the discipline of epistemology are not at all plausibly construed as versions of naturalism. Certainly they might be endorsed by naturalists, they might be among the consequences of naturalism, and they might serve well as statements of what is

---

[7] Goldman characterizes this as *radical* epistemological naturalism, or *scientistic* naturalism. He then goes on to characterize two other forms of epistemological naturalism, in each case providing a thesis about the discipline of epistemology.

involved in taking a naturalistic approach to epistemology. But I see
no reason to think that they are *versions* of naturalism. That is, I see no
reason to think that one could count as a naturalist simply by
endorsing some such thesis. The methodological dispositions that
characterize the naturalist tradition are much more far-reaching—
they have implications for many disciplines, not just epistemology. A
theist or a (contemporary) Platonist could accept 3.9; but few would
want to list theists and Platonists among the ranks of naturalists. To
say that 3.9 counts as a version of naturalism is, to my mind, much
like saying that atheism by itself counts as a version of naturalism.
Most naturalists *are* atheists; and, as we will see shortly, naturalistic
methodology, together with the current state of science, seems to
license if not prescribe belief in atheism. But to say that atheism is a
version of naturalism—that one could be a naturalist simply by
disbelieving in the God of traditional theism—goes too far.

Theses about knowledge or justified belief are more plausible
candidates for being versions of naturalism. After all, the methodological dispositions characteristic of naturalism do seem to favor
empirical ways of knowing over nonempirical ones. The trouble,
however, is that it is hard to see how epistemological theses like
3.10–3.12 could be presented *as versions of naturalism* without being
either self-defeating or otherwise unacceptable from a naturalistic
point of view. Before explaining why this is the case, however, I
would like to digress briefly and dismiss two objections against theses
like 3.10–3.12 that one might be inclined to raise but that I think are
ultimately unsuccessful.

One objection is that theses like 3.10–3.12 are defective because
epistemically circular. They clearly have no claim to being analytic (if
there even is any such thing as analyticity). They are obviously 'claims
about the world' rather than 'claims about the relations among our
concepts or ideas'. Thus, they are precisely the sorts of theses that by
their own lights must be justified empirically if at all. But each asserts
that the empirical methods of science issue in justified belief. Thus, to
offer any empirical support for such theses would be to argue in a
circle. To borrow a metaphor from Reid, offering empirical support
for such theses would be akin to appealing to a man's own word to
justify our belief that he is trustworthy.

Naturalists are well aware of this concern about theses like 3.10–
3.12; and typically they dismiss such concerns summarily as arising
out of a nonnaturalistic way of doing epistemology. As Quine puts it

in 'Epistemology Naturalized': 'If the epistemologist's goal is validation of the grounds of empirical science, he defeats his purpose by
using psychology or other empirical science in the validation. However, such scruples against circularity have little point once we have
stopped dreaming of deducing science from observation' (Quine
1968b: 75–6). The dream of providing a foundation for science—
i.e. the dream of justifying claims like 3.10–3.12 a priori—is a dream
left over from an epistemological project that the naturalist has
abandoned. Some naturalists seem to think that science is in no
need of justification. Dewey might be read in this way, since he rejects
questions about the possibility of empirical knowledge altogether as a
waste of time. Likewise for Quine. Just as often, however, naturalists
write as if science justifies itself. Quine himself sometimes writes this
way (as in the passage just quoted); though, as I indicated in Chapter
2, I think it is more plausible to attribute to him the other view. More
explicitly, Hilary Kornblith writes:

What does have priority over both metaphysics and epistemology, from a
naturalistic perspective, is successful scientific theory, and not because there
is some a priori reason to trust science over philosophy, but rather because
there is a body of scientific theory which has proven its value in prediction,
explanation, and technological application. This gives scientific work a kind
of grounding which no philosophical theory has thus far enjoyed. (Kornblith
1994: 49)

On his view, pretty clearly, science is a self-justifying enterprise.

I must admit that it is hard to accept the idea that science, or indeed
any discipline, could be self-justifying. But it appears that something
like this idea must be accepted by naturalists and nonnaturalists alike.
After all, nobody believes that we have infinitely many sources of
evidence, each being certified as reliable by sources at a higher level.
Thus, naturalists and nonnaturalists alike must believe that at least
some sources of evidence are appropriately trusted even in the absence of evidence certifying their reliability. (Roughly this same point
was defended earlier in a different way in Section 1 of Chapter 1.) We
might say, then, that at least some sources of evidence *stand in no need
of justification*. But we might just as well speak in terms of *self-
justification*, where a source is said to be self-justifying just in case
(*a*) it is trusted in the absence of evidence for its own reliability, and
(*b*) it delivers consistent outputs and fails to generate evidence that
leads to self-defeat. Such sources do not generate evidence that *confers*

epistemic justification upon the belief that they are reliable; but, crucially, neither do they generate evidence that eliminates the prima facie justification enjoyed by that belief. Thus, I am inclined to dismiss objections from epistemic circularity.[8]

The second objection that I want to dismiss is the objection that theses like 3.10–3.12 are self-defeating by virtue of their categorical nature. Recently, Paul Moser and David Yandell (2000) have raised exactly this sort of objection against the following pair of theses (the labels are theirs):

> *Core Ontological Naturalism*: every real entity either consists of or is somehow ontically grounded in the objects countenanced by the hypo- thetically completed empirical sciences (that is, in the objects of a natural ontology).

> *Core Methodological Naturalism*: every legitimate method of acquiring knowledge consists of or is grounded in the hypothetically completed methods of the empirical sciences (that is natural methods). (Moser and Yandell 2000: 10)

By way of objection, they write:

Neither individually nor collectively do [the empirical sciences] offer theses about *every* real entity or *every* legitimate epistemological method. The em- pirical sciences limit their theses to their proprietary domains, even if way- ward scientists sometimes overextend themselves with claims about every real entity or every legitimate epistemological method. Support for this claim comes from the fact that the empirical sciences, individually and collectively, are *logically* neutral on such matters as the existence of God, the reliability of certain kinds of religious experience, the objectivity of moral value, and the reality of thinking *substances*. Each such science thus logically permits the existence of God, the reliability of certain kinds of religious experience, the objectivity of moral value, and the reality of thinking substances. We have no reason to suppose that the hypothetically completed empirical sciences differ from the actual empirical sciences in this respect. Naturalists, at any rate, have not shown otherwise; nor has anyone else. (Moser and Yandell 2000: 11)

Moser and Yandell are obviously correct in saying that the sciences, neither individually nor collectively, offer theses about every real entity or every legitimate epistemological method. But, contrary to what they seem to think, this by itself does not disqualify Core Ontological

---

[8] On this point, see Alston (1993) and Bergmann (2000*a*). Thanks to Mike Bergmann and Joel Pust for helping me to see that the objection from epistemic circularity really ought to be dismissed.

Naturalism, Core Methodological Naturalism, or any of 3.10–3.12 from being justified by methods 'grounded in the methods of the hypothetically completed empirical sciences'. The reason is that even if the theories themselves do not include theses about every real entity or every legitimate epistemological method, we might still be able to infer such theses justifiedly from the theories in question. Even if no scientific theory *logically precludes* the claim that there are nonempirical sources of evidence (such as religious experience), we might still be able to infer from our scientific theories that there are not any such sources. I do not know of any scientific theory that logically precludes the existence of leprechauns; but I think I have a great deal of empirical warrant nonetheless for disbelieving in such things. And it seems that the naturalist might reasonably say the same about alleged non-sensory faculties. Such a naturalist might say that the empirical sciences (individually or collectively) provide warrant for believing that human beings have a certain inventory of cognitive equipment, that the equipment functions reliably in empirical domains, that there is no positive evidence for its reliable function in nonempirical domains, and that there are not any good reasons of a nonscientific sort for trusting religious experiences since (from a naturalistic point of view) there are not any good reasons of a nonscientific sort, period. Nonnaturalists will surely reject this line of reasoning, if for no other reason than that they will reject the supposition that scientific method is the only basic source of evidence. But, contra Moser and Yandell, I see nothing at all self-defeating in this line of reasoning.

So much for my digression. Now let us return to my reasons for thinking that 3.10–3.12 will not do as versions of naturalism. Suppose one of 3.10–3.12 is proposed as a version of naturalism. As such, it would have to be consistent with the methodological dispositions distinctive of naturalism. But then it must not be an empirical thesis. For, as we have already seen, theses refutable by science cannot plausibly count as versions of naturalism because naturalism involves, first and foremost, a commitment to follow science wherever it leads. Thus, 3.10–3.12 would have to be taken as theses justified, if at all, by methods *other* than the methods of science. But now they truly are self-defeating. For, as we have seen, by their own lights they are precisely the sorts of theses that *must* be justified by scientific methods if at all.

One might be tempted to suggest on behalf of the naturalist that 3.10–3.12 are in no need of justification. But this is implausible. Even

if we concede that we need no justification for believing that empirical methods issue in justified belief, still it is quite obvious that we
would need some justification for believing that *only* empirical
methods issue in justified belief. Thus, insofar as 3.10–3.12 are put
forth as theses intended to be consistent with the dispositions distinctive of naturalism, they cannot be taken as empirical theses and so
they are self-defeating. This, to my mind, constitutes decisive reason
for thinking that they cannot fairly be characterized as versions of
naturalism.

In light of all that has been said here, it seems clear that none of 3.9–
3.12 can plausibly be described as versions of naturalism. Furthermore, it seems that any thesis about how to do epistemology or about
the necessary or sufficient conditions for justified belief will suffer
from the same sorts of defects. Thus, I conclude that there is no such
thing as epistemological naturalism as it is ordinarily understood.

1.3. *Methodological Naturalism*

Our discussion of methodological naturalism can be brief. The theses
referred to by that label typically resemble either the theses that I have
called statements of metaphysical naturalism or the theses that I
have called statements of epistemological naturalism. Consider, for
example:

> (3.13) Naturalism in philosophy is always first a *methodological* view to
> the effect that philosophical theorizing should be continuous with
> empirical inquiry in the sciences. (Leiter 1998: 81)
>
> (3.14) Methodological naturalism holds that the best methods of inquiry
> in the social sciences or philosophy are, or are to be modeled on,
> those of the natural sciences. (Schmitt 1995: 343)
>
> (3.15) Methodological naturalism is the view that philosophy—and
> indeed any other intellectual discipline—must pursue knowledge
> via empirical methods exemplified by the sciences, and not by a
> priori or nonempirical methods. (Hampton 1998: 20)

I suspect that the reason for the overlap in labels is just that methodological assumptions generally are taken to be either background
presuppositions about what the world is like that guide and constrain
the process of inquiry, views about how inquiry should be conducted,
or views about what sorts of inquiry are likely to be fruitful. In other
words, methodological assumptions generally are either metaphysical
theses, theses about how inquiry in a particular discipline ought to be

conducted, or theses about know ledge or justified belief. But we have already seen that it is a mistake to take any such theses as characterizing a version of naturalism.

1.4. Combinations

I have argued that there is no such thing, properly speaking, as methodological, epistemological, or metaphysical naturalism. Thus, given that these are the main 'versions of naturalism' commonly identified, and given that the problems with the particular theses we have considered seem to generalize, it seems clear that no metaphysical, epistemological, or methodological thesis can plausibly count as a characterization of naturalism or of any version thereof. Furthermore, it seems equally clear that the problems described in previous sections will also affect any statement of naturalism that offers a combination of metaphysical, epistemological, or methodological theses. Thus, the following statement of naturalism offered by Alex Rosenberg is doubly defective:

> (3.16) So, we may characterize naturalism in philosophy as follows: [i] The repudiation of 'first philosophy'. Epistemology is not to be treated as a propaedeutic to the acquisition of further knowledge. [ii] Scientism. The sciences—from physics to psychology and even occasionally sociology, their methods and findings—are to be the guide to epistemology and metaphysics. But the more well-established the finding and method the greater the reliance philosophy may place upon it. And physics embodies the most well-established methods and findings. [iii] Darwinism. To a large extent Darwinian theory is to be both the model of scientific theorizing and the guide to philosophical theory because it maximally combines relevance to human affairs and well-foundedness. (Rosenberg 1996: 4)

Though Darwinism has been successful for over a century, it is surely at the mercy of further developments in science. Furthermore, the conjunction of (i) and (ii), insofar as each conjunct is to be construed as a substantive epistemological or methodological thesis (rather than, say, a nonassertoric prescription), is self-defeating.

2. Toward a Credible Naturalism

In the last section I examined sixteen different theses that have been offered in the literature as characterizations of naturalism or of some

version thereof. All suffered from crippling defects *qua* characterization of naturalism. Furthermore, I argued that the problem was quite
general: *any* substantive thesis would suffer from the same sorts of
crippling defects *qua* characterization of naturalism. Thus, it seems
clear that (insofar as we want to be charitable) naturalism should not
be understood as a definite philosophical thesis at all. Instead, it
should be understood as a research program. As I said in Chapter 1,
a research program is a set of methodological dispositions—a way of
conducting inquiry. One counts as a naturalist to the extent that one
shares the relevant dispositions and conducts inquiry in the relevant
way.

This view of naturalism—that it is not a thesis but a research
program—is now a minority view. But it is not without its proponents. As early as 1922 Roy Wood Sellars made the point that naturalism is not a thesis. He writes:

we are all naturalists now. But, even so, this common naturalism is of a very
vague and general sort, capable of covering an immense diversity of opinion.
It is an admission of a direction more than a clearly formulated belief. It is
less a philosophical system than a recognition of the impressive implications
of the physical and biological sciences. (Sellars 1922, p. vii; quoted with
approval in Kornblith 1994: 50)

This view seems to have been shared by the contributors to Yervant
Krikorian's widely discussed anthology *Naturalism and the Human
Spirit* (1944), as well as by many of those who commented on the
essays therein.[9] More recently Peter Forrest has explicitly adopted the
view that naturalism is 'a program rather than a thesis—the program
of understanding things by going beyond the natural sciences as little
as possible'.[10] Similarly, Ronald Giere proposes to characterize naturalism 'not in terms of theses about the world but in terms of a set of
strategies to be employed in seeking to understand the world'.[11] My
hope is that the arguments of this chapter will convince naturalists
and nonnaturalists alike that this view of naturalism is not an odd,

---

[9] See e.g. Edel (1946) and Murphy (1945).
[10] Forrest (1996: 89). Though it is doubtful that Forrest means quite the same thing by
'program' as I mean by 'research program'.
[11] Giere (1999: 70). However, Giere applies the label *methodological* naturalism to the
'form' of naturalism he takes himself to be characterizing, and distinguishes it from
metaphysical naturalism, which is 'any naturalism characterized in terms of theses about
the world supported by a priori arguments'. So I am not sure that he would be in general
agreement with my view that there are not many versions of naturalism.

out-of-the-way suggestion, but rather a compelling view in light of the intractable difficulties that face the formulation of naturalism as a substantive thesis.

I said in the Introduction that naturalism is a research program which treats the methods of science and those methods alone as basic sources of evidence. Notoriously, it is hard to say exactly what methods are supposed to count as *the* methods of science. But I think we will do well enough for present purposes if we say that the methods of science are, at the present time anyway, those methods (including canons of good argument, criteria for theory choice, and so on) regularly employed *and respected* in contemporary biology, chemistry, and physics departments. Reliance on memory and testimony is included in the methods of science, as well as reliance on judgments about apparent mathematical, logical, and conceptual truths. *Perhaps* saying the latter implies that naturalists are committed to treating the appearance of mathematical and logical necessity, as well as the appearance of conceptual truth, as basic sources of evidence. But even if this is so, it does not follow that naturalists are committed to treating the appearance of necessity *in general* as a basic source of evidence.

This understanding of scientific method is sufficiently conservative to rule out the various methods most naturalists want to rule out (e.g. the methods of astrology, phrenology, or iridology). But it is liberal enough to allow that the range of scientific methods might change over time. Presumably there are constraints: not just any method could count as scientific. But I see no reason to take a position on what those constraints are. Note that as the methods of science change, the total set of methodological dispositions shared by naturalists will change accordingly. But the heart of the shared research program—the disposition to treat as basic sources of evidence whatever methods count as scientific—will remain unchanged. Thus, naturalism is a stable shared research program, even though one and the same individual research program might count as naturalistic at one time but not at another.

Taking naturalism in this way puts it (rightly) at odds with two other research programs under discussion in this book: intuitionism and supernaturalism. The reason is that intuitionism treats rational intuition as a basic source of evidence, and supernaturalism treats religious experience as a basic source. Naturalism, however, involves a disposition *not* to treat these sources as basic. I will say more about both intuition and religious experience later on (in Chapters 8 and 9). But for now, a very brief discussion will suffice. For purposes of this book, an *intuition* is a conscious episode not involving sense perception, memory, or inference in which a proposition seems to be true.[12] A *rational* intuition is an episode of this sort in which a proposition seems to be *necessarily* true. A *religious experience* is an apparent direct awareness of either (*a*) the existence, character, or behavior of a divine mind, or (*b*) the fact that one of one's own mental states or a testimonial report communicated by others has been divinely inspired.[13] For naturalists, none of these belief sources are to be taken as basic sources of evidence. They can be treated as sources of evidence only after having been justified at the bar of scientific inquiry. At present, naturalists do not think that religious experience has been justified as a source of evidence by the methods of science. Nor do they believe that the methods of science have justified rational intuition as a source of evidence. In subsequent chapters I will follow the trend in assuming that the methods of science have not justified any of these sources as sources of evidence (though at the end of Chapter 8 I will suggest that empirical evidence might be thought to support the reliability of intuition in the ill-defined domain of mathematical, logical, and conceptual truths).

Taking naturalism as I have described it also respects the (relatively) uncontroversial things that philosophers are typically inclined to say about naturalism and helps us to understand better the source of disagreement on issues where there is controversy. Typically, disagreements arise either out of differing conceptions about what methods properly count as scientific (e.g. some might say that scientific method includes appeals to intuition in the case of logical or mathematical truths; others might not), or out of differing conceptions about what sort of ontology is indispensable for the truth of current scientific theories (e.g. some might say that belief in abstract objects is indispensable for the truth of our scientific theories; others might not).

---

[12] Here, and in my understanding of the term 'rational intuition', I follow the view outlined in Bealer (1998). See also Bealer (1987, 1993, 1996*a*, 1999), as well as Bonjour (1998).

[13] I leave open the question of what *divinity* consists in. Common usage allows the term to be applied to diverse kinds of beings—the God of traditional theism, the 'world soul' of Pythagoreanism, the gods of various pagan mythical systems, and so on. But I see no reason to think that, on this account, the term is vacuous or badly in need of technical definition.

Furthermore, my construal of naturalism helps us better to understand the close conceptual connections between naturalism, empiricism, physicalism, materialism, and atheism. As I noted in Chapter 2, naturalism is often identified with (or, as I would put it, confused with) those other doctrines; but if my own characterization is correct, we can see now that the identification is quite natural, even if misguided. Given that God and immaterial objects have no place in currently accepted scientific theories, and given that the positive doctrines of materialism and physicalism seem at least initially to find support from a survey of those theories,[14] it is quite natural to think that naturalists will, given the current state of science, be committed to physicalism and materialism. (But see Chapter 7 for arguments to the contrary.) Atheism will be a natural concomitant. Furthermore, given that current scientific methods are empirical methods, and given the general suspicions of a priori knowledge that are typical among naturalists, it is easy to see why at least some naturalists would appear to be, if not actually be, empiricists.

Is naturalism, on this construal, equivalent to *scientism*? As Peter van Inwagen uses the term, scientism involves an exaggerated respect for the physical and biological sciences and a corresponding disparagement of other ways of knowing (van Inwagen 1983: 215). Similarly, Kai Nielsen defines scientism to be the view that 'what cannot be known by science—and particularly the "hard" sciences—cannot be known' (Nielsen 1996: 26). The construal of naturalism that I am advocating is not scientistic in this sense. My own characterization of naturalism is, I believe, a Quinean characterization; and many philosophers (including Nielsen) accuse Quine of embracing scientism and then go on to try to distance their own version of naturalism from Quine's. But it should be clear from the discussion in Chapter 2 that, contra Nielsen and others, Quine did not embrace scientism as Nielsen understands it. There is more to science, on Quine's view, than the so-called 'hard sciences'; and much can be known that is not strictly part of their domain.[15] Granted, Quine might well be accused of an *exaggerated respect* for the hard sciences, particularly physics and biology. But that is a different matter. As we have seen, Quine thinks that philosophy is a part of science; and on his view, as on

---

[14] Again, I assume that physicalism and materialism are malleable enough to countenance energy, gravitational fields, and other such things that are posited by contemporary physical theories despite not being paradigmatic examples of material or physical objects.

[15] On this, see esp. Quine (1995*b*).

Dewey's, the task of philosophy is to pursue the project of developing theories that fill out the interstices of our scientific theories, all the while 'living within our means' by trying as much as possible to avoid believing in objects and properties whose existence cannot in any way be verified by scientific methods. Perhaps this view of what it means to 'live within our means' is properly labeled 'scientistic'; and if so, then there is at least one sense of the term in which naturalism *is* equivalent to scientism. But this sort of scientism is not the sort from which Nielsen and others try to distance themselves.

Let me emphasize, however, that in saying that Quine's naturalism is not scientistic in the sense described by Nielsen, I do not at all mean to suggest that Nielsen's 'naturalism' is in accord with Quine's. In fact it is not. Indeed, I think it is a mistake to consider Nielsen a naturalist at all. The reason is that Nielsen is a firm advocate of the 'method of wide reflective equilibrium'; and, though the method may be understood in ways compatible with naturalism, as Nielsen understands it, the method is more in accord with what I have called intuitionism. Let me digress briefly to explain why.

The method of wide reflective equilibrium was introduced by John Rawls as a method for theorizing in ethics and political philosophy.[16] According to Rawls, achieving *narrow* reflective equilibrium is a matter of bringing one's considered judgments into coherence with a set of moral principles. *Wide* reflective equilibrium comes when one has brought one's moral beliefs (including both principles and considered judgments) into coherence with whatever other background theories might relevantly impinge upon one's moral beliefs. The distinction, then, between narrow and wide reflective equilibrium is just the distinction between coherence in a particular domain (for Rawls, the domain of morality and political theory) and overall coherence.

Now, there is obviously nothing at all nonnaturalistic about striving for coherence among one's beliefs. Nor is there anything necessarily nonnaturalistic about including one's 'considered moral judgments' among the class of beliefs whose members one wants to bring into coherence. But the potential conflict arises when one asks about the nature and status of considered judgments. If one's considered judgments are, or are evidentially based upon, conscious episodes not involving perception, memory, or inference, in which a

---

[16] See Rawls (1951, 1971, 1975, 1980). For exposition and discussion of the method, see Brandt (1990), Daniels (1979, 1980), and DePaul (1986).

proposition seems necessarily to be true (as is plausibly the case with respect to our judgments about moral cases), and if one's considered judgments are being regarded as *evidence* in one's theorizing the way that observations are regarded as evidence for empirical claims, then to employ the method of wide reflective equilibrium as described above will be to employ a method more in accord with intuitionism or supernaturalism than with naturalism. On the other hand, if one's considered judgments are not rational intuitions or inferences there-from, then employing the method is perfectly consistent with natur-alism. Similarly, if one's considered judgments *are* rational intuitions but are *not* being treated as evidence—if, that is, one is striving for coherence with one's considered judgments for pragmatic reasons only—then, again, employing the method will be consistent with naturalism. In other words, whether the method of wide reflective equilibrium is compatible with naturalism depends upon whether using the method involves treating rational intuitions as a basic source of evidence.

As Rawls apparently understands the method, considered judg-ments are very much like rational intuitions, but they are *not* regarded as evidence.[17] Nielsen, on the other hand, does seem to think that considered judgments can and should be treated as evidence.[18] He is at pains to distinguish the method as he understands it from the sort of 'a priori intuitionism' that philosophers like Descartes were engaged in.[19] But in doing this, he does not deny that rational intuition (as it is here being understood) counts as a basic source of evidence. Rather, he simply emphasizes the idea that justification is holistic, and that no proposition, no matter how intuitive or apparently unrevisable, quali-fies as a certain or indubitable foundation for the rest of our beliefs. I should note here that Nielsen would emphatically disagree with my claim that the method of wide reflective equilibrium as he understands it is an intuitionist method rather than a naturalistic method. He thinks that the method is part of a *nonscientistic* naturalism. But I think that Nielsen's self-characterization is the result of conflating the naturalist tradition with the tradition of materialism and atheism.

Enough, then, about reflective equilibrium. Before closing this section, I would like to make one final point in favor of my

---

[17] Brandt (1990: 272); Rawls (1980: 519).
[18] Nielsen (1996, esp. 34–74).
[19] Nielsen (1996: 34–45, 69–74).

characterization of naturalism. More often than not, naturalists do not attempt to characterize their naturalism as a positive thesis; and when they do (as Quine sometimes does), they frequently offer slogans that can hardly be taken to be intended as serious and precise characterizations. So, for example, David Papineau (1993) declines to offer any definite characterization at all. Rather, he simply displays a naturalistic approach to various sorts of questions. Similarly, Hilary Kornblith offers the following partial description of such an approach:

In metaphysics, I believe, we should take our cue from the best available scientific theories. As Wilfrid Sellars so nicely put it, '...science is the measure of all things, of what is that it is and of what is not that it is not.' Current scientific theories are rich in their metaphysical implications. The task of the naturalistic metaphysician, as I see it, is simply to draw out the metaphysical implications of contemporary science. A metaphysics which goes beyond the commitments of science is simply unsupported by the best evidence. A metaphysics which does not make commitments as rich as those of our best current scientific theories asks us to narrow the scope of our ontology in ways which will not withstand scrutiny. For the naturalist, there simply is no extrascientific route to metaphysical understanding. (Kornblith 1994: 40)

This sort of description is representative; and it at least suggests that at the heart of naturalism is an *approach* to philosophical (and other sorts of) problems rather than a thesis. All I am doing is taking that suggestion seriously in refraining from trying to convert the description, and others like it, into a definite thesis.

3. On the Consequences of a Research Program

I have argued in this chapter that there is no *position*—no substantive thesis about metaphysics, epistemology, or methodology—that constitutes the heart and soul of naturalism. What unifies naturalists is just a shared set of methodological dispositions. Furthermore, these dispositions preclude naturalists from justifiably believing that their research program is one that *ought* to be shared by others, or that it is the only one that issues in justified belief. For to think such things is to suppose in part that the epistemic status of scientific reasoning is open for philosophical debate. But the project of using philosophy to justify science is a project that naturalists reject. Thus, given their methodological dispositions, they lack the resources for converting descriptions of their research program into theses about how inquiry ought to be conducted. Moreover, for reasons we have already seen, naturalists cannot identify their naturalism with any of the ontological claims to which they are committed by virtue of being naturalists. To do this (and to maintain a commitment to naturalism come what may) would, again, be to elevate philosophical reasoning over scientific investigation. None of this is a strike against naturalism. Rather, it is simply a recognition of the fact that the attempt to convert naturalism into a substantive philosophical thesis arises out of nonnaturalistic ways of thinking.

So naturalism is a research program. But now how will this book proceed? How do we draw out the consequences of naturalism if naturalism is not a thesis that can have consequences?

The consequences of a research program are just the views to which one is committed by virtue of adopting it. Of course, one might think that one has adopted a research program that one has not in fact adopted; or one might adopt a research program only intermittently, fluctuating back and forth between several different research programs. Thus, one can be a half-hearted naturalist, or an intuitionist in denial, or a Sunday supernaturalist. But we can ignore this complication here, leaving it to the naturalists to identify and chase down their heretics. For my purposes, the consequences of naturalism will be just those views to which one is logically or rationally committed by virtue of adopting the research program fully, consistently, and competently. The consequences of naturalism may change over time. Contrary to expectations, the range of scientifically respected modes of inquiry may expand or contract, or science may find a place for God, ghosts, or immaterial souls. If these changes came to pass, the consequences of naturalism would change and the conclusions of this book would become obsolete. But that does not matter. *Contemporary* naturalists aim to do metaphysics wholly within the bounds of *contemporary* science. My goal is simply to describe some of the radical and surprising conclusions that one is committed to by virtue of pursuing this project. As far as I am concerned, if science expands in such a way as to mitigate those consequences, so much the better for science, naturalism, and our view of the world in general.

PART II

ONTOLOGY

4

The Discovery Problem

... as we go forward on the road of knowledge we have *got* to let
ourselves be guided by the invisible hand of metaphysics reaching out to us from the mist, but ... we must always be on our
guard lest its soft seductive pull should draw us from the road
into an abyss.

(Erwin Schrödinger, *My View of the World*, 1964)

THE aim of Part I was to provide a fair and historically informed
characterization of naturalism. Now, in Part II, I turn to the task of
exploring some of the more surprising consequences of naturalism
for the metaphysics of material objects. In particular, my goal is to
show that commitment to naturalism forces one to reject both realism about material objects (RMO), and materialism, and that once
these two theses have been given up, standard arguments against
dualism threaten to undermine realism about other minds (ROM)
as well.

The focus of our discussion in this chapter and the following two
will be a problem that has been often raised in the literature but rarely
responded to in a way compatible with both naturalism and RMO.
The problem, which I will call the Discovery Problem, is just the fact
that intrinsic modal properties seem to be undiscoverable by the
methods of the natural sciences. Modal properties are properties
involving necessities or possibilities for the objects that have them.
They are properties like *being necessarily human, being possibly spher-
ical, being essentially such as to undergo mental activity,* and so on. As
I will make clear below in the process of motivating the Discovery
Problem, it is widely taken for granted that we are *somehow* able to
learn the modal properties of material objects; the difficult question
is *how.* Some of the answers to this question require that modal

properties be extrinsic. Others allow for the possibility that they are intrinsic. We will see that RMO requires that modal properties be intrinsic. But, of course, naturalism requires that they be discoverable (if at all) by the methods of science. Hence the Discovery Problem. Once the problem has been laid out, the remainder of the chapter will be devoted to explaining its significance, differentiating it from other problems with which it might easily be confused, and exploring the prospects for solving it. In fact, the prospects for solving it are dim—a point which will be defended over the course of this chapter and the following two. But, as I will argue below, if there is good reason for thinking that the problem cannot be solved, then naturalists cannot be justified in accepting RMO. And, as I will go on to argue in Chapter 7, if naturalists cannot be justified in accepting RMO, then they cannot be justified in accepting materialism; and this, in turn, puts ROM in danger as well.

1. A Difficult Epistemological Question

In an ancient comic play there appears a scene in which a man calls on a friend to collect a debt and receives, instead of his money, something like the following philosophical argument:[1]

As we all know, a human being is just a collection of particles. But, as we also know, if you add particles to or subtract particles from a collection of particles, you get a new collection. Now, this debt was contracted several weeks ago, and many of the particles that composed the person who contracted the debt have long since passed into the environment. So I am a different collection of particles from the one that contracted the debt. Thus, I am a different human being from the one who contracted the debt. Therefore, I do not owe you any money!

In the play the serious philosophical issues raised by this argument go sadly unappreciated by the creditor, who rebuts the argument with his fist. But, as is well known, subsequent philosophers have more than made up for his negligence.

The Debtor's Argument presents a puzzle about material constitution. Material constitution occurs whenever an object *a* and an object *b* (in this case, the debtor and the collection of particles that

---

[1] Adapted from David Sedley's description of the relevant scene in a play by the 5th century BC poet Epicharmus (see Sedley 1982: 255–6).

constitutes him) share all of the same material parts at the same time.[2] The phenomenon is puzzling because, typically, it is not clear just what the relationship is between the relevant *a* and *b*. In the argument above, the debtor assumes that he is identical with the collection of particles that constitutes him and concludes that he is not the same person as the one who contracted the earlier debt. We, on the other hand, might be inclined to agree with the creditor in denying this assumption, but if we do, then it appears that we are committed to the conclusion that there are two distinct objects (the debtor and the collection that now constitutes him) located in exactly the same place at the same time. But, as Harold Noonan has aptly put it, those who embrace *that* conclusion seem to 'manifest a bad case of double vision' (1988: 222). Surely there are not two objects located where the debtor is standing, but only one.

Puzzles like this are among the oldest, most widely discussed puzzles in the history of philosophy. They have appeared in the writings of Aristotle, Chrysippus, Abelard, Locke, Leibniz, Hume, and Hobbes, to name just a few, and they continue to be widely discussed in the contemporary literature. There are many different kinds of puzzles about material constitution. Some involve artifacts; others involve organisms. Some are supposed to show that growth, diminution, or part replacement is paradoxical; others are supposed to show that even shape change is paradoxical. Some are supposed to show that actual changes are paradoxical; others are supposed to show that the mere possibility of change is paradoxical. But *all* of them present us with scenarios in which it appears that an object *a* and an object *b* share all of the same parts and yet have different modal properties. This is what qualifies them as puzzles about material constitution; and the fundamental problem they all raise is what I have elsewhere called the *problem of material constitution*.[3]

In other work I have explored the question of how best to solve the problem of material constitution.[4] But there is another question

---

[2] For purposes here, constitution is to be understood as symmetric. That is, for any *x* and *y*, *x* constitutes *y* if and only if *y* constitutes *x*. This is nonstandard. More often people are inclined to say, for example, that a lump constitutes a statue but not vice versa. (See e.g. Baker 1997, 2000; Chandler 1971; Doepke 1982; and Thomson 1998.) However, it simplifies my presentation to take constitution as symmetric, and nothing substantial hangs on this decision. (I suppose I should also admit that I think it is *true* that constitution is symmetric; but I am not prepared to argue for that here.)

[3] Rea (1995).

[4] See especially Rea (1995, 1997, 2000c).

lurking in the neighborhood that is equally important: the question of how we could possibly learn (or acquire justified beliefs about) the truth or falsity of some of the crucial premises in puzzles that raise the problem. Consider, for example, the puzzle raised by the Debtor's Argument. The puzzle arises because, in the region allegedly occupied by our debtor, there exists matter that is arranged in at least two different ways: *collection-wise* and *human-wise*.[5] The debtor attempts to escape the debt by assuming, contrary to the creditor's assumption, that wherever one finds matter arranged in these two different ways, one finds an object that has the modal properties of a collection of particles and *not* an object that has the modal properties of a human being. To solve the puzzle, one must decide which, if either, of these assumptions is correct. Notice that, regardless of how one solves the problem, the presupposition all around is that we *can* make such a decision. Philosophers of every persuasion have devoted attention to the problem of material constitution, and virtually nobody responds to the puzzles that raise it by saying that we cannot have justified beliefs about the modal properties associated with various arrangements of matter. But the crucial question is *how* we can make such decisions in a way that results in justified belief.

Before discussing answers to this difficult epistemological question, let us make it a bit more precise. Some of the modal properties that we attribute to objects are trivial. For example: it is trivial that, for any property p, everything that has p is possibly such as to have p. It is also trivial that, for any property p, nothing is possibly such as to have both p and not-p. From these trivial truths, together with sufficiently liberal views about property extraction, we can infer that everything has the modal property *being necessarily such as not to have both p and not-p*, and that everything that has p has the modal property *being possibly p*. Such inferences are uninteresting. What is interesting is the fact that we also attribute *nontrivial* modal properties to objects. For example: for an object that has p, properties like *being necessarily p*, *being possibly not-p*, or *having intrinsically the property of being possibly p* would be nontrivial. Such properties play

---

[5] The property of being arranged collection-wise is, no doubt, trivial: all objects, however they are arranged, are arranged collection-wise. But that does not matter in the present context. What matters is just that (according to the debtor, at least) this trivial way of arranging objects has associated with it a set of modal properties that differs from the set of modal properties associated with human-wise arrangement. Mere collections can survive changes that humans cannot, and vice versa.

a load-bearing role in the debtor's argument; and typical responses to the problem of material constitution make it clear that most philosophers take themselves to have justified beliefs about the connections between such properties and various ways of arranging matter. In other words, we take ourselves to have justified beliefs that fit the following schema:

(MP) In any region containing matter arranged x-wise, there exists a material object with nontrivial modal property p.

For convenience, let us say that an MP-belief is any belief expressible by a sentence satisfying schema MP. Let us also, henceforth, take the term 'modal property' to refer to *nontrivial* modal properties unless otherwise qualified. The difficult epistemological question articulated at the end of the previous paragraph is equivalent to the question of how we acquire justified MP-beliefs. This is not quite the Discovery Problem; but discussing the various answers one might give to this epistemological question, and their bearing on RMO, leads us directly into the Discovery Problem.

2. Four Answers to the Epistemological Question

There are countless *possible* answers to the epistemological question, but only a few that have even a remote chance of being taken seriously by philosophers. For example, one *might* think that we acquire justified MP-beliefs by consulting astrological charts, bumps on the head, animal entrails, or the Delphic Oracle. But no respectable philosopher will take any of these answers seriously as having any hope of being correct. As far as I can tell, there are only four answers that are at all likely to be taken seriously. At any rate, no answers besides these four *have been* taken seriously in the literature; so I feel safe in restricting my attention to these.

2.1. Answer 1: Skepticism

One answer is that we *cannot* be justified in any of our MP-beliefs. As far as I know, nobody has defended this answer except indirectly by defending some much more general form of skepticism. Even anti-essentialists typically only direct their attacks against beliefs attributing *intrinsic* modal properties and not against MP-beliefs generally.[6] But, whatever its merits, this answer is not open to anybody who believes in material objects (mind-independent or not).

To see why, we need only reflect on the following truism: material objects have persistence conditions. By this I mean that, for every material thing, there are facts about what changes it can and cannot survive. A man over six feet tall cannot survive being crushed down to the size and shape of a sugar cube, and a sugar cube cannot survive its own dissolution in a cup of tea. On the other hand, a man usually can survive the sorts of changes normally undergone in the course of an afternoon stroll, and a sugar cube usually can survive the sorts of changes normally involved in the daily existence of a sugar cube (being in a bowl, being jostled as nearby sugar cubes are removed, and so on). Even for instantaneous objects (if there are such things) which do not last over time at all, there are nevertheless facts about whether and in what circumstances it is *possible* for them to last over time. If there are no facts at all about what sorts of changes a putative thing X can and cannot survive, then there is no such thing as X.[7]

Those who might doubt that material objects have persistence conditions are invited to consider the claim that there is such a thing as Socrates but literally *no fact at all* about whether Socrates could survive a trip to Macedonia or a trip through a meat grinder. The claim is patently absurd; and the same can be said for similar claims about other material objects. Many are willing to accept some indeterminacy in persistence conditions. Thus, for example, one might think that if we were to annihilate Socrates's constituent atoms one by one, there would be no fact about *which* atom was the one whose annihilation finally did him in. But accepting this kind of indeterminacy is not the same as accepting the view that Socrates lacks persistence conditions altogether. I know of no one who would say that there is no fact about whether Socrates could survive the simultaneous annihilation of *all* of his constituent atoms; and, again, similar remarks could be made with respect to any material object.

Having persistence conditions, then, is part of our concept of a material object—just as having boundaries is part of our concept of

---

[6] See e.g. Gibbard (1975) and Sidelle (1989).

[7] I assume that those who believe that persistence conditions are mind-dependent, and even those who believe that they are context-sensitive, will still say that there is always some fact (albeit a mind-dependent fact, or a contextually relative fact) about what some putative thing can or cannot survive. At any rate, if they were to deny this, I would find their position wholly unintelligible.

a geometrical figure. But notice that there is substantial ontological commitment lurking in the neighborhood. I have already indicated that persistence conditions are facts about what an object *can* and *cannot* survive. Thus, having persistence conditions is a matter of having modal properties. The commitment can be minimized by saying that modal properties are extrinsic rather than intrinsic (i.e. by saying that they are more like *being Fred's favorite number* than like *being bent*).[8] But the commitment is there nonetheless.[9]

If all this is right, however, then it follows that it is possible for belief in material objects to be justified only if it is possible for someone to have at least one justified MP-belief. The argument for this comes in three main steps.

Step One. The general belief that there are material objects can be justified only if some particular belief of the form '*this* is a material object' can be justified. After all, to say that the latter is impossible is to say that it is in principle impossible for us to detect material objects. But if material objects are in principle undetectable, how could we be justified in believing that there are any?

Step Two. A particular belief of the form '*this* is a material object' can be justified only if it is possible to be justified in believing that particular persistence conditions, or modal properties, are exemplified in the region supposedly occupied by the alleged material object. Since it is a conceptual truth that material objects have persistence conditions, it automatically follows from the fact that we can be justified in believing that a material object exists in some region that we also can be justified in believing that some persistence conditions or other are exemplified in the region. But that is not all that we can be justified in believing. For if we could have literally no idea at all *what* the object's persistence conditions were, we could have no grounds for saying that there is one object in the region rather than

[8] This minimizes the commitment because if modal properties are extrinsic then they might plausibly be understood in terms of more familiar, more obviously detectable natural properties and relations. For concrete examples, see Sect. 2.3 below.

[9] Unless one accepts a sparse theory of properties, as does David Armstrong (1978, 1989*a*, *b*, 1997). Then it may still be an open question whether modal facts are grounded in modal properties. Still, on this sort of view, the options will be pretty much the same: either modal facts will be grounded in intrinsic modal properties or they will be grounded in the relations between objects (or the stuff that composes them) and other contingent or merely possible beings. Thus, since there is no substantial difference between the latter alternative and a view according to which modal facts are grounded in extrinsic modal properties, and since accepting a sparse theory of properties will not rid one of commitment to modal facts, I will ignore this complication from here on out.

many or even none at all. After all, if you can't even answer questions like 'Could that thing survive being reduced to a pile of ash?' or 'Could that thing survive having its constituent molecules scattered to the outer reaches of the universe?' with respect to some putative thing, what could possibly justify you in believing that that 'thing' is really a single, unified object?

Step Three. If it is possible to be justified in believing that particular persistence conditions are exemplified in a region, then it is possible to have a justified MP-belief. One obvious reason is that, if nothing else, our MP-beliefs could be justifiably inferred from our beliefs about what persistence conditions are exemplified in what regions of spacetime. A more important reason, however, is that our MP-beliefs seem in fact to be more basic than our particular beliefs about persistence conditions. Apart from testimony, it is hard to see how we could possibly acquire justified beliefs about the persistence conditions, or modal properties, exemplified in a region without first acquiring some justified MP-belief. Suppose you travel to a foreign planet and encounter a region containing matter arranged in a wholly unfamiliar way; and suppose a fellow traveler asks you whether there's anything in the region that could survive a blast from your laser gun. How could you even begin to answer? You could take a shot at it with your gun, but how would you know whether your shot destroyed anything? Even if you produced a gaping hole in the putative object, apart from testimony (e.g. squeals of pain from the object, or a booming voice imploring you not to take another shot) and apart from some justified MP-belief, there would be no way of knowing whether you had damaged anything or simply rearranged some matter in an innocuous way. Perhaps God could have created organisms different from us who know such facts in a more basic way; but we appear not to.[10] Thus, it seems that if we have justified beliefs at all about the exemplification of modal properties in regions of spacetime, our having such justified beliefs depends either on testimony or on our having justified MP-beliefs. But obviously not *everyone's* beliefs about modal properties can come from testimony. So, our being justified in believing that particular essential properties are exemplified in particular regions of spacetime must ultimately

---

[10] Note, however, that even if I am wrong about this, the main point in this step of the argument still stands. For surely if we *were* able to know in a more basic way the facts about what modal properties are exemplified in what regions of spacetime, we would be able to infer justifiably at least one MP-belief from those facts.

depend upon someone's being justified in their MP-beliefs, and this too apart from testimony.

Conclusion. Therefore, by transitivity, it is possible to be justified in believing in material objects only if it is also possible for someone to have at least one justified MP-belief.

Thus, for those who believe we can be justified in believing in material objects, skepticism will not do as an answer to the question of how (if at all) we can acquire justified MP-beliefs.

2.2. *Answer 2: Concepts and Conventions*

Another answer to the epistemological question is that our MP-beliefs are grounded in apparent conceptual truths, or truths about our linguistic conventions, or both. If this is right, then, assuming we are always justified in accepting an apparent conceptual or conventional truth, it is easy to see how we could have justified MP-beliefs. There are, of course, problems with specifying exactly what it means for a proposition to be a conceptual or conventional truth; but for now we'll leave those aside.

This sort of view is commonly endorsed by empiricists, and it typically goes hand in hand with the view that modal properties are extrinsic. Thus, for example, Alan Sidelle (1989) holds that we can acquire justified MP-beliefs through our knowledge of linguistic conventions and relevant empirical facts, and he is quite explicit about the fact that his view implies that the world has no intrinsic modal structure. According to Sidelle, some of our MP-beliefs are analytic and others are derived from the conjunction of an analytic truth with an empirical truth.[11] 4.1 and 4.2 below are examples of each, respectively:

(4.1) Wherever there is matter arranged in the way distinctive of water molecules, there is a material object that is essentially such as to have the chemical structure of water.

(4.2) Wherever there is matter arranged in the way distinctive of water molecules, there is a material object that is essentially composed of H_2O.

Sidelle apparently holds that what *makes* the proposition expressed by 4.1 true is the fact that we have adopted linguistic conventions

---

[11] Never mind, for now, worries about analyticity. Let us simply suppose with Sidelle that the notion is well defined and not otherwise problematic.

governing the use of the words in 4.1 according to which that sentence has to be true, regardless of the empirical facts.[12] Knowing its truth, then, is just a matter of knowing the relevant linguistic conventions; and knowing the truth of 4.2 is just a matter of knowing both 4.1 and the empirical fact that water has the chemical structure H_2O. But if our conventions are what make propositions like that expressed by 4.1 true, then it follows that modal properties are exemplified in a region only if the matter in that region stands in particular contingent relations to human beings and their mental activity. Modal properties are therefore extrinsic rather than intrinsic. Sidelle embraces this consequence. Indeed, he defends his view in part by arguing that, if the world did have an intrinsic modal structure, that structure would be unknowable unless we had some mysterious faculty of intuition that was somehow sensitive to it. As it is, however, Sidelle thinks that MP-beliefs are justified, without help from rational intuitions, solely on the basis of our knowledge of the relevant empirical facts and linguistic conventions.[13]

Sidelle's view yields a conventionalist epistemology of MP-beliefs. Conceptualist epistemologies typically carry the same explicit commitment to modal antirealism (the view that modal properties are extrinsic).[14] Strictly speaking, however, conceptualist and conventionalist epistemologies of MP-beliefs can be separated from modal antirealism. There is nothing incoherent in saying that our MP-beliefs are grounded in conceptual or conventional truths while at the same time maintaining that the modal properties attributed by those beliefs are intrinsic. But, for present purposes, what is important to recognize is that *naturalists* cannot make this separation. Naturalists who embrace a conceptualist or conventionalist epistemology of modal properties will be committed to modal antirealism, even if the epistemology in question is strictly neutral on the question whether modal properties are extrinsic. The reason, in short, is that there is no naturalistically acceptable basis for thinking that reflecting upon conceptual or conventional truths is a way of acquiring

---

[12] Sidelle (1989, esp. chs. 2 and 3).

[13] One might object that rational intuition would have to play an important evidential role in justifying our beliefs about our concepts or linguistic conventions. If this is right, then Sidelle does not escape reliance on intuition after all. But I am not convinced that the objection is right. For more on this idea, see Ch. 8, esp. Sect. 5.1.

[14] See e.g. the view defended in Gibbard (1975). For discussion, see the introductory essay to Rea (1997).

information about the world's intrinsic modal structure. Examining some concrete proposals will help to illustrate this point.

In a recent article Michael Burke argues that we can discover the modal properties of material objects by determining (presumably by way of conceptual analysis) which of the many sortal concepts satisfied by a thing entails possession of the widest range of properties.[15] For example: According to Burke, wherever we find matter arranged human-wise, we find something that is *both* a human being and a collection of particles. But, he argues, *being a human being* entails a wider range of properties than *being a collection of particles*. (For example, the former entails possession of all of the same sorts of properties entailed by the latter; but the former *also* entails possession of biological properties, whereas the latter does not.) Thus, on his view, it follows that wherever we find matter arranged human-wise, we find something with the modal properties of a human being *and not* something with the modal properties of a mere collection of particles. We still do not have a story to explain how, if at all, we can know *what* the modal properties of human beings are. But presumably we can at least take it for granted that *being essentially human* is among them. Thus, we have an explanation for how we might justifiedly acquire at least one MP-belief, and it is an explanation according to which the belief is grounded in conceptual truths. Furthermore, as Burke himself points out, the view is strictly neutral on the question whether modal properties are extrinsic.

I am not inclined to accept Burke's view, and I have explained why in detail elsewhere (Rea 2000*c*). However, leaving aside questions about the view's plausibility, the thing to notice is that naturalists can have no basis for accepting it unless they assume that modal properties are extrinsic. If modal properties are intrinsic, it is very hard to see why they should be discoverable through a process of reflecting upon and comparing the ranges of properties entailed by the satisfaction of our sortal concepts. Prima facie, there is no more reason to think that this sort of procedure would be any more reliable in revealing intrinsic modal properties than it would be in revealing (say) intrinsic value. One could *say* that things of kind A are intrinsically more valuable than things of kind B just in case being a member of kind A entails a wider range of properties than being a member of kind B. But why believe it? In both cases the recommended criterion

---

[15] Burke (1994, sect. v).

bears no obvious connection to the properties we are trying to detect. Of course, Burke offers reasons for accepting his view; but, importantly, those reasons are just that his criterion yields *intuitively correct judgments* in a wide range of familiar cases, and there is no other plausible criterion in the offing. But citing these considerations as reasons presupposes that we have some intuitive access to modal properties; and if modal properties are supposed to be intrinsic, then the intuitions involved could not possibly be construed as intuitions about logical, mathematical, or conceptual truths. Thus, naturalists cannot take advantage of Burke's reasons for accepting his view.

One might be tempted to resist my assumption that it could not be a conceptual truth that (say) wherever there is matter arranged human-wise, there is something that is intrinsically such as to have the modal properties normally associated with human beings. But doing so would be of no use. If this were a conceptual truth, then our concepts of *human-wise arrangement* and *human being* would be modally loaded rather than purely phenomenal (as, I think, most are inclined to take them to be). So long as our concepts are purely phenomenal, it is a straightforwardly empirical matter whether they apply to the things to which we think they apply, and we face no difficult questions about how we could be justified in believing that they apply. On the other hand, if we take our concepts to be modally loaded, then we do face such questions. For example: Suppose it is a conceptual truth that human beings have the modal properties we normally associate with human beings. Let the concept of a *shuman being* be just like the concept of a human being except that it is a conceptual truth that shumans have the modal properties we normally associate with mere collections of particles. Now, what justifies us in believing that (say) in the region occupied by the debtor in the Debtor's Argument there is a human being rather than a *shuman* being, or matter arranged *human-wise* rather than *shuman-wise*? Naturally, there are stories to be told in response to this question. But the only plausible ones mirror three of the answers to the epistemological question that we are already in the midst of discussing. We could say that we are not justified in applying the concept 'human' (or any of our other sortal concepts), or that we are justified on the basis of rational intuition, or that we are justified on the basis of science. If the first, then we are not justified in believing that any of our sortal concepts correspond to intrinsic properties of things in the world; thus, we are not justified in accepting RMO. If the second, then our rational intuitions must be able to supply us with evidence in support of propositions that do not appear to be logical, mathematical, or conceptual truths. The reason is that it clearly is not a logical, mathematical, or conceptual truth that the modally loaded concept *human* is to be preferred over the modally loaded concept *shuman* in classifying the debtor. But naturalists cannot accept the claim that rational intuitions have evidential value outside the domain of logical, mathematical, and conceptual truths. Thus, they are left only with the third alternative. But the third is viable only if scientific methods can generate evidence in support of MP-beliefs attributing intrinsic modal properties; and I will argue later that they cannot. Thus, ultimately, resisting my assumption is a dead end.

So, returning to the main line of argument, naturalists cannot avail themselves of Burke's reasons for accepting his view. But neither can they have scientific reasons for accepting it. At any rate, they cannot if my arguments later on are sound. For, clearly enough, one could have scientific evidence for the claim that Burke's criterion provides a reliable way of detecting intrinsic modal properties only if one could have scientific evidence in support of MP-beliefs that attribute intrinsic modal properties. Thus, on the assumption that modal properties are intrinsic, Burke's view is naturalistically unacceptable.

On the other hand, suppose we assume that modal properties are extrinsic. More exactly, suppose we assume that whether an object has certain modal properties depends entirely upon whether our conceptual scheme associates those properties with it. We still might wonder whether Burke's criterion is reliable; but at least now we have a naturalistically acceptable way of checking. We need only check to see whether our conceptual scheme has the following two features:

(*a*) Sortal concepts are hierarchically arranged in the way that Burke takes for granted—i.e. distinct sortal concepts that can be satisfied by a single object are always such that one entails a wider range of properties than the other.

(*b*) Our conceptual scheme attributes to every object the modal properties that we associate with the highest-level sortal concept that is satisfied by the object.

If it does have these features, then Burke's view is correct; otherwise it is not. No appeal to intuition is required, and there are no residual mysteries about why the modal properties of things would be detectable in the way that Burke describes.

The second proposal I would like to examine appears in the work of David Lewis.[16] Consider again our sentences 4.1 and 4.2:

(4.1) Wherever there is matter arranged in the way distinctive of water molecules, there is a material object that is essentially such as to have the chemical structure of water.

(4.2) Wherever there is matter arranged in the way distinctive of water molecules, there is a material object that is essentially composed of H_2O.

According to Lewis, whether 4.1 and 4.2 express truths depends largely upon the context in which they are tokened; and knowing that they are true is largely a matter of knowing the salient facts about one's context—in this case, presumably, facts about the concepts of water, chemical structure, and so on, as well as one's interests and purposes in asserting 4.1 or 4.2.[17] Lewis's counterpart theory enters the picture too, however; and the truth of counterpart theory (or, at any rate, his brand of it) is not plausibly thought to be a purely conceptual matter. So, strictly speaking, Lewis's view seems not to be a thoroughgoing conceptualist proposal. But his view implies that, once the counterpart theoretic apparatus is in place, knowledge of concepts, linguistic conventions, and other relevant contextual features is sufficient to allow us to acquire justified MP-beliefs.

As with Burke's view, the bare skeleton of Lewis's view is strictly neutral with respect to the question whether modal properties are intrinsic. To see why, it will help first to review briefly the basic outline of counterpart theory. According to Lewis, the modal properties of an object are reducible to facts about the object's counterparts. To say, for example, that Socrates could have been a tax collector is to say that there are possible worlds that have Socrates-counterparts who are tax collectors. A counterpart of an object is just what you might expect from the label: it is an object sufficiently similar to the original to serve as a stand-in, or representative, for it in its absence. Thus, on Lewis's view, no individual object is a part of multiple worlds; but each individual thing is represented in multiple worlds by its counterparts. An object 'exists in a world' (or, better, exists *according to* a world) just in case it has a counterpart in that world; and it has a property P according to a world just in case it has a counterpart in

---

[16] I thank Andrew Cortens, David Lewis, and Ted Sider for helpful conversations about Lewis's view.

[17] Lewis (1986: 248–63).

that world that has P. So, in general, an object has the property of *being possibly P* just in case there is a world according to which it has P, and it has the property *being necessarily (or essentially) P* just in case it has P in every world according to which it exists at all.

Note that, though modal properties are reduced, on this view, to relations of similarity, nothing in Lewis's view up to this point is incompatible with the view that some modal properties are intrinsic. The exemplification of modal properties by an object depends on the relations of similarity it bears to its counterparts; thus, it depends on its relations to other things. But counterparts exist in other worlds. Hence, intrinsic resemblances among counterparts will be independent of accompaniment by other contingent things—assuming, anyway, that accompaniment is an intra-world relation and not an inter-world relation.

But something does not count unqualifiedly as one of your counterparts *simply* by standing with you in some (objective) relation of similarity. If it did, then everything in every world would automatically be your counterpart, since everything in every world is similar to you in some respect or other. You would have counterparts that are horses, rocks, atoms, electrons, and so on ad infinitum; and it would follow from this, on counterpart theory, that you have modal properties like *being possibly an electron* and *being possibly a rock*. But to affirm all of this without qualification would be to distort Lewis's view. Lewis does not deny that you are similar in various respects to electrons, rocks, and the like. But two elements are missing from the story so far. First, Lewis is not committed to the view that every similarity relation is a counterpart relation. Second, he thinks that modal claims are context-sensitive; and there may be no context in which it is ever true that you have electron-counterparts, rock-counterparts, and so on.

According to Lewis, all counterpart relations are similarity relations; but nothing in the view requires that all similarity relations be counterpart relations. Moreover, Lewis holds that *which* counterpart relations are relevant to the truth of a modal claim depends on features about the context in which the claim occurs; so even if you *did* have electron-counterparts, the electron-counterpart relation might never be in view when questions about your modal properties are being discussed. On this, he writes:

We have many and varied relations of comparative similarity. Some differ from others because they put different weights or priorities on different respects of (intrinsic or extrinsic) qualitative similarity; and even if they are alike in the respects of comparison they stress, they can still differ because one is more stringent than another. Any of these relations is a candidate to be expressed by the word 'counterpart'. Likewise many different relations, some more stringent and some less, some stressing some respects of comparison and others stressing others, have a claim to be called 'similarity'. The exact meaning of 'counterpart' or 'similar' is neither constant nor determinate. These words equivocally express a range of different semantic values, and the limits of the range are subject to pressures of context. Two things may be counterparts in one context, but not in another; or it may be indeterminate whether two things are counterparts. (Lewis 1986: 254)

Thus, it does not follow from the fact that you resemble rocks and electrons and so on that sentences like 'you have rock-counterparts' and 'you have electron-counterparts' are true in every or even any context of discourse.

At first blush it might appear that the contextualist element in Lewis's view straightforwardly commits him to modal antirealism. The property of being similar in this or that respect to other objects in other worlds may be intrinsic. But properties like *having round counterparts* or *having nonhuman counterparts* are apparently not intrinsic since what it is for something to be a counterpart is for it to be similar in some respect *relevant to the interests and purposes* that partially constitute the context in which the questions about modal properties are arising. Thus, since Lewis analyzes modal properties in terms of counterpart relations, modal properties cannot be intrinsic either. Thus, his view is apparently one according to which modal properties are mind-dependent.

But not so fast. Lewis says (in the passage quoted above) that there are many different relations of comparative similarity, each a candidate for being expressed by the term 'counterpart'. Elsewhere, he emphasizes that different counterpart relations correspond to different relations of similarity.[18] Thus, rather than holding that the property of being a counterpart is mind-dependent, he holds that there is no such thing as *the* property of being a counterpart. Just as there are many and varied relations of similarity, so too there are many and varied counterpart relations; and the role played by context is just to determine *which* of these many counterpart relations is being invoked by a particular modal attribution. On this view, all of the relevant

---

[18] See e.g. Lewis (1971, 1986: 255 ff.).

counterpart relations will be intrinsic. Thus, the corresponding modal properties will be as well. Still, it is clear that the basic elements of Lewis's view (contextualism cum counterpart theory) are compatible with modal antirealism; and it is for this reason that I say that the bare skeleton of Lewis's view is strictly neutral with respect to the question whether modal properties are intrinsic.

Insofar as Lewis believes in a multiplicity of counterpart relations, however, he is committed to the view that there are many different sorts of possibility and necessity. Keep in mind that, on Lewis's view, 'x has the property *being possibly p*' is equivalent to 'x has a counterpart that has p'. But there are many and varied counterpart relations. So, whereas there might be some counterpart relation R1 such that Socrates has a counterpart$_{R1}$ that is a horse, no doubt there is some other counterpart relation R2 such that he has no counterparts$_{R2}$ that are horses. (If you think that there is no context of discourse in which it could be true that Socrates has horse-counterparts, then substitute a different example.) But clearly it cannot follow from this that Socrates is intrinsically *both* possibly a horse and not possibly a horse. Rather, what must be the case is that, corresponding to the two counterpart relations, there are two different kinds of modality, so that Socrates is possibly$_{R1}$ a horse but necessarily$_{R2}$ not a horse.

Many will be uncomfortable with this consequence. One is obviously free to *say* that there are many different kinds of possibility. But what does that *mean*? I understand perfectly well the claim that Socrates could have been horse. But I do not understand the claim that there are multiple modalities such that Socrates could$_{R1}$ have been a horse but could-not$_{R2}$ have been a horse. The problem is not just that the subscripted modalities are as yet undefined. Rather, the problem is that my conceptual repertoire includes only one kind of modality rather than two (or more). Like many, I am prepared to recognize distinctions between (say) physical possibility and metaphysical possibility. But it is not that sort of distinction that Lewis is committed to by accepting a multiplicity of counterpart relations. Rather, once the distinction is drawn, it appears that he is committed to the view that there are multiple *metaphysical* modalities (and perhaps also multiple *physical* modalities, and so on). But, again, that is a view that I am unable to understand.

Still, setting aside this worry, we can readily see why Lewis's view might appear to provide the resources for an attractive answer to our epistemological question. On Lewis's view, we have modal plenitude.

The world is modally rich: every material object exemplifies countless intrinsic modal properties corresponding to many, if not all, of the conceivable ways of thinking about the thing that are both internally consistent and consistent with the empirical facts. The modal properties do not conflict because the modalities in question are of different kinds. Furthermore, so long as fairly liberal limits are set on what similarity relations qualify as counterpart relations, the reliability of our MP-beliefs is virtually guaranteed. Indeed, for those who accept the most extreme version of plenitude—saying that objects display modal properties corresponding to *all* of the conceivable and consistent ways of thinking about them—the reliability of our MP-beliefs is *trivially* guaranteed. (Though we are subject to massive unreliability in those beliefs of ours that conflict with plenitude.)

Whatever its merits, however, there is no way a naturalist could have grounds for accepting Lewis's view. There is, of course, the obvious worry that facts about counterparts would be inaccessible to the methods of science. But even if we set this worry aside, there is the additional problem of explaining how naturalists could be justified in accepting the commitment to modal plenitude. This commitment is what secures the reliability of our MP-beliefs. But, of course, a naturalist could have evidence in support of plenitude only if the methods of science could provide some independent evidence in support of particular MP-beliefs that attribute intrinsic modal properties. Again, however, I will argue later that the methods of science cannot provide such evidence.

We should pause here to observe that modal plenitude *can* stand alone as a way of accounting for the reliability of our MP-beliefs. Suppose we reject both counterpart theory and the idea that there are multiple different metaphysical modalities. Still, one might accept a suitably extreme version of modal plenitude according to which, in every filled region R of spacetime, there are countless objects in R corresponding to all of the conceivable, internally and empirically consistent ways of conceptually dividing the contents of R into objects with modal properties.[19] So far, the view is neutral on the question whether modal properties are extrinsic. But, again, the

---

[19] This sort of view (under the assumption that modal properties are intrinsic) is defended by L. A. Paul (2001) and was suggested to me independently by William Hasker and Robert Koons.

reliability of our MP-beliefs is trivially guaranteed. If we add to the view the claim that modal properties are extrinsic, we (probably) end up with rampant relativism. On the other hand, if we add the claim that modal properties are intrinsic, we have rampant colocation. But either way we avoid the consequence that there are multiple different kinds of metaphysical possibility and necessity. Still, as before, whatever the attractions of this version of modal plenitude, naturalists cannot accept it unless they can have scientific evidence for MP-beliefs that attribute intrinsic modal properties.

I have now surveyed a variety of different conceptualist and conventionalist views about how we might acquire justified MP-beliefs. We have seen, however, that even those that remain neutral on the question whether modal properties are intrinsic cannot be accepted by naturalists unless it is assumed that modal properties are extrinsic. The general problem is that, once we assume that modal properties are intrinsic, it is hard to see why reflecting upon conceptual truths would reveal them to us. The procedure seems ill suited to its task. One might try to offer an ontological story that explains why the procedure would be reliable. But, if it is to be believed, the story will have to be certified by evidence from rational intuition, science, or some other source. Since the story itself will not be a logical, mathematical, or conceptual truth, naturalists will be unable to accept intuitive evidence on its behalf. Thus, they must look for scientific evidence. But we can have scientific evidence for a story according to which reflection upon our concepts or conventions reveals the intrinsic modal structure of the world only if we can have scientific support for MP-beliefs that attribute intrinsic modal properties.

So it appears that naturalists cannot endorse a conceptualist or conventionalist answer to our epistemological question without committing themselves to the view that modal properties are extrinsic. But if modal properties are extrinsic, then RMO is false. Recall that RMO entails that at least some apparent sortal properties are intrinsic to the things they appear to sort. But sortal properties go hand in hand with modal properties. What a thing can and cannot survive depends on what kind of thing it is; and what kind of thing it is depends on what it can and cannot survive. Thus, if the facts about what a thing can and cannot survive depend upon its relations to other contingent things, then so also do the facts about what kind of thing it is. So, if accepting this second answer commits naturalists to modal antirealism, then it also commits them to the denial of RMO.

2.3. Answer 3: Intuition

Perhaps the most common answer to the epistemological question is that we acquire justified MP-beliefs by way of rational intuition. We know, for example, that wherever there is matter arranged cat-wise, there is something that can survive the loss of a tail but cannot survive the immediate scattering of all of its constituent atoms; and, according to the present answer, we know this on the basis of its seeming to be obviously and necessarily true.

Now, one *might* say that the reason our MP-beliefs seem obviously and necessarily true is just that they are grounded in conceptual truths. But, for those who say this, the present answer possesses the same virtues and vices as Answer 2. Naturalists might be able to accept it since (as I am prepared to grant) naturalists might have grounds for thinking that intuition is reliable in the restricted domain of logical, mathematical, and conceptual truths. But, in accepting it, naturalists will thereby commit themselves to the view that modal properties are extrinsic (for reasons already given in Section 2.2).

Typically, however, those who are willing to grant that MP-beliefs are justified on the basis of rational intuition are also adamant in denying that our MP-beliefs are grounded in conceptual truths. On this view, simply inspecting our concepts with attention to relevant empirical information is not sufficient to decide (say) the dispute between the debtor and the creditor in the Debtor's Argument. Consider the proposition (endorsed by the debtor) that wherever there is matter arranged human-wise there is something that has the modal properties of a mere collection of particles. According to most proponents of Answer 3 this is not a proposition whose truth can be discovered just by reflecting on and suitably unpacking our concepts of *human-wise arrangement, collectionhood,* and the like. Still, they say, insofar as it (or its denial) appears to be necessarily true, we can be justified in believing it (or its denial). But, quite obviously, this is *not* something that a naturalist can say, since naturalists reject the evidential value of intuitions about propositions that do not appear to be logical, mathematical, or conceptual truths. Thus, to the extent that it is substantially different from Answer 2, this third answer is incompatible with naturalism.

2.4. Answer 4: Science

The fourth answer is that we acquire justified MP-beliefs through scientific methods. This answer is obviously compatible with naturalism. The question is whether it can be fleshed out in a way compatible with RMO. Fleshed out one way, this answer might prove to be no different from the second answer discussed above. For if reflecting on conceptual truths or inspecting our linguistic conventions counts as scientific investigation, then one might embrace the present answer *simply* by embracing a conceptualist or conventionalist epistemology of modal properties. But, as we have seen, naturalists can accept a pure and unsupplemented conceptualist or conventionalist epistemology of modal properties only if they abandon RMO. Thus, the present answer will be compatible with RMO only if scientific methods can somehow reveal intrinsic modal properties. But can they? At first glance, it seems that the answer must be no. Empirical investigation tells us that water is H_2O. But it apparently does not tell us that every individual water molecule has intrinsically the property of being essentially H_2O. Whether a particular H_2O molecule could have been an atom of gold seems not to be a scientific question. So, on the assumption that this fourth answer is substantially different from the second, it appears (superficially, anyway) to be false.

3. The Discovery Problem and its Significance for RMO

In the last section 1 examined four different answers to the epistemological question raised in Section 1. The first was incompatible with belief in material objects (mind-independent or otherwise); the second was incompatible with the conjunction of naturalism and RMO; the third was incompatible with naturalism. Only the fourth held out any promise for a naturalistic answer to the question compatible with RMO. But the problem was that the intrinsic modal properties of material objects, if they exist at all, seem to be undiscoverable by scientific methods. This, again, is the Discovery Problem. Another way of putting it: Let us say that IMP-beliefs are beliefs expressible by a sentence satisfying schema IMP:

(IMP) In any region containing matter arranged x-wise, there exists a material object that has *intrinsically* the nontrivial modal property p.

The Discovery Problem, then, is just the fact that IMP-beliefs seem not to be (epistemically) justifiable through scientific methods.[20] Failure to solve the Discovery Problem involves conceding the appearances and admitting that material objects have no intrinsic modal properties discoverable by scientific methods. Solving the problem involves providing an account of how we could discover such properties by scientific methods.

The Discovery Problem is usually raised by empiricists as a reason for rejecting the view that objects have intrinsic modal properties. Surprisingly, however, relatively little has been done by way of exploring the options for solving it.[21] More often the problem is dismissed as unsolvable (by those who are inclined toward either modal antirealism or some brand of intuitionism) or simply ignored. I suspect that one reason for the latter response is that many philosophers believe that there is no connection between their being able to solve this problem and their being justified in accepting RMO. But this belief is mistaken.

Admittedly, one might be justified in accepting RMO without having a solution to the Discovery Problem. Most of your family and friends probably accept RMO (I know mine do), but probably none of them have a solution to the Discovery Problem. Are they unjustified in accepting RMO? Probably not. RMO seems to be one of those views that one is automatically justified in accepting, at least until one discovers that (*a*) accepting it involves substantially greater metaphysical commitment than accepting its alternative, and (*b*) there can be no evidence in support of it from the sources that one takes to be basic. However, upon making the latter discoveries, it seems clear that one's justification for accepting RMO is undermined. Thus, it is not my view that one needs to be able to *show* how one could be justified in accepting RMO in order to *be* justified in accepting it. However, it is my view that one cannot be justified in believing RMO if one sees that belief in RMO cannot be supported by evidence from her basic sources and involves substantially greater

---

[20] Whether they can be justified in some other sense is an issue that will be taken up in Ch. 6.

[21] Crawford Elder has come quite close to doing exactly this. His work is discussed in some detail in Ch. 4. Also, Robert Koons (2000*b*) has recently argued that at least some modal facts enter into causal relations. But it is not clear to me what relevance, if any, his work has to the Discovery Problem; for he says nothing to show that intrinsic modal properties might be empirically detectable, and I see no clear way of extending his arguments to show this.

metaphysical commitment than its alternative. That belief in RMO does involve substantially greater metaphysical commitment than its alternative is obvious. On RMO there are many mind-independent objects with mysterious intrinsic modal properties; on the alternative there are not. The Discovery Problem, in conjunction with the reflections laid out in Section 2 above, point strongly to the fact that belief in RMO cannot be supported by evidence from the sources that naturalists take as basic. Thus, if the Discovery Problem is unsolvable, reflective naturalists (i.e. those who reflect upon the issues enough to appreciate the facts laid out in this and the following two chapters) cannot be justified in accepting RMO.

4. Related Problems

Before attempting to show that the Discovery Problem cannot be solved, I want to take a moment briefly to distinguish it from some related problems with which it might easily be confused. The Discovery Problem is a problem about the discovery of intrinsic modal properties. But one might be tempted to see it simply as a generic problem about modal knowledge—as if showing that *some* modal truths can be known through scientific methods might be sufficient for solving the problem. Furthermore, since I have already acknowledged that modal properties and sortal properties go hand in hand, the Discovery Problem might just as easily be seen as some sort of classification problem. But seeing it this way makes it possible to confuse the problem with a variety of other classification problems. For example, many philosophers think that it has been reasonably well established that chemical kinds, but not biological kinds, sort objects in some sense according to their *real essences*. But essences are plausibly taken to involve essential properties; and essential properties are commonly taken to be modal properties. Thus, one might be tempted to infer that it has also been reasonably well established that at least chemical classification, if not biological classification, sorts objects according to their *modal properties*. If that is right, then the Discovery Problem is easily solved, at least in the case of objects studied by chemists; for presumably the methods by which chemists sort their objects of study into kinds are empirical methods. Similarly, since natural kinds in general are commonly thought to sort objects in some sense according to their essential properties, one might be tempted to think that naturalistic defenses of realism about natural kinds—i.e. naturalistic defenses of the view that we can discover genuine natural kinds in nature—are therefore also defenses of our ability to discover modal properties. All of these temptations ought to be resisted, however. In the remainder of this section I explain why.

To see why the first temptation ought to be resisted, we need only observe that solving the Discovery Problem requires much more than showing that some modal truths can be known through scientific methods. For example, consistency arguments or indispensability arguments (both of which are generally taken to be scientifically respectable) might justify us in the very general belief that *something* exemplifies intrinsic modal properties. Maybe such arguments could even yield the conclusion that certain nonmaterial objects exist and exemplify intrinsic modal properties. For example: Some philosophers have suggested that the idea of an external world wholly devoid of modal properties is incoherent.[22] But even if they are wrong, surely at least one mind would have to have intrinsic modal properties since not *everything* in the world can be mind-dependent. If so, then we have a consistency argument for the general belief that something exemplifies intrinsic modal properties (i.e. we have an argument for the conclusion that the denial of this general belief is incoherent). Similarly, Quine famously justified belief in abstract sets on the grounds that sets are indispensable for science; and perhaps one could also show that it is incoherent to suppose that the modal properties of sets are extrinsic. If so, then we have a combination consistency–indispensability argument for belief in intrinsic modal properties. But even if some or all of these arguments for modal realism are successful, it does not follow that intrinsic modal properties *of material objects* are discoverable by scientific methods, for belief in those might not be indispensable in scientific theorizing and denying their existence might not be logically incoherent.[23] Thus, the Discovery Problem is separate from more general epistemological questions about whether modal realism is justified or about whether belief in any intrinsic modal properties can be justified through scientific methods.

---

[22] See Blackson (1992) and Carter and Bahde (1998).

[23] At any rate, it does not follow if we assume that sets are not material objects. But see Maddy (1996) for arguments against this assumption. However, if sets *are* material objects, then there's no reason to think that consistency arguments can establish the conclusion that their modal properties are intrinsic.

The remaining two temptations arise out of a common tendency to conflate various different views about essences and essential properties.[24] According to Aristotle, for example, the essence, or nature, of a thing is, very roughly, a complex property of the matter composing it which (*a*) explains a large number of scientifically interesting features of the object—i.e. features of its outward appearance, behavior, natural development, and so on—and (*b*) is shared in common by other objects and provides a basis for sorting those objects into a kind that is definable in terms of necessary and sufficient conditions. For convenience, let us call essences that satisfy both of these conditions *Aristotelian essences*.

Locke, on the other hand, identified *two* kinds of essences: nominal and real. On his view, our sorting practices are purely conventional and are based on superficial resemblances which give rise to abstract ideas, like the idea of a cat or a human being. On Locke's view, the nominal essence of a thing is just the abstract idea that provides the basis for classifying the thing in the way we do. The real essence, on the other hand, is the underlying structure that explains the superficial features shared by objects having the same nominal essence. What this view has in common with the Aristotelian view is the idea that real essences are *explanatory*. However, unlike the Aristotelian view, it is no part of the Lockean view to suppose that real essences can, even in principle, serve as a basis for sorting objects into scientifically useful kinds that are definable in terms of necessary and sufficient conditions.

The three kinds of essences just described—Aristotelian, Lockean nominal, and Lockean real essences—are the ones most commonly talked about in the literature on classification and natural kinds. In that literature *essential properties* are widely taken to be properties that belong to an object's *Lockean real essence*, whereas *essentialism* (with respect to a particular science) is widely taken to be the view that the kinds recognized by that science are Aristotelian kinds, definable in terms of necessary and sufficient conditions.[25] As noted earlier, many philosophers are willing to believe that *some* material objects (for example, chemical compounds) have Aristotelian essences and therefore belong to Aristotelian kinds.[26] But it is also

---

[24] The discussion that follows is informed by Ayers (1981), Stuart (1999), and, to a lesser extent, Boyd (1991) and Hacking (1991*a*, *b*).

[25] See e.g. Dupré (1981, 1993), Hull (1965), and Sober (1980, 1993).

[26] But this is debated. See e.g. Dupré (1993).

common to believe that at least some material objects have essences that are not Aristotelian. For example, many philosophers now hold that some natural kinds are defined by *homeostatic property clusters*—indefinite families of properties whose members both tend statistically to be exemplified together or not at all and also lawfully explain many of the superficial features of the objects that have them.[27] The families are indefinite in the sense that an *exhaustive* list of the properties in each family cannot, even in principle, be given. Furthermore, on this conception of kinds, no particular property or cluster of properties in the family *must* be exemplified by an object in order for it to count as a member of the kind, though exemplifying any of a variety of different but overlapping clusters will be sufficient for membership in the kind. Indeed, necessary conditions for membership in the kind cannot even be specified by definite disjunctions of properties or property clusters. This is because the families of properties in terms of which these kinds are defined are of indefinite membership, and so any definite disjunction of properties or property clusters will inevitably omit properties or clusters that include some of the unspecified properties in the family. Thus, the properties that define the kind do not define an Aristotelian kind. Nevertheless, for any object belonging to a kind defined by a homeostatic cluster, there will be some set of properties it displays by virtue of which it qualifies as a member of the kind and which plays the explanatory role of a Lockean real essence. On this view, then, an essential property will not even be the sort of property that an object must have in order to belong to the kind it belongs to; rather, it will simply be an explanatory property that happens to be among the contingently related members of a vaguely defined family.

However, in the present context we must also keep in mind that the terms 'essence', 'essential property', and 'essentialism' are very often used in a way importantly different from that described above. Throughout the literature in contemporary metaphysics (and often in the literature on natural kinds as well) the term 'essential property' is used in such a way that a property *p* counts as an essential property of an object *x* if and only if it is impossible for *x* to exist and fail to have *p*.[28] 'Essentialism' is the view that objects have essential properties in

---

[27] For exposition and defense of the homeostatic cluster theory, see Boyd (1988, 1991) and Kornblith (1993). For an earlier characterization of the two conceptions of natural kinds, see Hull (1965).

[28] See e.g. Plantinga (1974).

this sense; and an 'essence' of an object x is any property (like *being identical to x*) that is both essential to x and such that it cannot be exemplified by objects other than x. (This is how I have been using these terms throughout this book, and it is how I will continue to use them outside of the discussion in the present section.) But notice that it does not at all obviously follow from the fact that a property is part of an object's *Aristotelian essence* that it is a property that the thing in question *could not possibly exist without*. Thus, even if 'essentialism in chemistry' has been empirically vindicated, it does not follow that essentialism in the sense just described has been empirically vindicated. But it is the latter sort of essentialism, and not the former, that would have to be empirically vindicated in order for us to have a solution to the Discovery Problem.

Understanding all of this makes it easy to see why the second and third temptations mentioned at the beginning of this section ought to be resisted. It is indeed true that many philosophers take it to have been established that 'essentialism' is true for chemical kinds but not biological kinds. But what is generally agreed upon here is not the thesis that chemical kinds but not biological kinds sort objects according to their *necessary* properties, but rather the thesis that chemical kinds but not biological kinds sort objects according to their Aristotelian real essences. Of course, many philosophers do believe the former claim. But, unlike the latter claim, it is not clear that there is empirical support for it. Similarly, it is also true that realism about natural kinds may imply a kind of realism about essence (depending upon one's conception of natural kinds).[29] But it is not obvious that realism about kinds will imply anything like realism about modal properties. At any rate, realism about Aristotelian or homeostatic cluster kinds will not imply any such modal realism; for, on the face of it, the question of whether there are properties that play the explanatory roles of Lockean or Aristotelian real essences seems wholly independent of the question whether modal antirealism is true.

As is well known, Kripke, Putnam, and others, in promulgating the 'new theory of reference' in the 1970s, explicitly stated that the Lockean real essences of things like water molecules are *both* empirically detectable *and* essential to them (in the sense of being properties they

---

[29] For further conceptions of natural kinds besides those described here, see Hacking (1991*a*).

cannot possibly fail to exemplify).[30] But in doing so, they offered no solution whatsoever to the Discovery Problem. For what they very definitely did not establish is the empirical justifiability of the belief that the Lockean real essence of a thing is essential in this strong sense. Why think that where we find matter arranged both in the way distinctive of H_2O molecules and in the way distinctive of mere collections of subatomic particles we find something that is essentially an H_2O molecule rather than something that is essentially a collection of subatomic particles? Indeed, why think that we find in that region anything with essential properties at all? These are questions not answered by the new theory of reference.[31] Kripke defends the claim that chemical structure is essential to a thing by appeals to intuition, not by appeals to science. Putnam (at least in some places) rejects intuition and presses for the conclusion that modal properties are extrinsic.[32] The Discovery Problem remains unsolved.

5. Prospects for a Solution

How then might we solve the problem? Toward answering this question, consider what it takes to acquire scientific justification for believing in *anything*. Broadly speaking, at least one of three things must occur: (*a*) we observe it, (*b*) we posit its existence to explain our observations, or (*c*) we discover that our theorizing is simplified or otherwise significantly pragmatically enhanced by supposing that it exists.

In saying this, of course, I am glossing over some complicated issues in the philosophy of science. For example, there really are no sharp distinctions to be drawn between observable entities, and explanatory posits; nor are there sharp distinctions to be drawn between the latter and objects whose existence is posited for pragmatic reasons. Furthermore, many empiricists will deny that we have scientific justification for believing in the existence of all of our theoretical posits. But for present purposes these concerns can be dismissed. Since I am mainly interested in showing what naturalists *cannot* believe in, no harm will be done in supposing that they can

---

[30] For a useful collection of and introduction to some of the most important work by and about Kripke and Putnam on these issues, see Schwartz (1977).

[31] This point receives detailed defense in Salmon (1981).

[32] See e.g. Putnam (1981*b*).

have epistemic justification for believing in *more* things than many empiricists will allow. Similarly, no harm will be done by supposing, for heuristic reasons, that there are distinctions to be made where in fact there are none. Despite recent work in the philosophy of science, most philosophers and scientists continue for the sake of convenience to talk as if there is a distinction between things we observe, things we posit to explain our observations, and background assumptions that we make to simplify or otherwise pragmatically enhance our theorizing. That is all I am proposing to do here; and nothing other than the relative complexity of our discussion will be affected by doing so.

A concern which is not so easily dismissed, however, arises from the fact that having scientific justification for believing something is not obviously equivalent to having *discovered* it to be true in the sense relevant to the Discovery Problem. For example, we have scientific justification for believing that simultaneity is relative and for believing that there are no 'hidden variables' to explain the relative frequencies of quantum phenomena. But can we really say that we have empirically *discovered* that these things are true when the main reasons for believing them are that their denials are empirically unverifiable and our theorizing is pragmatically enhanced by believing them? Saying that we have discovered that something is true seems to imply that we have epistemic justification for believing it. (At any rate, this is how I will be understanding the idea of discovery here and in what follows.) But one might well wonder whether pragmatic justification is sufficient for epistemic justification. This concern will be addressed in some detail in Chapter 6.

I assume that there will be no controversy over the claim that intrinsic modal properties are not directly observable. We cannot see, hear, smell, taste, or touch the fact that a rabbit cannot survive being flattened by a steamroller; for we cannot perceive the fact that the resultant mess is not the *same* object as the rabbit, just in a different form. Thus, if our beliefs about intrinsic modal properties are to be justified on scientific grounds, it must be because their truth provides the best (or at least a very good) explanation for some empirically detectable phenomenon, or because the supposition that they are true is somehow pragmatically useful as a background assumption. As far as I know, there are only two stories even hinted at in the literature about how we might acquire justified IMP-beliefs in either of the ways just mentioned. According to one story (which I will not attribute to anyone because it has only been hinted at and not developed in any detail), our IMP-beliefs are justified because their truth provides a good explanation for the existence of 'proper function phenomena' in nature. According to the second story, portions of which have been developed in some detail by Crawford Elder, our IMP-beliefs are justified because (*a*) the presupposition that there are intrinsic modal properties is justified on pragmatic grounds and (*b*) in light of this presupposition the truth of our IMP-beliefs provides the best explanation for the phenomenon of uniform clustering of explanatorily rich properties in nature.

One might think that an appeal to the method of wide reflective equilibrium might be an appropriate third alternative for explaining how we might acquire justified IMP-beliefs. Just as considered moral judgments might be thought to be justified once they are brought into coherence with various moral principles and relevant background theories, so too one might think that considered modal judgments (including considered IMP-judgments) could be justified in the same way. Recall, however, that in Chapter 3 we saw that the method of wide reflective equilibrium is compatible with naturalism only if the relevant considered judgments are not rational intuitions (or beliefs based on rational intuitions) or are not treated as evidence. If our considered MP-judgments are not rational intuitions (and are not inferred from rational intuitions), then it is hard to see why they would deserve to be treated as evidence for anything unless they were justified by way of something like inference to the best explanation. On the other hand, if our considered MP-judgments are rational intuitions (or are inferred therefrom) but are not being treated as evidence, then it is again hard to see why they should be taken seriously in the employment of the method of wide reflective equilibrium except for purely pragmatic reasons. In either case, then, naturalists are committed to thinking of our IMP-beliefs as being justified either by pragmatic arguments or by inferences to the best explanation. Appeal to the method of wide reflective equilibrium offers no help.

In Chapters 5 and 6, I will present in some detail both of the stories mentioned above according to which intrinsic modal properties are detectable via scientific methods, and I will argue that each is unacceptable. With respect to the first, I will argue that if there really are 'proper function phenomena' in nature, they are not empirically detectable; hence, an appeal to such phenomena cannot explain how our IMP-beliefs are *scientifically* justified. With respect to the second, I will provide some reason for doubting that uniform clustering is the mark of metaphysical import that Elder thinks that it is and, more importantly, I will provide general reasons for thinking that if the justificatory status of our MP-beliefs depends ultimately on their pragmatic usefulness (or on the pragmatic usefulness of other beliefs in light of which our MP-beliefs play some explanatory role), then our MP-beliefs are not epistemically justified and the Discovery Problem remains unsolved.

I realize that this procedure does not give me anything like deductive proof for the conclusion that the Discovery Problem is unsolvable. However, I do think that, together with the prima facie implausibility of believing that intrinsic modal properties are scientifically detectable, it will provide ample reason to believe that the problem cannot be solved. Those who remain unconvinced may take my overall argument in these chapters as a challenge to provide a different solution that does not fall prey to the objections raised against the ones presented here.

5

Proper Function

MANY people, philosophers and nonphilosophers alike, think that the world at least appears to contain objects some of whose parts have proper functions (i.e. functions those parts are objectively supposed to perform). If this is right, and if such appearances are plausibly thought to be grounded in perception rather than intuition, religious experience, or whatever, then these appearances might provide the basis for a naturalistic explanation of how we can acquire justified MP-beliefs.

Let us say that *proper function phenomena* appear in a region R of spacetime just in case R appears to contain an object whose parts have various functions they are objectively supposed to perform. Let us also say that such phenomena are *internal* just in case it appears that the phenomena in question supervene on properties that are intrinsic to objects in R. (So the fact that internal proper function phenomena appear in a region R does not by itself entail that there are any objects in R; nor does it entail that anything in R actually has a proper function. All it entails is that R *appears* to contain an object such that (*a*) its parts have proper functions and (*b*) the proper functions of its parts supervene on properties intrinsic either to the object or to its parts.) Now, consider a region R of spacetime in which proper function phenomena appear. One plausible explanation of this appearance is the supposition that R in fact contains an object whose matter is objectively supposed to be arranged in some particular way—most plausibly, a way that is jointly caused or sustained by the performance of the relevant proper functions. And this, in turn, might be explained by the supposition that R contains an object belonging to a kind whose members are essentially such as to have their matter arranged in the way in question. To the extent that the relevant appearances are perceptually based, MP-beliefs might then be thought to be justified by their role in explaining various empirical phenomena. Better scientific credentials could hardly be asked for. Furthermore, if the relevant proper function phenomena are internal, then they might also provide a basis for IMP-beliefs.

To illustrate, let us consider a pair of examples. In the region R_{car} apparently occupied by my car, there seems to be a system (i.e. the car) and the system seems to have parts (e.g. tires, a carburetor, windows) that have proper functions relative to the car. Furthermore, the evidence that explains these seemings is straightforwardly empirical. Not only do my senses report the fact that there is matter in R_{car} arranged car-wise, but various empirical sources inform me that the matter in R_{car} was arranged that way *for a purpose*. From this fact I might plausibly infer that the contents of the various subregions of R_{car} where parts of the car appear to be found are objectively supposed to contribute to the maintenance of the car-wise arrangement and automotive behavior of the matter that now occupies R_{car}. And from this latter claim I might plausibly conclude that there is an object in R_{car} that is essentially such as to have its constituent matter arranged car-wise and to be able to behave in an automotive way. Moreover, I might also conclude on the basis of my evidence that wherever I find matter arranged car-wise (or, at any rate, wherever I find matter that has been arranged that way for the relevant purposes) I find an object that is essentially such as to have its matter arranged car-wise. Thus, I have an empirical basis for at least one MP-belief. But, so far, there is no reason to think that the modal properties of the car are *intrinsic*. The empirical evidence does not tell me that the putative parts of the car could have their same proper functions without having been designed; and so I have no empirical basis for supposing that the car's modal properties are not similarly dependent upon the existence and activities of a designer. Hence, the proper function phenomena appearing in the region R_{car} provide me with no empirical basis for IMP-beliefs.

On the other hand, consider the region R_{cat} apparently occupied by my cat. As with R_{car}, R_{cat} appears to contain a system whose parts have proper functions relative to that system. Furthermore, these apparent proper functions seem to contribute to the maintenance of the cat-wise arrangement of the matter that now occupies R_{cat}. One plausible explanation of this phenomenon is the supposition that wherever we find matter arranged cat-wise, we find an object that belongs to a kind whose members are essentially such as to have their matter arranged cat-wise. Again, then, we have an empirical basis for MP-beliefs. Moreover, in the present case the relevant proper function phenomena are plausibly thought to be internal. Whether the putative parts of the cat are supposed to function in a way that contributes to the maintenance of the feline arrangement of the matter now occupying R_{cat} seems wholly independent of whether the alleged cat and its parts are accompanied by other contingent beings. But if this is right, then we seem to have empirical grounds for believing that wherever we find matter arranged cat-wise, we find a material object that is intrinsically necessarily such as to have its matter arranged cat-wise. In other words, we have an empirical basis for at least one IMP-belief; and so we have a solution to the Discovery Problem.

Even if it is successful, however, this solution has an important limitation. It is pretty clearly suited to explain how we might be justified in our IMP-beliefs involving biological organisms; but it does not at all seem to explain how we might be justified in IMP-beliefs involving nonliving natural objects like rocks, planets, water molecules, atoms, and the like. The reason is that neither planets nor water molecules nor any of their respective parts seem to have proper functions. Furthermore, since the proper function phenomena associated with artifacts are not internal, the solution also does not explain how we might have IMP-beliefs involving artifacts. Thus, at best, it seems to provide the naturalist only with a way of admitting living organisms into her ontology. It seems not to offer the resources for countenancing the wide variety of nonliving objects in which many of us believe.

There is a genuine concern here, but I do not think it is decisive. For one thing, some philosophers are content with an ontology that includes only living organisms and simples.[1] But even for those of us who like our rocks and cars and want to give them official ontological status, there may be a way for the view described above to provide what we want. Suppose one thinks (with Aristotle, for example) that living organisms are *paradigmatic* examples of material objects, and that our beliefs about proper function do indeed ground our beliefs in those paradigmatic items. One might then go on to argue that our beliefs in other things (like rocks, atoms, tables, and cars) are justified either by analogical extension or by their role in scientific theories. I will argue in the next chapter that the role of talk about such objects

---

[1] See e.g. Merricks (2001) and van Inwagen (1990).

in scientific theories is not sufficient on its own to justify belief in their existence or in material objects generally. But it is quite plausible to think that once we have already become justified in believing in some material objects by way of our beliefs about proper function, there is no longer any obstacle to believing in the many other sorts of objects that are talked about in our scientific theories. On this view, our beliefs about proper function give us reason to abandon an antirealist ontology in general; and once that is abandoned, it becomes legitimate to take all of our apparent talk about material objects at its face value.

So an appeal to proper function offers at least some initial promise as a way of solving the Discovery Problem. Indeed, it even offers promise as a way of solving a variety of other problems. The ordinary notion of proper function (the notion with which I am operating here) is an evaluative notion. To say that something has a proper function is, in ordinary parlance, to say that there is some function that it is absolutely *supposed to* perform—where the phrase 'supposed to' is taken in a way that implies that it would somehow be objectively bad, or wrong, or inappropriate if the thing in question did not perform its proper function. But that makes proper function precisely the sort of property that could ground attributions of moral and aesthetic properties. For example, we might say (following Plato and Aristotle) that morally wrong actions are those which in some sense manifest or contribute to the malfunctioning of human beings. And we might say that beautiful things are those which a properly functioning human being would aesthetically appreciate to some degree or other. To the extent that such claims (or suitably nuanced versions of them) might be plausible, and to the extent that proper function phenomena are in fact empirically detectable, we would then be well on our way toward a naturalistic ethics and aesthetics. But success depends on proper functions being empirically detectable; and here is where the appeal to proper function falls short.

In what follows I will argue that, except in the case of objects that are the products of design, proper functions are not empirically detectable. To be sure, various empirical phenomena may be *characterized* by us as proper function phenomena; but, so I will argue, whether some matter is objectively supposed to be arranged in a certain way, or whether putative parts of an alleged object are objectively supposed to function in the way that they function, is never an empirical matter. In making this argument, I will assume, for ease of exposition, the familiar common-sense ontology of mind-independent composite material objects. So, instead of continuing to talk about regions that apparently contain objects, I will just talk about objects; instead of continuing to talk about proper function phenomena, I will talk about proper functions; and so on. (I could make the argument without this assumption; but doing so would greatly increase complexity without significantly enhancing clarity or precision.) I will also focus my attention on *biological* proper functions. Biological organisms are the most likely candidates for being objects whose parts have *natural* (designer-independent) proper functions. Thus, my main goal will be to show that none of the available suggestions about what might make a function a *proper* function are compatible with the idea that biological proper functions are both natural and empirically discoverable. There is no reason to think that objects other than biological organisms have natural proper functions if biological organisms do not; and there is no reason to think that there are promising accounts of what might make a function a proper function that are not already available in the literature. Thus, I take it that by showing that natural biological proper functions are not empirically detectable, I will have done enough to establish the more general conclusion that internal proper function phenomena are not empirically detectable. Before presenting my argument, however, I must make some preliminary remarks about terminology.

1. Preliminaries

Almost everyone writing on functions agrees that function ascriptions are system-relative. In other words, statements of the form 'x has the function of doing φ' are always elliptical for statements of the form 'in system s, x has the function of doing φ'. The same is true for ascriptions of proper function. However, matters are complicated by the fact that sometimes we speak of whole systems (e.g. cats or cars) as functioning properly without meaning to imply that there is some larger system of which they are parts and relative to which they have some specific function they are supposed to perform. Thus, what we must keep in mind is that there are two very different things we might mean when we say that something is functioning properly. On the one hand, we might mean that the thing has a system-relative proper function which it is in fact performing. On the other hand, we might simply mean that it is healthy (or, for artifacts, in a state relevantly analogous to health), whether or not it has a function within some larger system. Toward keeping these notions of proper function separate, then, I will say that something has a *proper system function* just in case there is some way of functioning that counts as proper functioning (or health or a relevant analog of health) for that system, and I will say that something has a *proper function* or a *proper part function* just in case it has a function that it is supposed to perform within some larger system.

With this distinction in mind, we may now clarify the central question of this chapter. The question on which I intend to focus is *not* the question whether naturalists can believe that anything has a natural proper *system* function, but rather the question whether anything has a natural proper *part* function. Both questions are relevant, of course. But I focus on the latter because it would be redundant to discuss both, and most of the literature that talks specifically about 'proper function' is concerned with proper part function rather than proper system function.[2] For my purposes, a part of a thing has a proper part function just in case (*a*) it has a function, and (*b*) one of its functions is metaphysically privileged— i.e. the part is objectively *supposed* to have that function, or it abso- lutely *must* have that function, or its having that function contributes in some way to the Good (construed as absolute and objective), or something else in this vein. What I will ultimately argue is that whether or not a biological object satisfies condition (*b*) is not discoverable via empirical investigation.

2. Why Natural Biological Proper Functions are not Empirically Detectable

I will take it for granted that empirical investigation can reveal that something has a function. One might doubt this. For example, some philosophers think that an object has a function just in case it contrib- utes to a goal of some system of which it is a part; and some philoso- phers think that a system can be goal-directed only if it has been

---

[2] It would be redundant to discuss both questions because the strategies for giving an account of proper system function are not far different from the strategies for giving an account of proper part function; so the objections to the latter strategies have natural and obvious counterparts in objections to the former, and vice versa.

designed. If both views are correct, then it follows that biological objects have functions only if there is a cosmic designer.[3] But we are assuming that empirical methods cannot reveal the existence of a cosmic designer; hence, it is hard to see how (if this view were correct) those methods could reveal that anything has a function. If empirical investigation cannot reveal that anything has a function, then a fortiori it cannot reveal that anything has a proper function. Hence, I take it that in assuming that empirical science can reveal that some things have functions, I am simply giving the naturalist a running start.

There are various different views about what it is for something to have a function. Though it would certainly be interesting to do so, there is no need to canvass that territory here.[4] All that is important for present purposes is the fact that, no matter what view of functions ultimately turns out to be correct, in the literature on functions there are only three suggestions about what might make it the case that a function of a thing is also its proper function that are compatible with the idea that proper functions are empirically detectable. One suggestion is that statistical normality is what determines proper function. For example, one might think that X has F as its proper function just in case X belongs to a kind whose members (statistically) normally have F as their function. Another suggestion is that the etiology, or causal history, of a thing determines its proper function. On this view, roughly, what makes it the case that X has F as its proper function is the fact that X exists at all or exists where it is *because* it tends (or, better, because things of its type tend, or have tended in relevant circumstances) to do F.[5] The third suggestion is that the proper function of a part of a system is to perform whichever of its functions contributes to the well-being or flourishing of that system. Naturalists will obviously be uneasy with this third suggestion if it turns out that flourishing and well-being are not empirically detectable properties.

---

[3] Nissen (1997) offers a detailed argument for this conclusion.

[4] But see Melander (1997) and Nissen (1997) for comprehensive surveys.

[5] This is in fact a rough summary of Larry Wright's (1973) account of what it is for something to have a *function*. (For counterexamples, see Boorse 1976, Nissen 1997 and Prior 1985.) Nevertheless, many of those following Wright have adopted roughly this sort of view to explain what it is for something to have a *proper function*. In fact, many who write on proper functions make no real distinction between the notions of function and proper function (see e.g. Levin 1997; Maund 2000; Millikan 1989, esp. 293; Neander 1991, esp. 173).

But there is at least one proposal in the literature broadly in accord with this suggestion that seems to satisfy naturalistic scruples.

We should note at the outset that the first two suggestions suffer from the following defect: even if they are correct accounts of what it is to have a proper function, they have the consequence that biological proper function phenomena are not internal. This is a serious shortcoming in the present context. Suppose we attribute modal properties to a cat on the basis of how its matter is apparently supposed to be arranged. Suppose we also think that what makes it the case that the cat's matter is supposed to be arranged in a particular way is the fact that qualitatively similar matter is structured so as to maintain that sort of arrangement, or the fact that the arrangement has a particular ancestry. Then it looks as if our cat will lose all integrity as an object in its own right. Given the basis on which we attribute modal properties to the cat, we will have every reason for thinking that the facts about what it can and cannot survive, the facts about what kind of thing it is, depend importantly upon whether the cat is accompanied by other contingent things that stand to it in various relations of ancestry or comparative similarity. But if the cat's modal properties are extrinsic in this way (and if the modal properties of all other organisms are similarly extrinsic), it follows that biological organisms cannot exist alone—they can exist only in groups.

To see the oddity of this consequence, consider the world as it was (according to the standard evolutionary story) at the dawn of life. The appropriate reactions occur in the prebiotic soup and the first cell is formed. But wait: the cell exists only if it has modal properties, and (on the present view) its modal properties depend importantly upon the proper functions of its parts. But the proper functions of its parts, in turn, depend upon facts about the parts of similar cells (of which there are none) or cells in this cell's causal history (of which, again, there are none). Thus, contrary to initial appearances, our first cell's parts do not have proper functions after all and so the cell itself has no modal properties—in which case there *is* no cell.

I do not know whether this problem is surmountable. The view that modal properties depend on proper functions which, in turn, fail to be internal in one of the ways described above certainly appears to have some odd consequences. Strictly speaking, it is also incompatible with RMO (since RMO requires intrinsic modal properties). On the other hand, it is not a view according to which modal properties or sortal properties are *mind*-dependent. So there may be room for tinkering with the definition of RMO and its rivals in ways that make this sort of view realist enough for the purposes of common-sense ontology. Maybe. But there is no point in pursuing the issue, for all three views about proper function mentioned above suffer from a second problem. The problem is that none of these views provide plausible necessary and sufficient conditions for something's being objectively supposed to perform the function it in fact performs.

2.1. SN-Accounts

Let us begin by considering the suggestion that proper function is to be analyzed in terms of statistical normality. (And let us call accounts that conform to this suggestion 'SN-accounts'.) No one that I am aware of has explicitly proposed an SN-account; but, as Alvin Plantinga notes, this sort of account is 'widely popular in the oral tradition'.[6] Plantinga himself offers several counterexamples, but most of them seem directed against SN-accounts of proper system function rather than against SN-accounts of proper part function. So, for example, he writes:

Most 60-year old carpenters have lost a finger or thumb; it is not the case that those who have not have hands that are not normal and not capable of proper manual function.... Perhaps most male cats have been neutered; it hardly follows that those that haven't are abnormal and can't function properly. The vast majority of sperm don't manage to fertilize an egg; the lucky few that do can't properly be accused of failure to function properly, on the grounds that they do things not done by their colleagues. Most baby turtles never reach adulthood; those that do are not on that account dysfunctional. Obviously you can function properly even if you don't function the way most of your peers do. (Plantinga 1993: 200–1)

I take it that these examples do indeed show that statistical normality can't be the whole story about proper system function (and perhaps that is all they are intended to show). But none *directly* show that it is not the case that a thing X has F as its proper part function just in case X belongs to a kind whose members statistically normally have F as their function. The reason is that none of Plantinga's examples seem to provide us with an X that satisfies the right-hand side of the biconditional. Hands, no doubt, have functions; but it is not at all

---

[6] Plantinga (1993: 199). Plantinga also claims that the analysis is suggested, though not explicitly stated, in Pollock (1987).

obvious that *having a thumb* is among them. Sperm might also have various functions; but, again, we might well doubt that *fertilizing eggs* is among them. As I noted earlier, function ascriptions are system-relative. Thus, to say that sperm have the function of fertilizing eggs is to say that there is some larger system of which the sperm are parts and in which they have the function of fertilizing eggs. But what system might that be? Certainly not the male organism, for sperm do not fertilize eggs in the male organism. But not the female organism either, for sperm are not *parts* of a female. Perhaps there is such a thing as Shakespeare's beast with two backs, and perhaps *that* counts as a system of which sperm are parts and relative to which they have the function of fertilizing eggs. But such a system is not a biological organism, and it is not obvious that there are biological systems other than organisms. Hence, it is not clear that fertilizing eggs can count as a biological function of sperm, and many will doubt that sperm, as biological objects, can have any functions but biological ones. Similar reasoning will strongly suggest that cats and baby turtles lack functions as well.

Still, Plantinga's examples do have indirect bearing on SN-accounts of proper part function. They point out that there is no reason to think that what is statistically normal is metaphysically privileged in any way. Even if most male cats are neutered, it does not follow from this that being neutered is a metaphysically privileged way of existing for a male cat, or that male cats are supposed to be neutered in any deep and interesting sense of 'supposed to'. Similarly, then, it is hard to see why an object's belonging to a kind whose members normally have F as their function should imply that it is, in some metaphysically important sense, *supposed* to have F as its function. The proper function of a human optic nerve is to transmit information to the visual cortex. But this is not because it is statistically normal that it do so. If it became statistically abnormal for optic nerves to transmit information to the visual cortex, then malfunction of the optic nerve would be statistically normal. It would not be the case that optic nerves were no longer supposed to play the role in vision that they in fact play. Furthermore, if it became statistically normal for optic nerves to produce sensations of pleasure that stimulate philosophical creativity, it would not follow from this that producing such sensations is what optic nerves are supposed to do. Thus, SN-accounts of proper function will not do for our purposes.

2.2. Etiological Accounts

Turning now to etiological accounts, we should note first that what initially suggests itself as the most intuitive etiological account of proper function is also most likely to be unacceptable to a naturalist. The analysis I have in mind is this: the (or a) proper function of X is to F just in case X was designed to F. Though this analysis is quite intuitive, it commits naturalists to thinking that there are no biological proper functions.[7] Thus, if a naturalist wants to accept an etiological account and also to believe in natural proper functions, she will be committed to saying that it is some sort of natural etiology that confers proper function. As it turns out, the etiology of this sort that is universally invoked by naturalistic defenders of proper function is reproductive, or evolutionary, etiology. So, whereas no one explicitly defends an SN-account of proper function, almost everyone who explicitly defends a superficially naturalistic account of proper function defends a broadly evolutionary account. I will discuss only one such account—one proposed and defended independently by Karen Neander and Ruth Millikan.[8] This is not the only etiological account of proper function in the literature;[9] but it is the most prominent and the objections to it carry over to the others.

Millikan's 'In Defense of Proper Functions' offers the following brief summary of her account of proper function:

Putting things very roughly, for an item A to have a function F as a 'proper function', it is necessary (and close to sufficient) that one of these two conditions should hold. (1) A originated as a 'reproduction' (to give one example, as a copy, or a copy of a copy) of some prior item or items that, *due* in part to possession of the properties reproduced, have actually performed F in the past, and A exists because (causally historically because) of this or these performances. (2) A originated as the product of some prior device that, given its circumstances, had performance of F as a proper function and that, under those circumstances, normally causes F to be performed by *means* of producing an item like A. Items that fall under condition (2) have 'derived proper functions', functions derived from the devices that produce them. (1989: 288–9)

---

[7] Could a naturalist say that biological objects are designed by the forces of evolution, so that they are *designed* even though there is no *designer*? Some naturalists talk this way (see e.g. Kitcher 1993); but for present purposes I will assume that this way of talking is inappropriate except as metaphor. For argument to the effect that the forces of evolution should not be regarded as designing forces, see Schaffner (1993, ch. 8).

[8] Neander (1983, 1991); Millikan (1984, 1989).

[9] Cf. e.g. Griffiths (1993) and Melander (1997).

As Millikan indicates, this summary does not include all of the subtleties of the full presentation of her view that appears in *Language, Thought, and Other Biological Categories* (1984); but it will suffice for present purposes. Neander's account is quite similar, but more simply stated. She writes (under the assumption that the unit of selection in natural selection is a genotype): 'It is the proper function of an item X of an organism O to do that which items of X's type did to contribute to the inclusive fitness of O's ancestors, and which caused the genotype, of which X is the phenotypic expression, to be selected by natural selection' (1991: 174).

Before turning to objections, it is important to note that both Millikan and Neander deny that their theories are intended to *analyze* the *ordinary* concept of proper function.[10] Millikan eschews analysis altogether, claiming that she is giving a 'theoretical definition' of a 'technical term' that is of interest because of its usefulness in solving certain problems and not because of any relation it bears to ordinary notions of function or purpose.[11] Neander, on the other hand, embraces analysis but (*a*) denies that giving an analysis involves giving necessary and sufficient conditions and (*b*) claims that the concept of proper function that she is analyzing is a technical concept in biology, not our ordinary concept.[12] Despite initial appearances, then, it is doubtful whether either Millikan or Neander means to be giving an account of proper function as it is understood in the present chapter. Thus, the objections I will be raising should not at all be taken as objections to the projects that they intended to engage in. Rather, they should be taken simply as objections to the idea that their accounts of

---

[10] Even noting this, however, does not entirely remove the possibility of being misunderstood. For example, John Post accuses Alvin Plantinga of misreading Millikan; but, ironically, the accusation itself rests on a misreading of Plantinga. Post claims that 'Plantinga ... badly misreads [Millikan] as attempting an analysis, then tries to counter-example accordingly' (1998: 233). In fact, however, it is Post, not Plantinga, who is guilty of poor exegesis. Plantinga never suggests that Millikan is attempting an analysis, and he explicitly acknowledges that 'her project is not as it stands directly relevant to the question at issue: the question whether there is available a naturalistic understanding or analysis of proper function' (Plantinga 1993: 201.) He goes on to say that 'Millikan's account ... is subtle and challenging (and formidably difficult), and it is worth looking to see whether in fact it provides the materials for an adequate or accurate analysis of the notion of proper function' (1993: 202). But, of course, in light of his earlier remarks it is abundantly clear that Plantinga has not made the mistake of thinking that Millikan was *actually attempting* to provide 'the materials for an adequate or accurate analysis of the notion of proper function'.
[11] Millikan (1984: 17; 1989: 289–93).
[12] Neander (1991, esp. 168–73). Against the idea that the concept of proper function is a biological concept, see Boorse (unpublished: 26–34). See also Lewens (2000).

proper function in their sense(s) of the term could serve as adequate accounts of proper function in my sense of the term.

That the Millikan–Neander account will not do as an account of proper function in the ordinary sense can be seen by considering the now familiar example of reproductive clay crystals. In *The Blind Watchmaker* (1996) Richard Dawkins explains how natural selection could operate on a population of clay crystals.[13] He invites us to imagine a kind of clay that improves its own chances of being deposited by damming up streams. The streams form shallow pools which then dry up. The clay dries and is blown away as dust, only to be deposited in other streams. The new crystals reproduce themselves and dam up their respective streams. And the process begins anew. Here we have all of the elements of natural selection: the crystals reproduce, display random variation in the traits they possess, pass on traits to their descendants, and sometimes display traits that are either adaptive or maladaptive. But, of course, no one would want to say that there is any metaphysically important sense in which the crystals are *supposed* to dam up streams.[14] The reproductive history of an item makes no difference with respect to what it is supposed to do.

Granted, crystals are not biological organisms; so strictly speaking, though we do have a counterexample to Millikan's account (construed as an account of proper function in the ordinary sense), we do not have a counterexample to Neander's. Still, the example casts doubt on Neander's account. *If*, as we all want to say, the reproductive history of a population of clay crystals doesn't tell us anything at all about how those crystals are supposed to behave, why should we think that the reproductive history of a population of biological entities tells us anything at all about how those things are supposed to behave? There seems to be no relevant difference between the two cases.

We might put this point another way. Suppose we concede that Neander's view at least provides a materially sufficient condition for a biological object's having a proper function in the ordinary sense. That is, perhaps it is in fact the case that everything that satisfies her account also has a proper function. Still, that doesn't guarantee that her account is adequate, for it doesn't guarantee that there is any metaphysically or epistemologically important connection between

---

[13] Dawkins (1996: 150–4).
[14] Cf. Mark Bedau's discussion of this example in Bedau (1993: 36–42).

the properties by virtue of which something satisfies her account and the properties by virtue of which it counts as having a proper function. Furthermore, there is reason for thinking that in fact there is no important connection between the two sorts of properties. One reason is just the fact that clay crystals can exemplify many of the most important properties (namely, those involved in a natural-selective history) that Neander thinks guarantee proper function without themselves having a proper function.

Another reason for thinking that there is no important connection between reproductive history and proper function is that we can imagine cases where the two diverge. For example, we might imagine a world in which an incompetent demigod creates biological organisms that evolve in ways contrary to its intentions. In such a case, it seems clear that whatever we are inclined to say about what (if anything) counts as proper functioning for such organisms, we will not say that there is an objective, metaphysically privileged sense in which the organisms are supposed to function in the way that they evolved to function. Perhaps we will say that they are supposed to function in the way they were designed to function; or perhaps we will say that in this case there is no such thing as proper function for the organisms in question. But we will not say that the evolutionarily determined way of functioning is the objectively proper way.

Likewise, consider genetically engineered organisms. Will it be the objective, metaphysically privileged, proper function of a structure altered by engineering to display the reproductively established trait, the engineered trait, or neither? If one of the latter two, then there are cases where proper function and reproductive history *do* diverge and we have immediate counterexamples to Neander's view even as an account of *materially* necessary and sufficient conditions for proper function. If the former—if engineering always produces malfunction—then questions arise about what we should say about cases where an engineered trait becomes reproductively established. It seems clear that in such cases we should not say that a genuine malfunction has become a proper function. But if we should not say that, then, again, there are (or could be) cases where reproductive history and proper function diverge.

It should be clear that the problem here is quite general. Natural etiology might guarantee that there is some weak or analogical sense in which a thing is supposed to perform a certain function (and this largely to the extent that it guarantees that there is a weak or analogical sense in which the thing has been 'designed'). But natural etiology alone cannot guarantee that there is any strong, metaphysically privileged sense in which a thing is supposed to do anything. It simply does not follow from the fact that a thing has a certain kind of natural causal history that it is in some metaphysically important sense supposed to do whatever it is that its causal history has determined it to do.

2.3. Aristotelian Accounts

Finally, we turn to accounts according to which (roughly) the proper function of a thing in a system is to perform whichever of its functions appropriately contributes to the well-being or flourishing of the system. Let us call these 'Aristotelian accounts'. Aristotelian accounts are useless to a naturalist unless the property of flourishing is identified with, reduced to, or otherwise intimately connected with properties detectable by scientific methods. But the prospects for providing a naturalistic account of flourishing that could also support the sort of robustly normative notion of proper function under consideration here look dim.

The most fully developed and naturalistically respectable Aristotelian proposal in the literature appears in Robert Koons's *Realism Regained* (2000b).[15] There, Koons offers the following definition of 'proper function':

Aristotelian Definition of Proper Function: A state φ has the proper function ψ in kind υ if and only if (i) the fact that things in kind υ have state φ is causally explained (at least in part) by the existence of a causal law linking (φ & υ) to ψ as cause to effect; (ii) the system of functions (φ_i, ψ_i) meeting condition (i) for υ forms a mostly harmonious, mutually supportive whole, and the (φ, ψ) function contributes to this harmony; and (iii) the existence of things of kind υ is causally explained (at least in part) by the harmony mentioned in condition (ii). (Koons 2000b: 145)

Koons labels condition (i) 'Wright's Condition' because it is equivalent to the condition that Wright takes to be necessary and sufficient for φ's having the *function* of doing ψ in kind υ. Furthermore, he suggests that the well-being of a thing might plausibly be identified

---

[15] But see also Koons (1998). Others who defend broadly Aristotelian, or value-centered, accounts of function or proper function include Bedau (1992, 1993), Maund (2000), and Woodfield (1976). But, insofar as they all make some appeal to a primitive notion of goodness, none of these accounts would be acceptable from a naturalistic point of view.

with the nonaccidental harmonious and mutually supportive inter-action of the Wright-functions of the thing's parts (2000*b*: 144–5). Condition (ii) imposes the requirement of harmony and mutual sup-port; and condition (iii) imposes the nonaccidentality requirement. Koons also offers an account of harmony, but I will omit that here for the sake of brevity. For present purposes, our own pretheoretical understanding of that concept will suffice.

One advantage of Koons's definition is that it incorporates many of the causal–historical elements of standard etiological accounts while at the same time remaining immune to some familiar counterexam-ples. For instance, Alvin Plantinga has argued against Neander-style etiological accounts on the grounds that serious malfunctions can, pretty clearly, become reproductively established as a result of genetic engineering. For example, evil engineers might arrange for the visual apparatus of a population to produce nothing but searing pain and a uniformly blue visual field; but even if this trait became reproduc-tively established over time, it would not follow that displaying the trait was a sign of proper function (Plantinga 1993: 204). True enough; and Koons's definition, unlike Millikan's and Neander's, is able to accommodate this intuition. Though the gene responsible for the trait does indeed have a Wright-function, Koons says, this func-tion is not a contributing member of a harmonious and mutually supportive system of such functions (2000*b*: 144). Thus, the gene does not have the proper function of producing the trait.

But other counterexamples are not so easily dealt with. Consider Dawkins's clay crystals. These crystals exist where they are in part *because* they dam up streams. Thus, they apparently have the Wright-function of damming up streams. At any rate, they do if they are plausibly thought to be parts of a containing system—say, an ecosys-tem.[16] Koons's definition does not rule out the possibility that things might have proper functions relative to an ecosystem. Moreover, it is not implausible to think that the Wright-function of damming up

---

[16] If having a Wright function is treated as equivalent to satisfying Koons's condition (i), then it will probably be hard to show that clay crystals have the Wright function of damming up streams. But it will be equally hard to show that (say) hearts have the Wright function of pumping blood. What will be easiest to show is that the property *being a system that contains crystals of kind C* (or: *being an organism that contains a heart*) has the Wright function of *being a system some of whose streams are dammed up* (or: *being an organism whose blood is pumped*). But it seems absurd to cast the discussion in these terms for the sake of technical precision; and doing so will, in any case, have no substantive effect on the outcome. So, for now, I will ignore this complication.

streams contributes to the overall well-being (as defined by Koons) of ecosystems of the relevant sort. That is, it is not implausible to think that the crystals' function of damming up streams is a contributing member of a nonaccidentally harmonious and mutually supportive network of similar Wright-functions performed by other parts of the same ecosystem. But if that is right, then clay crystals have the proper function of damming up streams.

Likewise, lower organisms in a food chain are plausibly thought to owe their existence in part to the fact that they themselves serve as food for organisms higher in the chain. For example, in a marine ecosystem, zooplankton feed on phytoplankton and, in turn, serve as food for larger fish which are ultimately converted into nutrients that support phytoplankton. Thus, there is a clear sense in which zoo-plankton owe their existence in a marine ecosystem in part to the fact that they serve as food for larger fish. Thus, zooplankton apparently have the Wright-function of feeding larger fish. Furthermore, it is quite plausible to think that this Wright-function is a contributing member of a mutually supportive harmonious system of similar Wright-functions performed by other parts of the same ecosystem, and that the relevant harmony partly causally explains the existence of ecosystems of that sort. But then it follows that zooplankton have as their proper function the property of being food for higher organisms.

It is not obvious to me that Koons will be discontent with these consequences. He admits, for example, that 'seeds serve the purpose of feeding [birds]' and that 'the fat of [a] mouse serves . . . the extrinsic function of providing nutrition to [a] cat' (2000b: 142, 152). So perhaps he would be content also to say that the *proper* function of seeds relative to a certain ecosystem is to feed birds and the proper function of mouse fat relative to a certain ecosystem is to contribute to the health of cats. But to say this is, I think, to use the words 'proper function' in a way different from the way in which I intend to be using them here. For it is clearly absurd to say (without reference to a designer) that zooplankton are supposed to feed larger fish, or that clay crystals are supposed to dam up streams, or that mouse fat is supposed to contribute to the nutrition of cats.

So if I am right in thinking that the relevant activities of Dawkins's clay crystals and zooplankton satisfy Koons's Aristotelian definition of proper function, then it looks as if his definition does not provide a sufficient condition for having a proper function in the sense under consideration here. But we should also note that even if I am *not* right, there is still reason to be dissatisfied with the definition. For even if Dawkins's clay crystals do not have the proper function of damming up streams, clearly they *could* have if they were products of intelligent design.[17]

Suppose, contrary to what I have argued, that clay crystals and various elements of food chains do not satisfy the conditions Koons takes to be necessary and sufficient for having a proper function. Still, those things *could* have proper functions if they were the products of design. Clay crystals of a particular sort could be designed for the purpose of damming up streams; and organisms of a particular sort could be designed for the purpose of feeding other organisms. Intuitively, these functions would be *proper* functions—functions that are supposed to be performed—even if the performance of these functions made no contribution whatsoever to the well-being of the relevant ecosystem or food chain. Or consider an artifact whose overall design plan includes a self-destruct mechanism. Plausibly, a self-destruct mechanism is supposed to destroy the artifact of which it is a part—that is its proper function. But, except in contrived cases, self-destruct mechanisms make no contribution whatsoever to the overall well-being of the things of which they are parts. Thus, even if Koons's definition does provide a sufficient condition for having a proper function, it does not provide a necessary condition.

It might be objected that none of my examples thus far go any distance toward showing that Koons's definition (suitably modified) would not do as an account of *biological* proper function. But the examples in the last paragraph are readily modified to establish this conclusion. Organisms could have been designed by some demigod

---

[17] Surprisingly, Koons himself seems willing to concede that intelligent design confers proper function (see, esp. 2000*b*: 147–9). If so, then it is very implausible to attribute to him the view that his Aristotelian definition of proper function captures *the* ordinary sense of the term. Therefore, I do not attribute this view to him. I suspect that the apparent tension is to be resolved by attributing to him the view that the terms 'function' and 'proper function' are ambiguous, admitting of a variety of different, though in some sense appropriate, analyses. (His talk of 'Wright-functions', 'Woodfield-functions', 'etiological-functions', and so on seems to support this reading.) If that is right, then the point of the Aristotelian definition of proper function is not to capture the ordinary sense of the term, and the point is also not to provide a Millikan-style 'theoretical definition'. Rather, the point is to express what Koons takes to be one appropriate way among many of using the term. Be that as it may, the upshot of my criticisms is that the Aristotelian definition will not do as an account of proper function in the sense (which I take to be the ordinary sense) that is under consideration here.

to include a self-destruct mechanism; God could have designed human beings so that, from the very beginning, they displayed the unpleasant characteristics caused by Plantinga's vision-impairing genes; and so on. In such cases, again, there is pressure to attribute proper function even where there is no contribution to overall well-being.

2.4. Concluding Remarks

In light of the foregoing, we seem forced to the conclusion that the methods of science alone cannot reveal that any biological organism has a proper function.[18] Empirical investigation can reveal facts about statistical normality, facts about reproductive history, and facts about the nature and causal histories of harmonious systems of Wright-functions. But, as we have seen, there is no obvious epistemic or metaphysical connection between such facts and facts about proper function. Thus, there is no reason to think that in revealing such facts, empirical investigation reveals facts about biological proper function. Furthermore, there are no naturalistically acceptable alternatives on the horizon—which is just to say that there are no *other* empirically accessible facts that naturalists might reasonably take as indicative of biological proper function.

Naturalists might be tempted to object that all of my counter-examples ultimately rest upon my own intuitive judgments about what are and are not the proper functions of various things; and they might go on to point out that many—especially my opponents—may not share my intuitions. Why *not* say that, if the right sorts of changes occurred in human beings, the proper function of the optic nerve would be to produce pleasure and stimulate philosophical creativity? Why not grant that the proper function of (say) zooplankton is to feed larger fish, or that the proper function of certain kinds of clay crystals is to dam up streams?

In response to these challenges, I admit, I have nothing to offer apart from bare appeals to intuition. But it is important to note that, far from detracting from my overall argument, this admission only makes my position stronger. If natural proper functions really were empirically detectable, then parties on both sides of a dispute about what a biological object is supposed to do should, in principle, be able

---

[18] With the possible exception of genetically engineered organisms, as suggested above.

to provide empirical evidence in favor of their respective views. Perhaps the evidence would not be decisive. But, at the very least, the disputants should have something to offer besides appeals to intuition. In fact, however, we cannot even *imagine* empirical evidence that would resolve such a dispute. So, though I admit that I have nothing further to offer those who do not share my intuitions about natural proper functions, I also think that the fact that I have nothing further to offer (and, likewise, the fact that they have nothing further to offer) just counts as additional evidence in favor of my overall conclusion that *any* theory according to which natural proper functions are empirically detectable is doomed to failure.

3. Conclusion

Natural proper functions are not empirically detectable. Thus, even if the property of having a natural proper function is plausibly explained by the postulation of intrinsic modal properties, this fact is of no help in solving the Discovery Problem. We should also note that the reason why natural proper functions are not empirically detectable is that there is no empirically detectable property (or at least none that has been noticed by philosophers) that is plausibly seen as a 'mark of metaphysical import'—an indication that the matter in a region is, in any sense, objectively supposed to be arranged in some particular way. But if that is right, then, in light of the arguments in this chapter, it is highly doubtful that the Discovery Problem can be solved. For surely if modal properties could reasonably be posited to explain *any* empirically detectable phenomenon, that phenomenon would plausibly be taken to be a mark of metaphysical import. But no empirically detectable phenomenon seems to fit the bill.

Still, one might think that some empirically detectable phenomenon counts as a mark of metaphysical import not necessarily in its own right but perhaps in light of certain realist background assumptions. And perhaps the realist background assumptions could be justified on the basis of their pragmatic utility in simplifying or otherwise enhancing our scientific theorizing. It is this suggestion that will be considered in some detail in the next chapter.

6

Pragmatic Arguments

A COMMON strategy for defending realism about various kinds of problematic objects is to argue that belief in or talk about such objects is *indispensable* for science. For those not concerned about preserving RMO, this strategy would also be promising in the case of our MP-beliefs. No doubt it *would* be impossible to engage in scientific theorizing as we know it without presupposing the existence of material objects; and, as we have seen, belief in material objects carries a commitment to modal properties. Thus, one might argue that our particular MP-beliefs are justified on the grounds that we *have to* form some MP-beliefs or other, and the ones we in fact form have allowed us to formulate a wide variety of very successful scientific theories.

The trouble, however, is that what the defender of RMO needs but cannot get out of this line of argument is some reason for thinking that IMP-beliefs—MP-beliefs attributing *intrinsic* modal properties—are somehow indispensable for science. Even if it is true that we cannot engage in scientific theorizing without forming some MP-beliefs or other, the obvious fact is that we *can* engage in such theorizing without attributing intrinsic modal properties to the objects we classify. Material objects do not have to be regarded as mind-independent in order for science to proceed. Nobody worries that if the antirealists win the day, science will grind to a halt. And even if we agree (as seems reasonable) that theories that quantify over familiar material objects like cells or atoms are in some sense committed to the existence of such things, there is no reason to think that simply by quantifying over such things a theory is committed to any philosophical thesis about what those things are. In particular, no scientific theory is committed by virtue of quantifying over *x*s (for any *x*s) to the philosophical thesis that *x*s have intrinsic modal properties.

Some philosophers (myself included) think that it is incoherent to believe that idealism is false but that no intrinsic modal properties are exemplified in (or by) the external world. But even though this might provide us with a consistency argument for the general claim that *there are* intrinsic modal properties, it does not solve the Discovery Problem since it does not provide us with any reason for thinking that we can *detect* particular modal properties. It provides no grounds for IMP-beliefs, and hence no reason for thinking that material objects exemplify intrinsic modal properties. So, strictly speaking, indispensability arguments on their own offer no comfort to those who wish to solve the Discovery Problem.

But where indispensability arguments fail, somewhat weaker pragmatic arguments might succeed. One might press the point that, though science *could* proceed without the assumption that the objects quantified over in scientific theories have intrinsic modal properties, it would be very *difficult* for it to do so. Perhaps it is easier or more natural for human beings to think about the world as if it were a world that contains material objects with intrinsic modal properties than to think otherwise. If that is right, then doing away with the presupposition may be extraordinarily difficult, if not practically impossible, and the belief that there are material objects with intrinsic modal properties might then acquire the status of a pragmatically justified background assumption.

Still, this does not yet tell us how, if at all, our *particular IMP-beliefs* are supposed to simplify or otherwise pragmatically enhance our theorizing. Consider, for example, a case where we judge that a region contains something with the intrinsic modal properties of an oak tree rather than a heap of cellulose molecules, or a case where we judge that a region contains something with the intrinsic modal properties of a human being rather than a lump of microparticles. We may grant for the moment that our theorizing about these regions is simplified by our supposing that the regions in question are filled by *some* material objects or other that have intrinsic modal properties. It is much easier to formulate theories in terms of human beings, trees, lumps, or atoms than it is to formulate them in terms of matter arranged tree-wise, human-wise, lump-wise, or atom-wise. But how does it simplify our theorizing to make the particular MP-judgments we make—namely, that the objects occupying these regions are objects with the essential properties normally associated with oak trees and human beings (respectively) rather than objects with the essential properties normally associated with mere heaps, lumps, or collections? Initially, it would seem that such judgments do not simplify our theorizing. We could do just as well by supposing that *nothing* has the essential properties normally associated with human beings or oak trees—that wherever we seem to find such things, really there are only lumps of tissue or collections of microparticles contingently displaying a humanoid or arboreal organizational structure. But if that is right, then we do not have a pragmatic solution to the Discovery Problem after all.

As one might expect, there is much more to be said here. What we have so far is a pragmatic argument for engaging in the general practice of forming IMP-beliefs. What we are still looking for, however, is some explanation of how we could be justified in making the *particular* MP-judgments we make. In a series of recent articles defending various kinds of realism (realism about necessity, realism about culturally generated kinds, and realism about various kinds of 'medium-sized' objects), Crawford Elder defends a story that fills in some of these missing details.[1] In the next section I will present this story and then summarize the total solution to the Discovery Problem that emerges once it is conjoined with the considerations I have just presented. Subsequent sections will show why this solution, and pragmatic solutions in general, are inadequate.

1. Aristotelian Essences and Essential Properties

Very roughly, Elder's view is that Aristotelian essences (as defined in Chapter 4) are indeed empirically detectable for some kinds, and that there is good reason for thinking that the property of having a particular Aristotelian essence is always an essential property of its bearer (in the sense of being the sort of property that an object cannot fail to have if it exists at all). Elder does not express his view in quite this way, however; and the view is developed over a series of articles which address a variety of different questions. Thus, a bit of textual support is in order.

According to Elder, objects are to be sorted into kinds on the basis of their microstructural properties (properties like *being H_2O* or *being jadeite*) or on the basis of their proper functions (understood

---

[1] See Elder (1989, 1992, 1995, 1996a). Of relevance also are Elder (1994, 1996b).

in Millikan's technical sense, as described in Chapter 5 above). Thus, he writes:

Jade is actually two different minerals, namely jadeite and nephrite. These are alike in respect of several of their superficial properties, but have quite different microstructures. Now, the question is, is jade a single natural kind—a single kind of substance which, in some samples, has one microstructure, and in others another? Or is jadeite a different natural kind—a different kind of substance—from nephrite? Perhaps most philosophers, in this post-Kripkean era, will find that their intuitions incline them toward the latter answer. In any case, there appear to be good reasons for preferring it. For one thing, it seems that uniformities observed to hold true of jadeite cannot warrantedly be projected for nephrite.... Moreover, it is likely that jadeite will prove to have, by nature, yet other features which nephrite has only sometimes or not at all.

As microstructure is to kinds of substance, so history is to kinds of copied device. Suppose male sticklebacks on Twin Earth develop a dance indistinguishable...from the mating dance male sticklebacks perform here on Earth—but suppose the dance gets established in their behavioral repertoire just because it has historically served, often enough, to mesmerize tasty flies. Should we say that 'one and the same biological device'...has arisen in the two populations? Or that different, though superficially similar, devices have arisen? The local 'mating dance' has a history of having been performed, at least often enough, in the presence of female sticklebacks genetically disposed to respond with eggs...but the same pattern cannot warrantedly, nor even accurately, be predicted to show up in the case of the Twin Earth stickleback dances.... H_2O is a single natural kind. Jade is not; it is the union of two different natural kinds, and to each of them, a particular microstructure is essential. Stickleback dances, if developed here and on Twin Earth because of different historical successes, likewise belong to two different natural kinds. In general, to each natural kind of copied device, a particular proper function is essential, and so is an historically proper placement. (Elder 1996*a*: 195–6, 198)

The point being emphasized here and elsewhere in the article is that microstructural properties and Millikan-style proper functions lawfully explain many of the superficial features of the objects that have them. Moreover, Elder seems pretty clearly to think that these features of objects not only are the basis on which they are sorted into kinds, but also provide necessary and sufficient conditions for kind membership. Thus, they qualify as Aristotelian essences; for, as we saw in Chapter 4, Aristotelian essences are sets of properties that provide (*a*) necessary and sufficient conditions for kind membership, and (*b*) lawful explanations for other interesting superficial features of the objects that have them.

So, on Elder's view, objects are sorted into kinds on the basis of their Aristotelian essences;[2] and since these essences are just micro-structures or particular kinds of causal histories, they are readily empirically detectable. But how does Elder get to the conclusion that Aristotelian essences are essential to the objects that have them? How do we move, solely on the basis of empirical evidence, from the premise that (for example) there is an H_2O molecule in a region of spacetime to the conclusion that there is something that is *essentially* an H_2O molecule (rather than something that is contingently an H_2O molecule but essentially a collection of subatomic particles) in the region? Elder clearly thinks that this conclusion is true. But in the work just cited, I see no answer to the question how one arrives at the conclusion that Aristotelian essences are essential.

However, in other work Elder does offer an answer. In defending realism about necessity, Elder argues that the empirical indicator of the fact that a property P is essential to things belonging to a kind F is the fact that objects of kinds closely related to F (e.g. kinds belonging to a common genus with F) uniformly have some competitor of P. He writes: 'What suggests that gold essentially has a melting point of 1063°C is that each of the other metals itself uniformly possesses just one competing melting point; what suggests the scientific claim that water is essentially H_2O is that various acids and bases, which science treats as substances generically similar to water, uniformly possess their own alternative chemical structures'. (Elder 1992: 325). Of course, this view all by itself does not tell us anything about how we manage reliably to identify the *relevant* competing kinds. For

---

[2] In other work (Rea 2000c) I have distinguished between two ways of belonging to kinds. An object belongs to a kind in the nominal way just in case it displays the superficial features distinctive of members of that kind; it belongs to a kind in the *classificatory* way just in case terms referring to that kind are metaphysically better answers to the question 'What is that thing?' than terms referring to any other kind. Here and elsewhere (unless otherwise noted) when I talk about things being 'sorted into kinds', I have in mind classificatory sorting and not merely nominal sorting. Similarly, unless otherwise noted, I will take it for granted that *classification* is a process of trying to sort objects into kinds in a way that reflects the metaphysically best answers to the 'What is it?' question for those things. This is not to say that the process presupposes that there is a uniquely best classificatory scheme. But, as I am understanding it, it does presuppose that some are better than others from a metaphysical point of view. Sorting objects without attention to the metaphysically best answers to the 'What is it?' question is, in my terminology, not classification but merely nominal sorting.

example, it does not tell us how we know that the competing kinds with gold are other *metal* kinds rather than other *lump* kinds (like lump of clay, lump of flesh, lump of pizza dough, and so on). But presumably we can settle such issues by an appeal to Aristotelian essences as outlined above.

Thus, what emerges from Elder's work is a view according to which uniform clustering of explanatorily rich properties—itself a straight-forwardly empirically detectable fact—not only provides a basis for sorting objects into natural kinds but also constitutes a mark of metaphysical import. The fact that these sorts of properties cluster in the ways that they do is explainable (and, presumably, best ex-plained) by supposing that the matter exemplifying the properties in question composes an object which has those properties essentially. If this view is right, then it is easy to see how we might have empirical grounds for particular MP-beliefs. We observe that a certain way of arranging matter uniformly exemplifies certain explanatorily rich properties, and so we infer (as a kind of inference to the best explan-ation) that wherever we find matter arranged in the way in question, we find an object that is essentially such as to exemplify the relevant explanatory properties. Nothing so far provides a basis for thinking that the essential properties of the objects we identify are intrinsic; but this lack is made up for by the pragmatic considerations outlined at the beginning of the present chapter.

This last point bears emphasizing. Elder's view *presupposes* rather than justifies our belief that the objects of scientific investigation are material objects with intrinsic modal properties. This is not necessar-ily a defect; but it is important for us to observe in the present context lest anyone think that Elder's view might be able to stand alone, apart from the pragmatic arguments mentioned earlier, as a solution to the Discovery Problem. Consider, for example, the case of a gold atom. On Elder's view, the fact that gold's microstructure explains its super-ficial properties, and the fact that objects sorted into competing kinds on the basis of their microstructural properties uniformly possess different superficial features, is evidence of two things: first, that gold atoms are to be classified as such (that 'gold' is the metaphysically best answer to the 'What is it?' question for a gold atom) and, second, that they have essentially the properties lawfully entailed by the possession of their microstructural properties. But why should we accept this view? Elder has given us an a priori argument (based, presumably, on something like conceptual analysis) for the conclusion that *if* a region containing matter arranged gold-atom-wise contains a material object with empirically detectable intrinsic modal properties, then those properties can be detected in the ways that he describes. But there is nothing in Elder's work to explain why we are justified in making the realist starting assumption. The fact that some of the properties exemplified in a region are explanatorily richer than others and are uniformly clustered together in a way that mirrors the uniform clustering of 'competing' sets of properties is no reason all by itself for thinking that there is a material object in the region that has any of those properties essentially. One might just as easily suppose that the phenomena Elder describes occur simply because of relations (necessary or contingent) among the properties involved and not at all because those properties are exemplified by material things that have any of them essentially. In other words, the phenomena that on Elder's view undergird our MP-judgments might just as easily occur in a world devoid of material objects and mind-independent modal properties; and there is nothing in Elder's work to explain how we might justifiably believe that our world is not devoid of such things. Again, as far as Elder's own projects are concerned, this is probably not a serious worry. But it does show that Elder's view cannot stand alone as a solution to the Discovery Problem.

I should note that I do not endorse, as a general rule, the principle that whenever our evidence is compatible with two conflicting possibilities, we cannot know which of the two conflicting possibilities is actual. Down this road lies skepticism. But there are really only two ways of avoiding it. One way is to say that the gap left by the empirical evidence is bridged by our rational intuitions; but this is not the way of naturalism. The other way is to say that the gap is bridged by pragmatic considerations; and this is precisely the sort of bridge that I have been arguing that Elder's view needs if it is going to provide the foundation for a solution to the Discovery Problem.

What I have described in this section, then, is a twofold solution to the Discovery Problem. According to this solution, our practice of forming IMP-beliefs is justified on pragmatic grounds, and the empirical cues that guide the formation of those beliefs are those that Elder has described. Furthermore, we are justified in taking the empirical cues as reliable because, *given* the (pragmatically justified) assumption that RMO is true and that some IMP-propositions or other must be true, the story that Elder tells is indeed the best explanation for the phenomena that supposedly guide our judgments. In the next section I will raise some concerns about Elder's contribution to the solution. In subsequent sections I will raise concerns about the pragmatic component.[3]

2. Concerns about Elder's View

Let us assume for the moment that the pragmatic component of the solution is wholly unproblematic. Still, it is not at all clear that the solution just described can give us what we really want. For one thing, there is reason to doubt that it can support realism about individual organisms (which, presumably, is what proponents of RMO are, by and large, most interested in saving). Furthermore, there is reason to doubt that the solution is really as naturalistic at its core as it purports to be on its surface.

Before turning to these objections, however, there is one natural objection to Elder's view that I would like to set aside. One might object on the grounds that, in some cases, it seems that we can classify objects *without* knowing what properties best explain their behavior. For example, one might think that people knew that a region containing matter arranged water-wise contained something classifiable as a body of water before they knew that water was H_2O and hence before they knew that the exemplification of the property *being H_2O* was what best explained the behavior of the matter in such regions. But this objection is misguided. Notice that, prior to knowing what it was to be water, either people knew that the property of being water best explained the behavior of the matter in regions occupied by bodies of water or they did not. If they did, then they did know what property best explained the behavior of those bodies; they just did not know exactly what was involved in exemplifying that property. On the other hand, if they did not know that the property of

---

[3] Recall that I am here ignoring the fact that there are no precise distinctions to be drawn between pragmatic arguments on the one hand and inferences to the best explanation on the other. Most would agree that pragmatic criteria play a large role in determining what counts as the 'best' explanation for a given phenomenon. Thus, it is misleading (though very convenient) to talk as if 'Elder's contribution' can be neatly separated from the 'pragmatic component' of the solution. Note too that, insofar as pragmatic criteria do enter into the process of inference to the best explanation, my arguments later against the epistemic value of pragmatic arguments will count against the epistemic value of inference to the best explanation as well.

being water best explained the behavior of the matter in the regions occupied by bodies of water, it is not at all clear how they could possibly have known that bodies of water were indeed to be classified as such. Suppose things had turned out this way: the property *being a clear liquid* is the salient explanatory property in all regions occupied by bodies of water (as well as in regions occupied by bodies of other clear liquids like 7–Up and vodka), and 'clear liquid' refers to a natural kind whereas 'water' does not. If things had turned out this way, bodies of water would not have been classifiable as such. Rather, it seems, bodies of water, bodies of 7–Up, bodies of vodka, and the like would all have been classifiable as bodies of clear liquid.

A more serious objection to the solution described above is that, as Elder himself admits, though his view may support realism about biological organs (like hearts) and various kinds of artifacts, it is not clear that it will be able to support realism about individual organisms. The reason is that there seems to be no basis for believing that individual organisms have Aristotelian essences. This is a familiar point, standardly supported by appeal to the fact that biological species (the most obvious candidates for being biological natural kinds) are not definable in terms of necessary and sufficient conditions.[4] Thus, Elder writes:

On the current view, genetic accidents and mutations will ensure that any features confined to one biological species will be absent from at least some members of that species, and the only features shared by all the members will also be found outside the species. The problems posed by intra-specific genetic variation cannot, it is widely held, be removed even by confining attention to 'healthy' or 'normal' members of a species. (1996*a*: 200)[5]

The implication, then, is that there is no empirical basis for sorting individual organisms into groups whose members *uniformly* possess some distinctive set of properties. Indeed, he says, even the kind *individual organism* is biologically suspect.

. . . just what properties is it that every individual organism is bound to have, and that nothing that is not an individual organism can have? Perhaps one is willing to defy speculations about strange forms which life might take in distant galaxies and maintain (for example) that any organism is bound to

---

[4] See e.g. Dupré (1993), Sober (1980, 1993), and Hull (1965).
[5] In personal correspondence Elder reports that he has since abandoned the view expressed here. But, as I will argue below, it is doubtful that abandoning the view will help to preserve realism about individual organisms.

contain amino acids. Even so, one must tell a careful story about what 'containing' amino acids amounts to, since in one perfectly ordinary sense, test tubes can contain amino acids. The chief obstacle here is that there seems to be no one sort of functional organization which is mandatory for absolutely every individual organism. (1996*a*: 200)

If this is right, then Elder's criterion for detecting essential properties cannot be applied to living organisms. Hence, on the assumption that his criterion gives the correct account of how we detect essential properties in material objects, the implication is that we cannot detect any essential properties in individual organisms.

Note also that it will not help matters to drop the assumption that natural kinds are defined by sets of properties that provide necessary and sufficient conditions for kind membership. Suppose we say that biological kinds are definable in terms of properties shared by 'typical' members, or by way of indefinite disjunctions of conjunctions of properties as described in Chapter 4. In adopting one of these views, we preserve realism about biological kinds, but we lose any basis for saying that the properties in question are essential to the objects that have them. The reason is that, on these views about kinds, for any property P in terms of which a kind K is defined, an object can belong to K without possessing P; so there is no reason to think that the members of K who do possess P possess it essentially. Similarly, we also lose any basis for saying that kind membership is essential. For if we have no basis for thinking that any of the properties in terms of which a kind is defined are essential to the things that have them, it is hard to see how we could have any reason for thinking that membership in the kind is essential. Of course, this is not to say that objects *must* have Aristotelian essences in order to have essential properties. But it is to say that the story that Elder tells about how we detect particular modal properties empirically offers no way of explaining how we could detect the essential properties of objects that lack Aristotelian essences.

But by not offering any way of detecting the essential properties of individual organisms, Elder's view fails to offer any support to realism about individual organisms. As I have said, Elder himself acknowledges this implication and (in his 1996*a* paper, anyway) seems content with it. But it is not clear that a naturalist should be any more content with this sort of ontology than with an ontology that rejects RMO altogether. After all, what good is it to have material objects in one's ontology if one cannot have the objects we most care about—namely, human beings?

One might also object to Elder's view on the grounds that it takes for granted the claim that there is no distinction to be made between what is metaphysically necessary and what is necessary simply as a matter of natural law. For example, Elder's criterion for essentiality has the implication that the melting point of gold is essential to it; but one might think that, had the laws of nature been different, gold might have had a different melting point. Of course, there is controversy over the question whether the laws could have been different. Some philosophers believe that nomological necessity is equivalent to metaphysical necessity; others do not.[6] I have nothing to add to this debate. But the question that seems worth pressing in the present context is the question of how one could possibly *know* whether nomological necessity is equivalent to metaphysical necessity. Elder's view, as I have said, presupposes that it is; but how is the presupposition justified? In 'Laws, Natures, and Contingent Necessities' (1994), Elder argues that we should believe that nomological necessity and metaphysical necessity are equivalent because (*a*) we cannot give a clear and consistent account of a genuine necessity weaker than metaphysical necessity, and so (*b*) we have reason not to assign evidential weight to the intuitions that suggest that nomological and metaphysical necessity might diverge. But what justifies the supposition that nomological necessity is a 'genuine' form of necessity at all? Why think it is anything other than brute regularity? As far as I know, the only arguments available for the conclusion that there is any such thing as nomological necessity appeal either to intuitions or to pragmatic considerations. There is no straightforwardly empirical evidence for the conclusion.[7] But appeals to intuition are not the way of naturalism, and pragmatic arguments will fall prey to the criticisms below.

3. Pragmatic versus Epistemic Justification

The most obvious objection to the foregoing defense of our practice of forming IMP-beliefs is that the fact that it is in our best interests

---

[6] Others besides Elder who believe that metaphysical and nomological necessity coincide include Shoemaker (1980*a*, *b*) and Swoyer (1982). Against this view, see e.g. Armstrong (1983, ch. 11).

[7] Cf. van Fraassen (1989), which argues in detail along these lines for the conclusion that the notions of natural law and nomological necessity ought to be discarded.

(theoretically speaking) to engage in those practices is no reason for thinking that the beliefs involved in those practices are true. So, in effect, the pragmatic defense solves the Discovery Problem only by misconstruing it. The problem is to figure out how we could be *epistemically* justified in forming IMP-beliefs. But the solution shows, at best, only how we could be *pragmatically* justified in doing so.

I endorse this objection. However, two features of it deserve extended comment, and an apparently obvious reply must be laid to rest. First, the objection suggests that the pragmatic arguments given in Section 1 might not even succeed in showing that we are *pragmatically* justified in forming IMP-beliefs. I will explain why this is so in Section 3.1. Second, the objection presupposes that pragmatic justification is not sufficient for epistemic justification. This presupposition seems to me to be true. However, some philosophers will be tempted to question it. In Section 3.2, I will explain why naturalists at any rate should resist the temptation. Third, one might think that the obvious reply to the objection is that naturalists do not need to justify the epistemic value of pragmatic arguments because pragmatic arguments are integral to scientific reasoning, and naturalists treat scientific reasoning as a basic source of evidence. In Section 3.3, I will show why making this reply only helps my argument for the conclusion that naturalists are committed to rejecting RMO.

3.1. The Limits of Pragmatic Arguments

In order to see why the pragmatic arguments described in Section 1 do not even provide pragmatic justification for our IMP-beliefs, we must first examine the distinction between pragmatic and epistemic justification and some of the examples that motivate the distinction.

The distinction between pragmatic and epistemic justification is of a piece with the distinction between pragmatic and epistemic rationality. The latter distinction is that between what it is rational to do given the goal of furthering one's overall best interests and what it is rational to believe in light of one's evidence given the goal of believing in accord with the truth. In both cases rationality is understood as a matter of adopting strategies of action or belief formation that are appropriate or reliable means of achieving one's goals. Accordingly, the distinction between pragmatic and epistemic justification may be characterized simply as the distinction between what is permissible or fitting from the point of view of pragmatic rationality and what

is permissible or fitting from the point of view of epistemic rationality.[8]

The motivation for drawing the distinction between pragmatic and
epistemic rationality typically comes from cases where believing in
the way best suited to arriving at the truth seems to be inconsistent
with furthering one's overall best interests. In such cases it is very
tempting to say that believing in accord with one's best interests is a
rational thing to do, all things considered, *despite* the fact that it is not
rational to do from the point of view of trying to reach the truth.
Below is a representative sample of examples from the literature that
are designed both to illustrate and to motivate the distinction:

Ed and Edna

Consider the following not unlikely situation. Ed and Edna have been
devoted partners in marriage and business for the past twenty years. Lately,
however, Ed has acquired strong evidence indicating that Edna is disloyal to
him in both the marriage and the business. For instance, Edna's own parents,
who are trustworthy friends of Ed's, have recently informed Ed of Edna's
privately confessed disloyalty toward her marriage and business relationships
with Ed. In addition, Ed recently has found several very recent love letters
addressed to Edna by an unknown author. Moreover, Ed has just discovered
Edna's hitherto undisclosed involvement in some very dubious business
transactions which violate the ground-rules on which their business partnership was founded. Such evidence, we may plausibly suppose, makes likely to
be true, and so epistemically justifies, for Ed the proposition that Edna is
disloyal in both the marriage and the business. But given the past twenty
years, Ed is heavily dependent upon his marriage and business relationships
with Edna. Indeed, without these relationships, Ed would be psychologically
as well as financially devastated; and Ed painfully realizes this. What's more,
Ed is well aware that his believing that Edna is disloyal would have at least
two undesirable consequences: it would result in the breakup of his marriage
and business partnership with Edna, which in turn would spell his psychological and financial doom, and it would bring him to despise and even to
mistreat Edna. (And it is easily imaginable that Ed's merely refraining from
believing that Edna is loyal would have similar undesirable consequences.)

---

[8] I say permissible or fitting because some philosophers understand epistemic justification in deontological terms as involving a kind of epistemic duty fulfillment whereas others
do not. But I take it that those who would reject talk of epistemic permissibility would be
content with understanding justification in terms of 'fitting one's evidence'. Cf. Bergmann
(unpublished).

Consequently, it would not be surprising for Ed to refuse to believe that Edna is disloyal, and to persist in his belief that Edna is a model of loyalty. (Moser 1985: 212–13)

Alpine Climber

... think of an Alpine climber who, because of an avalanche and a blinding blizzard, is stranded on a desolate mountain path facing a chasm. The climber cannot return the way he came because of the avalanche, yet if he stays where he is, he will freeze as the temperature plummets. The climber's only real hope is to jump the chasm, the width of which is obscured by the blizzard. The climber knows himself well enough to realize that, unless he believes that he can make the jump, his attempt will only be half-hearted, diminishing his chance of survival. In circumstances like these, one is clearly justified in relying upon pragmatic reasons, since survival is practically possible only given belief. The point of the Alpine climber case is that pragmatic belief-formation is sometimes both morally and rationally permissible. (Jordan 1996: 412–13; see also James 1956: 31, 59, from which the example was adapted)

Lobsters and Helen

Epistemic permissibility must be distinguished from both moral and prudential permissibility. For example, because beliefs can have important consequences for the believer, it may be prudent to hold beliefs for which you have inadequate evidence. For instance, it is popularly alleged that lobsters do not feel pain when they are dunked alive into boiling water. It is extremely doubtful that anyone has good reason to believe that, but it may be prudentially rational to hold the belief because otherwise one would deprive oneself of the gustatory delight of eating boiled lobsters. Conversely, it may be imprudent to hold beliefs for which you have unimpeachable evidence. Consider Helen, who has overwhelming evidence that her father is Jack the Ripper. It may be that if she admitted this to herself it would be psychologically crushing. In such cases people sometimes do not believe what the evidence overwhelmingly supports. That is prudentially reasonable but epistemically unreasonable. (Pollock and Cruz 1999: 12–13)

Each of these authors is also concerned to show that there is nothing *morally* inappropriate about forming beliefs in accord with pragmatic considerations. (Indeed, Moser thinks that in the case of Ed and Edna, Ed's dispositions are such that he might even have a moral *obligation* to believe that Edna is not disloyal.) But we may leave that issue aside for now. The main point here is that all of these examples

offer strong prima facie reason for thinking that one may be pragmatically justified in believing something that one is not at all epistemically justified in believing.

Before continuing, we should probably observe that it is a bit of an
oversimplification to say that pragmatic rationality is just a matter of
believing what it is in one's own best interests to believe. It might be in
my own best interests to believe that there is a pot of gold in my basement because believing this would lead me to go down there sooner
than otherwise and going down there sooner than otherwise would
lead me to discover a dangerous gas leak. But, having no awareness of
the second counterfactual, and (unfortunately) lacking any evidence
at all for the claim that there's a pot of gold in my basement, it could
not possibly be rational for me, pragmatically or otherwise, to form
the belief anyway and to run home to check my basement. On the
other hand, it might *not* be in my own best interests to go down into
my basement because (unbeknownst to me) the basement has been
booby-trapped with trip wires and poisoned darts; but clearly if I
smell gas coming from the basement, it is both pragmatically and
epistemically rational to believe that it is a good idea to go down
and check it out. Thus, it is probably more accurate to say that in
order to be pragmatically justified in believing that *p*, one must at least
believe that it is in one's own best interests to believe that *p*, and
perhaps one must also be epistemically justified in believing that it is
in one's own best interests to believe that *p*.[9] Both conditions seem to
be satisfied in each of the quoted examples above. And it is the
satisfaction of these conditions, rather than the mere fact that believing in the ways described in the examples is advantageous, that
explains why the beliefs in question seem to be pragmatically justified.

But *are* they pragmatically justified? The answer is less than clear.
Consider Ed, from Moser's example, who believes (with epistemic
justification) that it is in his own best interests to believe that Edna is
loyal. Furthermore, suppose (as seems plausible) that Ed believes he is
not epistemically justified in believing that Edna is loyal. Is it even
possible for Ed voluntarily to form the *sincere* belief that Edna is loyal
while at the same time maintaining the belief that he is not epistemically justified in believing that she is? My inclination is to think that
this is not possible—at least not without serious cognitive malfunction on Ed's part. To believe a proposition while at the same time

---

[9] Cf. Foley (1987) and Mills (1998).

appreciating the fact that one has no epistemic justification for believing it is consciously to ignore evidential considerations in belief formation. Of course, people sometimes do ignore evidential considerations. But sane people typically do so by not attending to those considerations rather than by attending to but flagrantly disregarding them. Thus, it is hard to see how a person not suffering from serious cognitive malfunction could believe a proposition for which she consciously takes herself to have no epistemic justification. But if this is right, then it would appear that Ed is pragmatically justified in believing that Edna is loyal only if (*a*) contrary to our supposition, he believes that he *is* epistemically justified in believing that Edna is loyal, or (*b*) he is suffering from serious cognitive malfunction. Similar remarks apply to the other examples. But a surface glance at the examples would seem to suggest that the protagonists in each are *not* supposed to be cognitively malfunctioning or mistaken about the epistemic status of their beliefs. If this is so, however, then the examples do not establish the point they aim to establish.[10]

We should also observe that if the foregoing remarks are correct, then another, more interesting conclusion also follows—namely, that *regardless* of what the above examples show, if pragmatic and epistemic rationality can diverge at all, they can diverge only in those people who suffer from serious cognitive malfunction (i.e. the sort of malfunction that makes one remarkably able to ignore or devalue evidential considerations in forming beliefs) or in those people who mistakenly believe that an epistemically unjustified belief is epistemically justified. But if this is right (and if we persist for the moment in the assumption that pragmatic arguments do not yield epistemic justification), then pragmatic arguments alone will not yield any justification at all for the IMP-beliefs of ordinary, reflective naturalists. At best, they will justify only the IMP-beliefs of those naturalists who suffer from serious cognitive malfunction or are sufficiently nonreflective to escape noticing that their IMP-beliefs are not epistemically justified.

This is an important point, but it is not the main point that I wanted to press in this section. To make the main point, I will assume for the sake of argument (and contrary to what has just been said) that the examples quoted above *do* unproblematically establish the fact

---

[10] Eugene Mills (1998) argues along related lines and in greater detail for the conclusion that examples like those quoted above do not establish the thesis that pragmatic and epistemic justification might diverge.

that pragmatic and epistemic justification might diverge for sane, epistemically attentive individuals. Still, neither they nor any other example that I am aware of in the literature even come close to establishing that the pragmatic arguments given in support of our IMP-beliefs might provide us with pragmatic justification for those beliefs.[11] The reason is this: in all of the standard sorts of examples, the protagonist has good reason to believe that the benefit to be gained by believing the epistemically suspect proposition can be had *only* by believing it and not simply by *acting as if* the proposition were true. Consider Ed and Edna again. If Ed had good reason to believe that all the same psychological and financial benefits could be had simply by acting as if his wife were loyal and not by believing it, would there be anything at all to be said for his 'going the extra mile' and actually believing it? No. Indeed, practical rationality would seem to demand not believing it. Why *cultivate* a tendency to believe contrary to one's own evidence when one does not have to? Why spend the extra energy trying to produce belief in a proposition one has good reason to doubt when doing so is unnecessary? One might think that no extra energy would need to be spent: continually acting as if certain propositions are true might naturally lead us to believe those propositions. Or maybe in some cases the easiest way to act as if something is true is simply to believe that it is true. But if so, then practical rationality would seem to require us to resist what comes most easily or naturally. For, again, we have very good reason to believe that, as a general rule, it is in our own best interests to resist processes that unnecessarily inculcate beliefs in us in a way that is insensitive to evidential considerations. But, of course, similar remarks apply in the case of our IMP-beliefs. Given that all the theoretical benefits associated with our usual classificatory practices can be had by acting as if the sentences that express our IMP-beliefs are true without actually believing them, practical rationality seems to demand that the reflective naturalist cease believing them (again, assuming that pragmatic arguments do not yield epistemic justification and assuming that there is nothing beyond pragmatic arguments to be given in their defense).

Could it be that it is simply *impossible* for us to conceptualize our world in a way that does not involve making IMP-judgments? If so, then I think we probably do have pragmatic justification for making such judgments. But I find it extremely implausible to think that this

---

[11] In addition to these, see e.g. Nozick (1993: 69–70) and Foley (1987: 210–11).

is impossible. After all, the debate between realists and antirealists about modal properties is a serious and ongoing debate in philosophical circles. For many people, it seems altogether too easy to avoid forming IMP-beliefs. Of course, appearances can be deceiving. Peter van Inwagen (1983) has argued convincingly that the denial of the thesis that we have free will is literally unbelievable, and this despite the fact that some very good philosophers profess to believe it. But antirealism about modality seems different. Those who profess modal antirealism do not manifest beliefs to the contrary with their every action in the way that deniers of free will manifest beliefs to the contrary with their every action. But if it *is* possible for us to conceptualize our world in a way that does not involve making IMP-judgments, it is hard (for reasons just outlined) to see how we could have pragmatic justification for doing otherwise. Thus, the pragmatic arguments described in Section 1 do not provide us with pragmatic justification for our IMP-beliefs.

3.2. Do Pragmatic Arguments Yield Epistemic Justification?

Until now we have been presupposing that pragmatic arguments yield, at best, pragmatic justification for believing their conclusions. The reason: pragmatic considerations have nothing at all to do with the *truth* of a view. Intuitively, the fact that our classificatory practices simplify our theorizing is no reason for thinking that the beliefs involved in those practices are true. The mere fact that it is convenient for us to think and act as if those beliefs are true is no evidence for their truth.

Surprisingly, however, some philosophers are inclined to reject this line of reasoning. According to some, there is an intimate connection between what is true and what is convenient or useful in some sense for us to believe. Indeed, some philosophers go so far as to define truth (roughly) as acceptability or assertibility under ideal conditions, where 'ideal conditions' are spelled out partly in terms of pragmatic considerations. Such 'pragmatic theories of truth' have been endorsed by, or at least commonly attributed to, William James, C. S. Peirce, Hilary Putnam, Richard Rorty, and Crispin Wright, among others. But if some such theory of truth is correct, then the door is wide open for saying that pragmatic considerations are truth-relevant; and if they are truth-relevant, then pragmatic arguments might confer epistemic justification upon our beliefs after all.

For this reason, one might think that a pragmatic theory of truth is a natural and welcome supplement to the solution described in Section 1. Furthermore, there are other benefits to be gained by a naturalist from accepting such a theory of truth. Most importantly, one solves the rather difficult problem of explaining how it is that we are epistemically justified in believing that our *scientific* theories are true. Scientists apparently make free and heavy use of pragmatic considerations in the process of theory construction and theory choice; but if they do, and if pragmatic considerations are not truth-relevant, then it is hard to see why the overall success of a scientific theory (as measured by a mixture of pragmatic and nonpragmatic criteria) should provide any reason for believing that it is true.[12] Nonnaturalists might appeal to rational intuition for evidence of the fact that success of this sort is an indicator of truth; but naturalists cannot. A pragmatic theory of truth, however, will also do the trick. Thus, it is easy to see why naturalists might be attracted to one.

But the attraction should be resisted. One reason is that pragmatic theories of truth are apparently incompatible with RMO. If truth itself depends importantly upon what is useful or convenient for human beings to believe, then it would appear that property exemplification depends upon the existence of human beings. If, for example, it cannot be a *truth* that a thing x has property p unless it is somehow useful or convenient for human beings to believe that x has p, then it is hard to see how x could have p in a world that does not include human beings. So pragmatic theories of truth seem to imply (perhaps absurdly) that every property is extrinsic. Hence, they also imply that modal and sortal properties are extrinsic. Thus, they are incompatible with RMO.

This fact is sufficient to show that a pragmatic theory of truth cannot be included in any viable solution to the Discovery Problem. But in light of the strong historical and methodological connections between pragmatism and naturalism, I think it is worth digressing briefly to observe another, more interesting problem. It turns out that a pragmatic theory of truth is, from a naturalistic point of view, a Trojan horse. The reason is that pragmatic theories of truth, insofar as they really are *theories* of *truth*, imply epistemic truth equivalences; and epistemic truth equivalences imply something very much like

---

[12] This is a familiar point, marshaled most recently by Robert Koons (2000*a*) in defense of the conclusion that naturalism and scientific realism are incompatible.

theism.[13] Of course, I have already made it clear that naturalism is not in principle incompatible with theism; but theism (or something like it) is not the sort of thing that a naturalist would want to accept simply as a consequence of a theory about truth. Thus, insofar as pragmatic theories of truth carry this consequence, naturalists would do well to avoid them. To see why pragmatic theories of truth entail something very much like theism, a little stage setting is in order. I will begin with some terminology.

Near-theism is the thesis that (i) there exists a necessarily existent rational community and (ii) necessarily there exists an omniscient community. (By 'rational' I just mean 'capable of thought or reasoning'; and, for the sake of simplicity, I am pretending that the term 'community' may be applied both to single individuals as well as groups.) Near-theism is entailed by theism, since theism holds that God constitutes a necessarily existent, necessarily omniscient community. But it does not entail theism. In particular, though it entails that there is a necessarily existent rational community, it does not entail that this community is omnipotent or omnibenevolent, nor does it entail that this community is necessarily omniscient (there might be worlds in which the necessarily existent community is not omniscient, but some other community is omniscient).

An *epistemic truth equivalence* (or ETE for short) is any claim that asserts that there is a necessary equivalence between what is true and what would be believed by a rational agent or community of agents under certain specified conditions. More exactly, an ETE will be any thesis that conforms to the following schema:

(E) Necessarily: p is true $\equiv$ if there were a rational community that satisfied condition C with respect to p, then there would be a rational community that both satisfies condition C with respect to p and accepts p.

'Condition C' refers to what we might call 'the acceptance condition'. It is a schematic term that takes as substitution instances descriptions of the conditions that must be satisfied by a rational community in order for its acceptance of p to be necessary and sufficient for the truth of p. I add the 'with respect to p' qualifier to take account of the

[13] The argument that follows is a somewhat simpler (and cleaner) version of the argument that appears in Rea (2000*b*). I thank Robert Koons for suggestions that led to the changes.

fact that what counts as satisfying the acceptance condition might vary from proposition to proposition. Such would be the case if, for example, the acceptance condition is satisfied only if the community in question possesses all *and only* the evidence relevant to *p*. I have constructed the right-hand side of the biconditional in E as a counterfactual conditional because that is the sort of conditional that stands on the right-hand side of the biconditional in the most plausible ETEs. However, with minor modifications the argument that follows does equally well in showing that E-style claims involving material or indicative conditionals also entail near-theism.

Finally, I will say that a being or community is *omniscient* just in case it accepts all and only true propositions or, equivalently, just in case it accepts a proposition that tells the whole truth about whatever world is actual. There is some debate about whether this view of omniscience is coherent.[14] But for present purposes I will leave that debate aside.[15] Moreover, I will leave aside debate about what are the necessary and sufficient conditions for saying that a multi-membered community accepts a proposition. (For example, one might wonder whether a simple majority is required, or a two-thirds majority, or consensus, or simply consensus among the most informed members of the community.) If it turns out that there is no coherent way to spell out what it takes for a multi-membered community to accept a proposition, then so much the worse for those ETEs that presuppose that this sort of thing can be spelled out.

In addition to the terminology, I will need two assumptions and two theorems. Here is the first assumption:

> (SC)   For any true ETE: Let C be its acceptance condition and let α be the proposition that there exists a community S such that, for every proposition *p*, S satisfies C for either *p* or the denial of *p*. Then: Necessarily, if there is a community that satisfies C with respect to α, then α is true.

At first blush SC may seem rather difficult to evaluate. We have, at best, a handful of suggestions as to possible acceptance conditions;

---

[14] See e.g. Kvanvig (1986) and Plantinga and Grim (1993).

[15] Even if this view of omniscience is not coherent, surely there is *some* sort of true proposition (perhaps a large conjunction of propositions) acceptance of which would suffice for being either actually omniscient or as close to omniscient as logically possible; and if there is, then my argument will imply that, necessarily, there exists a community that accepts some such proposition.

thus, it is initially hard to see how we could possibly make a reasonable judgment about what *must* be the case if the acceptance condition of a true ETE is satisfied with respect to α. But upon closer inspection it turns out that there is good reason to think that SC is true.

Note first that, for any true ETE, either the acceptance condition for a proposition *p* requires ideal reasoning with respect to *p* on the part of the community in question, or it does not. Suppose it does not: the condition can be satisfied by a community S with respect to *p* even if S reasons in a less than ideal manner with respect to *p*. In such a case, clearly the fact that S would or would not accept *p* is not going to be logically sufficient for the truth or falsehood of *p*. For to say that S reasons in a less than ideal manner with respect to *p* is just to say that S reasons in such a way that it might accept *p* even if *p* is false, or might fail to accept *p* even if *p* is true.[16] So, any true ETE will be such that its acceptance condition for a proposition *p* does require ideal reasoning with respect to *p* on the part of the community whose acceptance of *p* is relevant to its truth. Furthermore, for the same reason, the acceptance condition for a true ETE will also require the community in question to have ideal evidence about *p*, if *p* is the sort of proposition that an ideally reasoning community would accept or reject only on the basis of evidence.

Once this is clear, it is easy to see why SC must be true. I take it that only an omniscient being could be directly aware of the truth of α (presumably by being directly aware of its own omniscience). If this is right, then an ideally reasoning community satisfies C with respect to α only if (*a*) it is omniscient, in which case α is true, or (*b*) it has ideal evidence in favor of α. But since we are assuming that some ETE is true, we must also assume that ideal evidence is *infallible*. The reason is that an *ideally* reasoning community would accept any proposition for which it had ideal evidence; hence, if ideal evidence were fallible, it would follow that a community's accepting a proposition for which it satisfied the relevant acceptance condition would not be logically sufficient for the truth of that proposition. Thus, it follows directly from the fact that a community has ideal evidence in favor of α that α is true.

---

[16] Note, then, that an ETE that incorporates a condition requiring less than ideal evidence will turn out to be necessarily false. So, given that a necessarily false proposition entails every proposition, it follows that every such ETE entails near-theism.

Though the point is not strictly germane to my argument, we may note in passing that, if ideal evidence must be infallible, then it is impossible for a community to have ideal evidence *against* α. The reason is that, in order for a community to have ideal evidence against α, at least one of the following conditions must be satisfied: (i) α is incoherent, or (ii) the community has ideal evidence and engages in ideal reasoning about what other communities exist, about what evidence every community has for every proposition, about how every community reasons with respect to every proposition, and about what constitutes ideal evidence and ideal reasoning. There is no reason to believe that α is incoherent.[17] Thus, ideal evidence against α is possible only if it is possible for some community to satisfy (ii). But a nonomniscient community could not possibly satisfy (ii).

In order to satisfy (ii), a community would have to know, for every proposition that anyone believes, whether that proposition is true or false. It would also have to know how every true proposition that anyone believes bears evidentially on every other proposition. As an ideal reasoner with respect to its evidence, its beliefs would be closed under entailment; thus, if any mathematical or logical propositions are among those known, it would know every mathematical or logical truth. Moreover, it is hard to see how it could possibly have ideal evidence for philosophical claims (such as claims about what counts as ideal reasoning and ideal evidence) unless it were omniscient with respect to matters philosophical as well. Furthermore, in order to have ideal evidence about what other minds exist, it would have to have access to facts about the contents of every region of space-time that could possibly contain a mind and it would also have to have ideal access to facts about what (if any) immaterial minds exist. In addition, in order to satisfy (ii) it would have to have ideal information (i.e. information that is at least as good as first-person information) about what every mind believes and about how every mind reasons with respect to what it believes. *Perhaps* it is possible for a nonomniscient reasoner to do all of this that I have just mentioned; but in order to satisfy (ii) in a way that would enable it to conclude that α *is* false, the community in question would have to

---

[17] One might think there are general Cantorian worries to be raised about any proposition that quantifies over every proposition. (See Plantinga and Grim 1993 for a discussion of such worries.) But this is no special problem for α. In fact, it will plague ETEs as well.

be able to do all of this and more *at an instant.* For the physical universe is always changing; the contents of minds are always changing; hence, even if a community managed to inspect the universe and the minds of its own members well enough to have ideal evidence for the conclusion that α *was* false, it could never be sure— unless it somehow had direct access to all of the universe at once— that, in the time it took to complete its investigation, α did not become true as a result of some change in a far corner of the universe that was inspected early on but not afterward. In short, then, only a community that satisfies α could possibly satisfy the conditions required for it to acquire ideal evidence for the falsehood of α; but in such a case, it *could* not acquire such evidence since α would be true. Hence, ideal evidence against α is impossible.

Here is the second assumption:

(NCB) Possibly: There are no contingently existing rational beings.

NCB is controversial among theists. Those who endorse a Leibniz-ian Principle of Plenitude, for example, will not be at all inclined to accept it. But such controversies may be left aside in the present context. If theism is false, NCB is eminently plausible. The probability of life evolving in a universe like ours, even if high, is still clearly less than one. Furthermore, the probability of *rational* organisms evolv-ing is even lower. Thus, given the denial of theism, there seems to be no reason to reject the bare possibility of there being a universe that contains no contingently existing rational beings. And if theism is assumed, then there is no need for NCB since the conclusion of this section could then be established by a different route. Theism, if true, is necessarily true, and (as I have already explained) it entails near-theism; thus, it follows directly that every ETE entails near-theism.

So much for assumptions. Now for the theorems:[18]

(T1) $\Diamond\Box P \Rightarrow \Box P$

(T2) $[\Box(P \equiv Q\Box\!\!\rightarrow R) \,\&\, (Q \Rightarrow P)] \Rightarrow \Box P.$

T1 is a theorem of the **S5** modal system. That system is controver-sial; however, since it is the system that seems to accord best with the

---

[18] Following standard conventions, I use '≡' as the symbol for the material 'if and only if', '$\Box\!\!\rightarrow$' as the symbol for counterfactual implication, and '⇒' as the symbol for strict implication. '$\Box$' is the necessity operator and '$\Diamond$' is the possibility operator.

modal beliefs of most contemporary philosophers, I expect that T1 will have fairly wide appeal despite the controversy. Moreover, rejecting T1 will have little effect on the main argument. Without T1, I will not be able to show that every ETE entails near-theism; but (as the reader can verify) I will be able to show that every ETE entails the thesis that necessarily there exists an omniscient community.[19]

T2 is derivable in the **S4** modal system, but not in any weaker system. Here is the proof: Suppose the antecedent of T2 is true and suppose, for *reductio*, that there is a possible world W at which P is false. From the first conjunct of the antecedent, it follows that, at W, $Q\Box\rightarrow R$ is false. This, in turn, implies that there is a world W* at which Q is true and R is false. (If there were no such world, $Q \Rightarrow R$ would be true in every world; hence, $Q\Box\rightarrow R$ would be true in W.) But if Q is true and R is false at W*, then $Q\Box\rightarrow R$ is false at W* as well. Furthermore, it follows that P is true at W*. This is because (*a*) according to the antecedent of T2, Q entails P, (*b*) Q is true at W*, and (*c*) in **S4**, the accessibility relation among worlds is transitive. Thus, at W*, P is true whereas $Q\Box\rightarrow R$ is false. But, given the antecedent of T2, this is impossible. QED.

We are now ready for the argument. The first premise I have already asserted earlier: pragmatic theories of truth entail epistemic truth equivalences. Below are some representative examples:

True ideas are those that we can validate, corroborate, and verify. (James 1907: 142)

The opinion which is fated to be ultimately agreed to by all who investigate, is what we mean by the truth . . . . (Peirce 1878: 139)

. . . truth is an *idealization* of rational acceptability. We speak as if there were such things as epistemically ideal conditions, and we call a statement 'true' if it would be justified under such conditions. (Putnam 1981*a*: 55)

Truth is superassertibility, or 'assertibility which would be durable under any possible improvement to one's state of information'. (C. Wright 1992: 75)

Pretty obviously, each of these claims taken as a theory of truth is equivalent to a thesis that satisfies schema E. Granted, one might argue (quite convincingly in some cases) that these authors did not *really* mean to be giving a theory about what truth is. Since my aim is not exegesis, I will not enter into this debate. Suffice it to say that the

---

[19]   The same is true for NCB: without it I cannot establish the first component of near-theism, but I can establish the second.

views above are such that *if* they were theories of truth, they would clearly be pragmatic theories and they would imply ETEs. Moreover, I see no way in which a theory of truth could plausibly count as pragmatic without implying an ETE. Some theories (e.g. deflationary theories) that do not imply ETEs are compatible with pragmatism; but there is nothing distinctively pragmatic about such theories, for they do not have as a consequence the claim that truth is importantly tied to what is useful for humans to believe.

Crispin Wright has suggested that problems related to those that I am raising here might be avoided by rejecting ETEs altogether in favor of conditionals of the following sort:

> (W) Were P to be appraised under (constructively specified) sufficiently good epistemic conditions, P would be true if and only if P would be believed. (C. Wright 2000: 350)

Such conditionals, Wright argues, serve to constrain the notion of truth in the ways that pragmatists typically want without suffering from some of the problems that plague ordinary ETEs. Maybe this is right; and if W-style conditionals were theories of truth, or were entailed by theories of truth, then here we would have a plausible counterexample to the claim that pragmatic theories entail ETEs. But the fact is, conditionals like this are not theories of truth, and I am not aware of any non-ETE-entailing theories of truth that would have a W-style conditional as a consequence.

Admittedly, we could just stipulate that W-style conditionals count as theories of truth; and we could perhaps justify the stipulation on the grounds that they *do* say something important and controversial about truth. Furthermore, we could insist that some such conditional is true despite the fact that there is no more general theory of truth, no analysis of truth, to be had that entails it. But now we have a mystery. Why should truth behave in the way described by W? Short of some account of what truth is that implies that truth behaves in that highly counterintuitive way, it is hard to see how we could have any basis for believing that it *does* behave in that way. But, again, it seems that any account of what truth is that would have W as a consequence would also have some ETE as a consequence.

So pragmatic theories of truth—genuine theories of truth that are distinctively pragmatic and not merely compatible with pragmatism—imply epistemic truth equivalences. But, as I will now show, epistemic truth equivalences imply near-theism.

Let EC below be any *true* ETE (if such there be); let C be EC's acceptance condition; let α be the proposition that there exists a rational community S such that, for every proposition p, S satisfies C with respect to either p or its denial; let β be the proposition that there exists a rational community that satisfies C with respect to α; and let γ be the proposition that there exists a rational community that both satisfies C with respect to α and accepts α. We then have:

(EC) Necessarily: p is true $\equiv$ if there were a rational community that satisfied condition C with respect to p, then there would be a rational community that both satisfies condition C with respect to p and accepts p. (Premise)

(6.1) Necessarily: α is true $\equiv$ if β were the case then γ would be the case. (From EC, by substitution)

(6.2) $\beta \Rightarrow \alpha$ (From SC)

(6.3) Necessarily: α. (From 6.1, 6.2, T2)

From 6.3 it is a short step to the conclusion that there exists a necessarily existing rational community. 6.3 implies that it is necessarily true that there exists a rational community; but, according to NCB, it is possible that there are no *contingently existing* rational beings. So NCB and 6.3 together imply that there is a possible world w that contains a rational community but no contingently existing rational beings. Thus, w must contain a necessarily existing rational community. But this claim in conjunction with T1 implies that there in fact exists a necessarily existing rational community.[20] Thus we have the first component of near-theism.

But what of the second component—the claim that, necessarily, there exists an omniscient community? Here again the argument is simple. According to 6.3, it is necessarily true that there exists a rational community S such that, for every proposition p, S satisfies C with respect to either p or its denial. But this in conjunction with EC implies that it is necessarily true that, for every *true* proposition p^*, there is a rational community that both satisfies C with respect to p^* and accepts p^*. Hence, it follows that, necessarily, there is a rational community that accepts a proposition that tells the whole truth about

[20] Here are the steps: Let W be a world with no contingently existing rational beings and let $E_1 \ldots E_n$ be the members of the rational community that exists in W. We then have:

(1) $\Diamond \Box (E_1 \ldots E_n \text{ exist})$.

(2) Therefore: $\Box (E_1 \ldots E_n \text{ exist})$.

whatever world is actual.[21] Thus, necessarily, there exists an omniscient community.

If my argument is sound, pragmatic theories of truth entail near-theism. Theists, of course, will not be bothered by this conclusion, for their view entails near-theism and (typically) is motivated by considerations independent of a commitment to an epistemic account of truth. Naturalists, on the other hand, ought simply to reject epistemic accounts of truth; hence, they ought also to reject pragmatic theories of truth. One might avoid the commitment to near-theism by rejecting one of the assumptions or rules laid out at the beginning of this section; but that will not do much to elevate the reasonability of accepting a pragmatic theory of truth. For no matter how one ultimately responds to the argument in this section, the upshot is that pragmatic theories of truth carry substantial metaphysical baggage. If a proponent of some pragmatic theory of truth refuses to accept near-theism as a consequence of her theory, then she must accept some other substantial consequence: that S5 is not the correct modal system, that the most prominent views about counterfactuals are false, that necessarily there exist contingently existing rational beings, etc. But surely these are not the sorts of claims that one wants to accept *simply* as a consequence of one's theory of truth.

3.3. *Pragmatic Arguments as Basic Sources of Evidence*

Throughout Section 3, I have been pressing the objection that pragmatic arguments yield, at best, pragmatic justification for their conclusions, and I have argued that there is even reason to doubt that they yield that. However, I have also noted that scientists appear to make heavy use of pragmatic considerations in the construction and assessment of their theories. In light of this, one might think that there is an obvious reply to the objection ready at hand. Naturalism is a research program which treats the methods of science as *basic* sources of evidence. Furthermore, epistemic justification is plausibly relativized to a research program in the sense that one is automatically at least prima facie epistemically justified in believing propositions that are sanctioned by her basic sources of evidence. Indeed, for this very reason one is also plausibly at least prima facie justified in

---

[21] Or, if there is no such proposition, then at least this much follows: necessarily, for any true proposition that *approximates* telling the whole truth about the world, there is a rational community that accepts it.

believing that her basic sources of evidence are truth-conducive. Thus, perhaps naturalists need no argument in support of the claim that pragmatic arguments are truth-conducive; and, by virtue of their role in the sciences, perhaps pragmatic arguments automatically yield prima facie epistemic justification for naturalists.

Fair enough; I do not propose to take issue with any of this. But we can still ask what would be the best explanation for the reliability of the sources we take as basic. In the worst cases, such lines of questioning turn up reasons to believe that the sources we take as basic are probably unreliable or, at any rate, not appropriately treated as basic. In those cases, our research program defeats itself. In the present case, however, such questions simply lead us away from RMO.

Suppose it is true, as it certainly seems to be, that pragmatic considerations play a large role in the assessment of scientific theories. Suppose also that we are epistemically justified in accepting the ontological commitments of scientific theories that meet suitably high standards of assessment. We can infer from the fact that we are *epistemically* justified in accepting these commitments that pragmatic considerations are reliable guides in ontological matters: theoretical virtues like simplicity, elegance, and compatibility with entrenched views are somehow sensitive to the truth or falsity of the ontological commitments incurred by our theories. Now, what would be the best explanation for this fact? One possibility is that someone or something in the universe is somehow guaranteeing that pragmatic criteria for theory choice will be truth-conducive. Another possibility is that constructivism is true. If constructivism is true, then we *make it the case* that a particular ontology is true by conceptualizing the world in whatever way we do. Thus, so long as we conceptualize the world in a way that is empirically adequate (as our scientific theories aim to do) there is no real question whether the ontological commitments we thereby incur will be true. We make them true. It is hard to imagine (plausible) explanations other than these for why pragmatic criteria ought to be truth-conducive in matters of ontology. As a theist, I am sympathetic to the first. Naturalists, I suspect, will prefer the second.

Thus, on the supposition that pragmatic arguments are an integral part of scientific theorizing and a source of epistemic justification, and on the further supposition that naturalists will not be attracted to something like theism as an explanation for why pragmatic arguments are reliable in matters of ontology, naturalists are straightforwardly committed to constructivism. In fact, the only reason for not advertising and developing this argument as the main one in favor of the conclusion that naturalists are committed to constructivism is that I am not prepared to defend in proper detail the first supposition just mentioned. In the present context, however, where that supposition is being invoked as an 'obvious reply' to the main argument of the present chapter, there is no need for defense. But, clearly enough, invoking the assumption only helps my argument; and so the 'obvious reply' turns out to be a dead end.

4. Conclusion

In light of the foregoing, it seems clear that pragmatic solutions to the Discovery Problem are doomed to failure. One worry is that the most natural such solution (one erected on the foundation of a view like that described by Elder) does not manage to provide us with the sort of realism (i.e. realism about human beings and other biological organisms) that naturalist proponents of RMO are likely to be after. But the more important problem is that (short of accepting a pragmatic theory of truth and near-theism along with it) pragmatic arguments generally do not provide us with epistemic justification for their conclusions and, furthermore, they do not even seem to be able to provide us with *pragmatic* justification for our IMP-beliefs. One might try to dodge this problem by claiming that pragmatic arguments are integral to scientific theorizing and that they therefore constitute basic sources of evidence for a naturalist. But, as we have seen, going this route only makes the commitment to constructivism (or something like theism) all the more straightforward.

7

What Price Antirealism?

> What happens if a philosopher is (1) an anti-aprioristic natur-
> alist, who (2) allows that there is such a thing as the synthetic
> identity of properties, and (3) also has a hard-line realist view of
> truth? I wish to claim that such a philosopher will find himself
> confronted with serious epistemological difficulties.
>
> (Hilary Putnam, *Reason, Truth, and History*, 1981)

IN Chapter 4 we saw that if there is good reason to think that the
Discovery Problem cannot be solved, then naturalists cannot be
justified in accepting RMO. This is not to say that naturalists, or
anyone else, must be able to give an account of how their IMP-beliefs,
or any other beliefs, are justified in order actually to be justified in
holding them. But if one has good reasons for thinking that a particular kind of belief *cannot* be justified by any of the sources that one
takes as basic, and if one has no evidence that defeats those reasons,
then one cannot then be justified in holding beliefs of that kind. Such
is the situation of the naturalist with respect to IMP-beliefs.

We have seen in Chapters 5 and 6 that there is no reason to think
that any empirical phenomenon is best explained by the truth of IMP-
beliefs, and that an appeal to pragmatic arguments is of no use in
saving RMO. But, as we saw in Chapter 4, it is hard to see how else our
IMP-beliefs could be justified via the methods of science. Thus, the
Discovery Problem appears to be unsolvable. Intrinsic modal properties cannot be detected by scientific methods, and so anyone who
takes the methods of science to exhaust our basic sources of evidence
has no justification for IMP-beliefs and hence no justification for
accepting RMO.

But what are the implications of giving up RMO? This is the
question that will occupy us in the present chapter. I will begin by

explaining why, in giving up RMO, naturalists are committed to accepting constructivism. I will also suggest reasons for thinking that, though naturalists are not committed to idealism, neither can they rule it out. I will then go on to explain why those who reject RMO must also reject materialism, and why rejecting materialism makes it difficult for naturalists to accept ROM.

1. Constructivism and Idealism

In Chapter 1, I defined constructivism as the thesis that none of the properties that appear to be sortal properties of nonabstract, nonmental objects are intrinsic. I said that constructivism is compatible with idealism, but does not entail it. I also said that, on the assumption that idealism is false, constructivism implies that the apparent sortal properties of nonabstract, nonmental objects are extrinsic properties involving relations between a human mind or group of human minds and the stuff that supposedly constitutes the objects in question.

Giving up RMO is not equivalent to accepting constructivism. One might be a thoroughgoing skeptic about the nature of modal properties, believing that we cannot know one way or the other whether the modal properties we are naturally inclined to attribute to material objects are intrinsic to anything. If so, then one will be committed not only to withholding belief in RMO (since RMO requires the positive belief that modal properties *are* intrinsic) but also to withholding belief in constructivism (since constructivism requires the positive belief that modal properties are extrinsic). To show that naturalists are committed to *accepting* constructivism is therefore to establish a somewhat stronger conclusion than the conclusion that naturalists must give up belief in RMO.

The main reason for thinking that naturalists are committed to constructivism is that it is hard to see how science could possibly get along without the supposition that we can have knowledge of modal properties. For one thing, scientific theories regularly quantify over material objects and sort them into kinds. Biological theories quantify over organisms, chemical theories quantify over chemical compounds, physical theories quantify over atoms and subatomic particles, and so on; and each of these disciplines also offers some sort of taxonomy of the objects it studies. But, as we have seen, if we are justified in believing in material objects and sorting them into kinds, then we are justified in believing in modal properties and in forming various MP-beliefs.

Admittedly, some say that, contrary to initial appearances, material objects really are not *indispensable* for science. Quine, for example, suggests that all we really need in our ontology are filled regions of spacetime.[1] But regions cannot exist apart from modal properties any more than material objects can. For any region of spacetime, there will be facts about whether it could have been bigger or smaller, facts about whether it could have been unfilled or filled differently, and so on. And, again, for purposes of science we would need to do some sorting, which would, in turn, involve us in the practice of forming MP-beliefs.

Could we do away with regions as well, and move to an ontology of stuff? Not for scientific purposes. The world appears to exemplify many different properties in many different places, and it is part of the business of science to discover the lawful relations among these appearances. But to do this, scientists will need to posit multiple properties with multiple bearers; and a pure stuff ontology lacks the relevant bearers. Thus, the ontology of science cannot be a pure stuff ontology.

So naturalists are committed to thinking that there are material objects or regions of spacetime, and they are committed to thinking that we can have knowledge of modal properties. But, because the Discovery Problem is unsolvable, they are also committed to thinking that our knowledge of modal properties cannot be knowledge of intrinsic modal properties. Thus, they must think either that idealism is true (there is no external world, and so our knowledge of modal properties just amounts to knowing the relations among our ideas) or that modal properties are extrinsic. But, as we have already seen, if modal properties are extrinsic then so are sortal properties. Thus, naturalists are committed to constructivism.

But what about idealism? Must naturalists accept it, reject it, or withhold belief on the matter? At first glance, the third alternative seems to be the correct one. To see why, think about the typical naturalistic response to skepticism. One of the most prominent themes in the naturalist tradition is the rejection of the traditional epistemological project of refuting the skeptic. The reason is simple.

---

[1] Quine (1976).

Naturalists respect the methods of science as our only ways of acquiring information about the world. But those methods can tell us only about the relations among our representations. They cannot tell us what those representations represent, whether they represent correctly, or even whether they represent at all. In short, naturalists abandon the project of refuting the skeptic because the skeptic *can't* be refuted by the sources of evidence they take as basic.[2] To find out what our representations represent, whether they represent correctly, or whether they represent at all, we must look somewhere other than science. But, according to the naturalist, there is nowhere else to look.

Saddling naturalists with skepticism about the external world is not quite so simple as this, however. On the one hand, it does seem right that idealism cannot be ruled out by scientific evidence. On the other hand, there are many other theses that seem not to be ruled out by scientific evidence but that we seem to be perfectly justified in rejecting anyway. For example, there is the thesis that we are brains in vats, the thesis that we and the rest of the world were created just five minutes ago but designed to look and think as if we had longer histories, the thesis that there are legions of leprechauns in our midst that are so clever about hiding themselves that we can and will never detect them even with the best instruments we could possibly imagine, and so on. Some might see here the seeds of an argument against naturalism. If such theses are *not* ruled out by scientific evidence, then naturalists must either admit that we are not justified in rejecting them (which is bizarre) or they must recognize other basic sources of evidence besides the methods of science (which is to abandon naturalism). But naturalists rarely take either of these alternatives; and presumably whatever they would have to say about theses of this sort could also be said about idealism.

A proper survey of the possible replies naturalists might give to the threat of idealism would require more space than I am prepared to devote to that task in this book. So, we will have to make do with a severely abbreviated, and accordingly inconclusive, discussion.

At a very general level, two main options seem to be available to a naturalist for ruling out the idealist hypothesis (or any of the other scenarios just mentioned). One is to appeal to pragmatic

---

[2] Of course, I don't mean to suggest that the skeptic definitely *can* be refuted by appeal to sources taken as basic by (say) intuitionists or supernaturalists. But adherents of those research programs can at least find room for optimism about the success of some sort of limited Cartesian antiskeptical project in a way that naturalists evidently cannot.

considerations. This, in fact, seems to be the option that would be favored by Dewey, Quine, and many other naturalists. But in taking that option, one falls prey to the considerations raised against pragmatic arguments in Chapter 6. The other option is to try to show that we are justified in rejecting idealism (along with claims like the brain-in-a-vat hypothesis, the five-minute hypothesis, and the leprechaun hypothesis) on the basis of some general epistemic principle sanctioned as a part of 'scientific method'. For example, we might reject them on the grounds that such theses are vastly improbable, or on the grounds that the success of our theorizing is extremely unlikely on the supposition that the thesis is true, or on the grounds that we ought to reject any hypothesis that we have absolutely no reason to accept. The trouble, however, is that it is not at all clear that, from a naturalistic point of view, we can have grounds like this in support of the denial of idealism. The probability of idealism, or of our theorizing being successful if idealism is true, will be impossible to determine without some sort of appeal to intuition. And, given that 'reasons' for accepting a view must, on naturalism, be empirical reasons, there is not obviously any more reason to accept realism about the external world than there is to accept idealism. Thus, by the lights of the last thesis, *both* ought to be rejected.

So, in sum, naturalists are committed to constructivism, and it is not clear that they can rule out idealism. But, of course, there is no reason to think that they would be *committed* to idealism either. Nothing in science suggests that an external world *can't* exist. And, indeed, the very considerations that suggest that naturalists cannot rule out idealism also suggest that they cannot accept it.

2. Against Materialism

Materialism is the thesis that nothing exists except for spacetime, material objects and events in spacetime, and the properties exemplified by spacetime and the objects and events therein. Materialism is obviously incompatible with idealism; therefore, if I am right in thinking that naturalists must withhold belief about idealism, it follows trivially that they must also withhold belief about materialism. But I do not want my argument for the conclusion that naturalists must give up materialism to rest on the claim that naturalists must withhold belief about idealism. One reason is that, as I admitted in the last section, I have not provided anything like a properly thorough argument for that claim. The more important reason is that a stronger conclusion can be established: materialism is incompatible with constructivism.

To make this argument, I will need two assumptions: that there are minds, and that mental activity cannot occur except in a mind. As with most claims that seem obviously to be true, both of these have been disputed by serious philosophers. However, I will pass over such rumblings in silence, partly because I have nothing illuminating to say in defense of these two theses and partly because I think most naturalists will not take any comfort in knowing that they can avoid giving up materialism by giving up either the thesis that there are minds or the thesis that mental activity cannot occur outside of a mind.

Suppose, for *reductio*, that both materialism and constructivism are true. From materialism it follows that, if there are minds, then minds are either material objects or events. There are no other alternatives. However, if either of these alternatives is correct, then no mind can exist unless some material object exists. Constructivism, however, implies that no material object can exist unless some stuff stands in some particular relation to a mind. Moreover, by all accounts, if constructivism is true then the relevant relations involve or presuppose some mind's being able to think of the matter in question as falling under a sortal concept. But now we have a problem. For it follows from what has just been said that no mind can exist unless some mind is able to think of some matter as falling under a particular sortal concept. But thinking of matter in terms of sortal concepts is a fairly advanced mental process—the sort of process that presupposes a great deal of *prior* mental activity which (by our assumption above) could not have occurred *outside* of a mind. So, if minds are material objects or events, then minds cannot *come into existence* unless some minds *already* exist and develop to a point where they can conceive of matter in the ways necessary to bring minds into existence. But, of course, this scenario is impossible. Therefore, constructivism and materialism cannot both be true. Hence, insofar as naturalists are committed to constructivism, they must give up materialism.

One might object that this argument overlooks a possibility. To explain the possibility, I need to introduce two additional philosophical doctrines. *Eternalism* is the view that there are some past objects, there are some future objects, and there neither were nor will be objects that do not exist. (Eternalism is opposed to presentism, the view that it always has been and always will be the case that there are no actual but nonpresent objects.) The *doctrine of temporal parts*, or *perdurantism*, is the thesis that objects *perdure* rather than *endure*— that is, they persist over time by having parts (or, as some have it, counterparts) at every time at which they exist rather than by being wholly present at every time at which they exist. On one way of understanding this view, objects are extended in time in just the same way as they are extended in space. Just as your arm (now) is the sum of a bunch of 'two dimensional' spatial slices, so too *you* are the sum of a bunch of momentary 'three dimensional' temporal slices. On this way of thinking, you are not identical to any of those slices; rather, they are parts of you, and you are the four-dimensionally extended object composed of them.[3] On another way of understanding perdurantism, however, you *are* identical to your present temporal slice and the other temporal slices of your career simply stand in for you as your counterparts at other times. According to this view, you have temporal properties (like having been less than four feet tall, or having had tomatoes for lunch) in the same way that counterpart theorists about modal properties say that you have modal properties: you *were* less than four feet tall just in case you have a counterpart at some other time who *is* less than four feet tall.[4] Either way, perdurantism implies that the life history of every adult human includes numerous distinct objects existing at different times, each of which possesses a fully developed human brain. And eternalism implies that none of these objects, strictly speaking, come into or pass out of existence; they all simply exist—as does everything else that ever did or ever will exist.

Suppose, now, that both eternalism and the doctrine of temporal parts are true. Since there is no objective *becoming*, we no longer have the problem of understanding how minds could *come into existence*. From the point of view of eternalism and perdurantism together, it has always been and will always be true that among the things that exist *simpliciter* there are numerous fully developed adult human brains—or, at any rate, there is the stuff of which those brains are composed and the properties exemplified by that stuff that explains all of the thoughts occurring in the brains. Of course, the brains only

[3] See e.g. Heller (1990).
[4] Cf. Sider (1996, 2001). On counterpart theory, see Lewis (1986) and Sect. 2.2 of Ch. 4 of this book.

count as such by virtue of the relations between their matter and other human minds. But why should this be a problem? Why not think that all material objects, *including all human minds*, are mind-dependent, and that minds themselves might be mind-dependent simply by virtue of standing to one another in relations of *mutual* dependence. The picture looks promising. We might suppose that the world timelessly includes stuff arranged mind-wise that is *thinking* about the world in a way that makes it a world containing material objects, some of which are minds that do the thinking. So no thought actually has to occur outside of a mind; and materialism might still be true because it might still be the case that any possible world in which *all* of the relevant physical facts obtained would be a world which included stuff arranged mind-wise that thinks about the world in the ways that our minds think about the world.

Nevertheless, I think that this is the wrong way to try to save materialism. The intuitions that motivate materialism strongly suggest that if materialism is true, then, for any time t, the property *being a mind at t* naturally supervenes on what the world is like at t.[5] In other words, whether or not a mind exists does not seem to depend on any facts outside of the time at which the mind exists. But if this claim is added as a premise, then it is easy to show that materialism cannot be saved in the way just described. For the view just described implies that many minds—in particular, those that existed prior to the emergence of minds that engaged in the practice of applying sortal concepts to the world—count as minds only by virtue of their relations to things existing at other times. Hence, there will be possible worlds that duplicate our world and its natural laws at those times which do not include minds, thus violating the restricted principle of supervenience described above.

It is worth noting here that not only is materialism incompatible with constructivism, but so too is *any* view according to which minds are material objects or events. Thus, it would appear that naturalists are committed to some kind of dualism.[6]

---

[5] A-facts at a time naturally supervene on B-facts at a time if and only if all of the B-facts at that time, in conjunction with the natural laws, determine all of the A-facts at that time. For present purposes, I leave open the question of whether a time is to be understood as an absolute instant, a set of simultaneous objects or events in a frame of reference, a set of space-like separated objects or events, or whatever. I also leave open the question whether times might have some small degree of temporal thickness.

[6] For purposes here, 'dualism' means the same as 'substance dualism'.

3. Against Realism about Other Minds

Commitment to dualism will not sit well with most naturalists. The reason is that dualism is widely regarded as having been thoroughly discredited by the empirical study of the mind. Empirical research reveals, among other things, that changes in the brain are intimately correlated with changes in the mind. Substances that affect the brain also affect the mind, physical damage to the brain damages the mind, brain development correlates with mental development, and so on. Furthermore, the supposition that nonphysical minds exist offers no empirical explanatory advantage over the hypothesis that the mind is identical to the brain. These considerations, together with a general appeal to simplicity considerations (e.g. 'do not posit entities above and beyond what is necessary to account for the empirical data') constitute the main scientific reasons for rejecting dualism.[7] As dualists will point out, these considerations do not *refute* dualism. But for those who regard scientific evidence as the only evidence there can be for a hypothesis, these considerations are virtually decisive—as evidenced by the fact that the naturalistic community is virtually unanimous in thinking that dualism ought not even to be taken seriously any more.

Of course, if the arguments of the previous section are correct, naturalistic attitudes toward dualism will have to change. But what I want to focus on here is the fact that *if* the naturalistic arguments against dualism are really as good as naturalists take them to be, then even though the arguments will no longer suffice to rid naturalists of the specter of dualism, they will suffice to rid naturalists of the specter of other minds.

The reason is simple. Introspection reveals to us the existence of our own minds. Reflection on the nature of material objects and the necessary conditions for the existence of a mind (as described above and in the foregoing chapters) reveals that, if there are minds at all, they must be nonphysical. Thus, on the basis of introspection and reflection upon conceptual truths about material objects and so on, we arrive at the conclusion that there exists at least one nonphysical mind. Materialism is falsified. But, importantly, we have not falsified materialism by introducing any role for nonphysical minds to play in

---

[7] This sort of argument is ubiquitous in the literature. For a succinct and forceful presentation, see Churchland (1988: 18–21).

directly explaining *empirical phenomena*.[8] Thus, the considerations that normally count against dualism now count strongly against the supposition that other human beings have minds. For if we had no reason before to suppose that nonphysical minds had any role to play in explaining the behavior of human beings, we have no reason now to suppose this either.

This conversion of an antidualistic argument into a skeptical argument might seem puzzling at first. The skeptical argument relies on the premise that the hypothesis of other minds is a *nonexplanatory* hypothesis. However, the now standard naturalistic argument *in favor* of realism about other minds makes the hypothesis that other minds exist rest on an inference to the best explanation. On this view, the supposition that there are other minds *is* an explanatory hypothesis, and it constitutes the best explanation for various facts about the behavior of other human beings.[9] Hence the puzzle: is the other minds hypothesis explanatory or not? And, we might add, if it is not explanatory (as the common antidualistic argument seems to suggest) then why would naturalists ever have been attracted to the idea that skepticism about other minds could be rebutted by an inference to the best explanation?

The solution to the puzzle lies in spelling out the relevant premises in a bit more detail. The antidualistic argument takes as a premise the claim that *nonmaterial* minds have no role to play in explaining the manifest behavior of human bodies. The antiskeptical argument takes as a premise the claim that *material* minds *do* have a role to play in explaining the manifest behavior of human bodies. Once this is clear, we see that the two arguments are no longer in tension. But we also see that, insofar as naturalism is committed to the denial of materialism, the antiskeptical argument is no longer of any use in saving ROM.

Are there other arguments a naturalist might invoke to preserve ROM? This is doubtful. The other main argument in the literature— the argument from analogy—is widely taken to be unsound.[10] In

---

[8] Does this mean that we have not falsified materialism in a *scientific* way and, hence, that naturalists are not committed to rejecting it after all? No. Recall that in Chs. 1 and 3 I noted that commitment to naturalism is not incompatible with the practice of drawing conclusions on the basis of reflection upon our concepts. Plausibly, that is all that is required to establish the conclusions of this book thus far.

[9] Cf. Chihara and Fodor (1965), Churchland (1979, 1988), Melnyk (1994), Pargetter (1984), Price (1938), and Ziff (1965).

[10] Among the most well-known defenders of the argument are J. S. Mill (1889: 243–4) and Bertrand Russell (1948).

basic outline, the argument from analogy holds that we are justified in
believing in other minds on the basis of a kind of inductive inference.
As Russell puts it:

It is clear that we must appeal to something that may be vaguely called
'analogy.' The behavior of other people is in many ways analogous to our
own, and we suppose that it must have analogous causes. What people say is
what we should say if we had certain thoughts, and so we infer that they
probably have those thoughts. They give us information which we can
subsequently verify. They behave in ways we behave when we are pleased
(or displeased) in circumstances in which we should be pleased (or displeased). We may talk over with a friend some incident which we have both
experienced, and find that his reminiscences dovetail with our own; this is
particularly convincing when he remembers something that we have forgot-
ten but that he recalls to our thoughts. Or again: you set your boy a problem
in arithmetic, and with luck he gets the right answer; this persuades you that
he is capable of arithmetical reasoning. There are, in short, very many ways in
which my responses to stimuli differ from those of 'dead' matter, and in
all these ways other people resemble me. As it is clear to me that the causal
laws governing my behavior have to do with 'thoughts,' it is natural to infer
that the same is true of the analogous behavior of my friends. (Russell
1948: 4)

On this view, the other minds hypothesis is justified exclusively on
the basis of a single-case induction. Just as, upon observing a myriad
black crows and no white ones we infer that all crows are black, so too
here, upon observing that various features of our own behavior are
caused (or, at any rate, attended) by various mental states, we infer
that similar behaviors in all human beings are caused (or attended) by
similar mental states. I take it that the main difference between this
view and the view that the other minds hypothesis is justified on the
basis of an inference to the best explanation is just that on this view
the resemblance between ourselves and other human beings and the
information we obtain about ourselves via introspection constitutes
our *total* evidence for believing in other minds, whereas on the other
view the supposition that others have minds is an empirical theory
that is holistically confirmed and testable in a variety of different ways.
As many have pointed out, however, one main problem with the argument from analogy is that a single case constitutes pretty shaky
grounds for an inductive inference.[11]

---

[11] For further, more detailed, criticism of this argument, along with references to other
critical discussions of it, see Plantinga (1967).

Christopher Hill (1991) has recently tried to revive the argument from analogy. But the way he revives it is by suggesting a revision—namely, that we add the hypothesis that we ourselves are biologically normal members of our species. Thus, his version of the argument goes like this:

When I consider my own conscious experiences, I find that they play essential roles in all of my sensory explorations of the external world, and also that they are causally linked to all or almost all of the patterns of behavior in my behavioral repertoire. Further, I find that many of the sensory explorations and behavioral ventures that depend on my conscious experiences are essential to my physical well-being and survival. And, finally, when I compare my basic sensory and behavioral capacities with those of other people, I find that they are biologically normal, in the sense that they are shared by almost all other members of my species. Hence, probably all other biologically normal members of my species enjoy conscious experiences like my own. Moreover, it is likely that the experiences of such beings are linked to other factors in perceptual processes and to patterns of behavior by laws that are quite similar to the laws I have found to hold in my own case. (Hill 1991: 212)

True, in this version as in the last, we are still inferring from a single case. But, Hill argues, single-case inductive inferences might be warranted when one has reason to believe that the sample is a normal member of a kind (Hill 1991: 217–19).

But, whatever its merits otherwise, Hill's argument will not do in the present context since it presupposes materialism. If materialism is false, mental states are not biological properties; thus, the fact that our bodies are biologically normal members of the species 'human being' does nothing to support our single-case inference to the conclusion that other human bodies have minds associated with them. ROM remains in danger.

There are, of course, other arguments in the literature. But most either fall prey to objections of the sort raised above or else appeal to intuitions that naturalists would find objectionable.[12] Of course, this is not the last word: I have not shown that it is *impossible* to defend ROM. But at this stage, the project does not look promising.[13]

---

[12] Cf. Buford (1970), as well as Burge (1998) and Vendler (1984).

[13] One might insist that naturalists are justified in believing in other minds on the grounds that psychology is a science and psychology quantifies over other minds. Fair

4. Conclusion

In closing this chapter, I think it is important to acknowledge that the theses I have said naturalists must give up are theses that many philosophers, naturalists in particular, will be very reluctant to give up. In a way, this is worrisome; for, if the history of philosophy is any guide, arguments for conclusions that people are very reluctant to accept have an extremely poor track record with respect to actually convincing anybody. Hume was unable to remain a skeptic outside of his study, and even Pyrrho was forced to admit that it is hard to be a skeptic while being attacked by dogs.

Nevertheless, I must emphasize here that in arguing for the conclusions that I have defended in this part of the book, I have not at all been pressing for the conclusion that the theses that people will be reluctant to give up (RMO, materialism, and ROM) are *false*. I have not even been arguing for the conclusion that those theses cannot justifiably be believed. Instead, I have simply argued that *naturalists* cannot justifiably believe them, and this only because they have made a rationally indefensible decision to restrict themselves to the methods of science alone in developing their theories about the world. Of course, naturalists typically *want* to believe these theses. And they very often write as if one *can* justifiably believe them while at the same time maintaining commitment to naturalism. But here we have a shell game. We are told that if only we look in the right places we will find everything we want: realism about material objects, realism about other minds, materialism for those who want it, and much more. But when all the shells have been turned over, we find that we have been duped, and nothing is there.

enough; this is one way out of the problem. But notice the strategy of the present section. I start by taking it for granted that standard materialist arguments against dualism are strong. Given that assumption, those arguments count heavily against ROM. One response to this might be to treat other minds as convenient fictions for the purposes of simplifying psychology and ordinary life. Another response is to affirm the commitment to minds and to discount the weight of standard antidualist arguments. I have assumed that naturalists would prefer the former response; but I would be just as happy to see them endorse the latter.

PART III
ALTERNATIVES

8

Intuitionism

MY exploration of the ontological consequences of naturalism is now complete. We have seen in the last four chapters that naturalists as such cannot reasonably accept realism about material objects or materialism. We have also seen that, in giving up RMO and materialism, naturalists will probably have to give up realism about other minds as well. Needless to say, these are not the happiest of consequences. RMO and ROM are both intuitively well entrenched, and materialism is almost universally regarded as de rigueur for any self-respecting naturalist. The price of naturalism is high, and not at all widely advertised. Couple this with the fact (observed in the Introduction and Part I) that it can be no part of naturalism to say that anyone *ought* to be a naturalist, or that accepting naturalism is more rational from an epistemic point of view than adopting any other research program, and one naturally finds oneself casting about for alternatives. Embracing naturalism might make sense if you are already an antirealist, a dualist, and a solipsist; but anyone else ought to think twice before jumping on the already overcrowded naturalistic bandwagon.

But what are the alternatives? Naturalism requires its adherents to treat the methods of science alone as basic sources of evidence. Thus, strictly speaking, there will be as many alternatives to naturalism as there are nonscientific ways of investigating the world. Many of these (for example, research programs treating the methods of phrenology or the methods of fifteenth century alchemists as basic sources of evidence) may be dismissed out of hand—not necessarily because it is irrational to adopt them (though it might be), but because no reflective, intelligent person nowadays is likely to adopt them. However, two programs deserve special consideration. The first, intuitionism, takes rational intuitions and the methods of natural science, but nothing else, as basic sources of evidence. The second, supernaturalism, takes at least the methods of science and religious experience as basic sources.

The present chapter focuses on intuitionism. I will argue that intuitionism is self-defeating unless it gives rise to evidence that warrants belief in a cosmic designer. I will begin by explaining in more detail my use of the terms 'intuition' and 'rational intuition'. I will then argue that, absent evidence for the existence of a cosmic designer, intuitionists—at any rate those with what I take to be 'ordinary' or 'normal' beliefs and intuitions—have a defeater for the belief that intuition can rationally be treated as a basic source of evidence. If this is right, it implies that intuitionism is, by its own lights, irrational. I will go on to examine some of the most persuasive considerations in support of the claim that intuition is a reliable source of evidence; however, it will shortly become clear that, though these considerations may provide good reason for thinking that our intuitions are reliable in certain restricted domains, they do not support the thesis that intuition can rationally be treated as a basic source of evidence. We will also see that these considerations do not support the thesis that our intuitions about IMP-propositions are reliable; hence they offer no solace to anyone hoping to co-opt them in the service of helping naturalism to avoid the ontological consequences described in Part II.

1. Intuition

As noted in Chapter 3, I follow George Bealer in taking intuitions to be conscious episodes, not involving memory, sense perception, or inference, in which a proposition seems to be true.[1] For example, it seems to many people that modus ponens is valid, that all red things are colored, that there must be a set of all sets, that the behavior characteristic of human beings is evidence that they have minds, and so on. Furthermore, in most people these seemings are conscious episodes that are not the products of sensation, memory, or inferential reasoning. Thus, for most they qualify as intuitions.

Notice that, as far as the definition is concerned, intuited propositions may be true or false, and they may have their truth values

---

[1] See e.g. Bealer (1987, 1993, 1996*a,b*, 1998, 1999). Bonjour (1998) takes a similar approach. The only real difference between my approach and Bealer's is that Bealer does not explicitly state that intuitions must be noninferential episodes.

necessarily or contingently. Note also that hunches are not intuitions in the sense under consideration here, though they are sometimes described as if they were intuitions. For example: a juror may decide before the trial begins that she will register a 'guilty' vote simply because the defendant 'seems to be guilty'; and she may even say that she had the intuition that he was guilty. Or a mother may wake up in the night with the strong conviction that her son is in danger; and, again, she may later describe it as an intuition to the effect that he was in danger. As Bealer points out (1998: 210), these sorts of episodes seem to be better described as ungrounded convictions rather than as intuitions. The reason is that they appear not to be genuine *seemings* at all. The phenomenology is different. One cannot just see, or seem to see, that a defendant is guilty or that one's absent son is in danger in the way that one sees that modus ponens is valid or in the way that one seems to see that there must be a set of all sets. Furthermore, as Bealer also points out, ungrounded convictions, unlike genuine intuitions, are automatically displaced as soon as one appreciates evidence to the contrary. Note too that, just as intuitions are different from hunches, they also are different from beliefs or judgments. I have the intuition that there must be a set of all sets; but (because I am aware of the relevant paradox) I do not believe that there is a set of all sets. Finally, we should observe that, in addition to seeming to be true, a proposition might seem to be necessarily true. Following Bealer again, I hold that one's intuition that *p* is a *rational intuition* only if *p* seems to be necessarily true; otherwise it is a *physical intuition*.[2] Except where otherwise indicated, talk about intuitions in this book is always meant to be taken as talk about rational intuitions.

So, as I will understand it, treating rational intuition as a source of evidence is precisely a matter of treating the *appearance of necessity* as evidence in favor of a proposition. Intuitionism therefore presupposes that it is possible for some propositions to be justified a priori. For this reason, it is tempting to identify intuitionism with rationalism; and, on some definitions of rationalism, such an identification is appropriate. However, I have shied away from this identification because there are other ways of drawing the distinction between empiricism and rationalism according to which the identification is inappropriate. For example, one might characterize rationalism

---

[2] Thus, 'rational intuition' as I use the term is akin to what Laurence Bonjour calls *rational insight* (Bonjour 1998).

simply as the view that a priori knowledge is possible. On this characterization, intuitionism would be a species of rationalism, but not identical to it (since one could believe that a priori knowledge is possible without treating the appearance of necessity in general as evidence).

There are, of course, other definitions of 'intuition' in the literature. For example, Jerrold Katz (1998) holds that intuition is the immediate apprehension of the structure of an abstract object; Alvin Goldman (1999) holds that (philosophical) intuitions are conscious spontaneous beliefs or judgments typically about whether particular concepts apply to particular hypothetical examples; and Ernest Sosa (1998) defines intuitions as dispositions to believe particular abstract propositions upon fully understanding them. All of these definitions are at least plausible; and, importantly, all will give rise to somewhat different characterizations of intuitionism since all will give rise to different understandings of what is involved in treating intuitions as evidence. Thus, one might reasonably wonder what justifies me in focusing exclusively on 'Bealer-intuitions' in discussing intuitionism as one of only two noteworthy alternatives to naturalism.

The answer is that defining intuitionism in terms of Bealer-intuitions is the best way to give my discussion the appropriate scope. With a few exceptions, it is very implausible to think that contingent truths could be known a priori; and the exceptional cases are not cases that would be of help to an intuitionist in avoiding the arguments of the present chapter.[3] On the other hand, as I will explain in more detail later, the sorts of necessary truths (IMP-propositions) that we would have to know a priori in order to avoid the ontological consequences of naturalism are *not* abstract propositions, nor are they propositions about the structures of abstract objects or about the applicability of our concepts to hypothetical cases. Thus, defining intuitionism in more restricted terms, as we would be doing if we followed someone like Katz, Goldman, or Sosa in our definition of intuition, seems to cast the net too narrowly.

Of course, one might worry that there are arguments in support of the evidential value of intuitions as understood by Katz, Goldman, or Sosa that *could* be extended to support the claim that we can have a

---

[3] Alleged exceptions include propositions like *I exist, I am here, the standard meter stick is one meter in length, the time is now*, and so on.

priori knowledge of IMP-propositions but that do not support the evidential value of Bealer-intuitions. Thus, one might worry that potential support for intuitionism, or at least for the reliability of intuition with respect to IMP-beliefs, might be overlooked by focusing on Bealer-intuitions. But such a worry would be misguided. Any defense of the evidential value of intuitions as defined by people like Katz, Goldman, and Sosa is readily taken to be a defense of the prima facie evidential value of Bealer-intuitions *in certain restricted domains*. The reason is that all of the propositions that Katz, Goldman, and Sosa recognize as the proper objects of intuition are propositions that typically appear to us to be necessarily true if they appear to be true at all; and, as a general rule, the appearance of necessity gives rise to belief except in those cases where we have acquired specific reasons for withholding belief.

In the next three sections I will present my argument against intuitionism. My argument is inspired by and in some important respects resembles Alvin Plantinga's widely discussed 'evolutionary argument against naturalism'. Thus, it is only natural to preface my argument with a brief discussion of Plantinga's. Before doing that, however, I must begin by introducing some terms, assumptions, and qualifications.

2. Preliminaries

As Plantinga defines it, *naturalism* is the view that there is no such being as God or any other supernatural designing agent. Obviously, then, his understanding of naturalism is very different from mine. On his view, naturalism is not a research program, but rather a kind of extended atheism. Thus, for the sake of clarity, I am going to use the label 'atheism' to refer to the view that Plantinga refers to with the label 'naturalism', and I will henceforth refer to Plantinga's argument as an evolutionary argument against atheism. Still, to the extent that naturalists are presently committed to atheism, the argument may have implications for naturalism after all.

An important ingredient in Plantinga's argument is the concept of a *defeater*. Roughly, one has a defeater for a belief B just in case one has beliefs or experiences that somehow undermine one's justification for believing B. Typically, philosophers recognize two kinds of defeaters: rebutting and undercutting. As I will understand these notions, a person has a rebutting defeater for a belief B just in case she takes herself to be justified in believing that B is false, and she has an undercutting defeater just in case one of the following two conditions is met: (*a*) she believes B on the basis of other beliefs or experiences, but she takes herself to be justified in believing that those beliefs and experiences do not confer epistemic justification on B; or (*b*) she does not believe B on the basis of other beliefs or experiences, and she takes herself to be justified in believing that it is epistemically irrational to believe B without believing it on the basis of other beliefs or experiences.[4] Note that one might take oneself to be justified in believing *p* without yet believing *p*. Thus, defeat does not require the occurrent belief that the defeated belief is either false or inadequately supported. All it requires is that one see that one would be justified in so believing. Note too that *falsely* taking oneself to be justified in believing the denial of B or that one has inadequate grounds for B will be sufficient to provide a defeater for B. The reason is that, as most contemporary epistemologists agree, one cannot be justified in holding a belief that one takes to be unjustified.[5] Finally, I assume that one can take oneself to be justified in believing something without doing so under that description. Nonphilosophers surely acquire defeaters for various beliefs, but it is doubtful that in so doing they ever explicitly employ the concept of epistemic justification. Still, it makes sense to think that they have the concept, and that in acquiring defeaters they are, in some meaningful sense, taking themselves to lack appropriate justification for the defeated belief.

Since one might acquire evidence on both sides of a disputed matter, defeaters themselves might be defeated. For example: Suppose your friend has been accused of a crime. You believe that she is innocent, but you then acquire forensic information pointing to her guilt. Later, however, she insists with all fervor and sincerity that she is innocent and offers plausible explanations for the forensic information. Furthermore, you have every reason to believe that her testimony on this matter is completely trustworthy. Assuming you take all of this evidence at face value and treat it as having justificatory force, the forensic information (absent her testimony) defeats your belief that she is innocent, whereas her later testimony defeats that defeater

---

[4] This is closely in accord with the account of defeaters offered in Plantinga (1994). For somewhat different views, see Bergmann (1997*a,b*, 2000*b*); Pollock (1995); and Pollock and Cruz (1999).

[5] On this, see Bergmann (1997*a*).

by undermining your justification for believing that the forensic information is evidence of her guilt.

As I am understanding these notions, once a defeater is defeated it ceases to be a defeater. Thus, upon hearing your friend's testimony and appreciating its evidential force, you do not have both a defeater for your belief that she is innocent and a defeater for that defeater. Rather, the second defeater simply cancels the first. If, upon appreciating your friend's later testimony you take yourself to be justified in believing that the forensic information does not justify belief in your friend's guilt, it is hard to see how, at the same time, you could take yourself on the basis of the forensic information to be justified in believing that your friend is guilty. Maybe it is possible for someone (suffering from serious cognitive malfunction) to think in this way; but even if it is, I am going to assume for purposes here that it never happens. This allows me the convenience of saying that having a defeater for a belief makes it epistemically irrational to persist in holding the belief. I would not be able to say this if it were possible to have at the same time a defeater for a belief and a defeater for that defeater.

Another important ingredient in Plantinga's argument is the notion of objective probability. As Plantinga himself notes, this is a notion widely employed but difficult to analyze. On the one hand, we have statistical probabilities. For example, an actuary might report that the (objective) probability of a German male dying before the age 41 is 0.01106; but this report will be equivalent to something like the claim that the proportion of men insured by the age of 40 and satisfying various other criteria who were dead before their 41st birthday is 0.01106.[6] These sorts of probability claims are relatively unproblematic. On the other hand, we sometimes talk about object-ive probability in single cases, where it makes no sense to suppose that the sort of probability we have in mind is statistical. For example: the objective chance of a fair coin coming up heads is 0.5, and this even if it is flipped only once and it is the only coin in the world. Each of the six sides of a fair die has a 0.17 chance of landing face up, and this even if it is rolled only once and there are no other dice. The objective probability that evolutionary processes would give rise to human beings apart from intervention by a cosmic designer is astronomically low. The objective probability that Mars will not depart significantly

---

[6] The example is due to von Mises (1957: 16–17).

from its orbital path today is extremely high. It is these sorts of statements that raise difficulties.

It is tempting to try to understand objective probability in terms of proportions of possible worlds. Intuitively, the probability of a fair coin landing heads is 0.5 because half of the *relevant possibilities*—i.e. half of the worlds that share our history up to the time of the flip, our natural laws, and so on—are worlds in which heads appears. Likewise, the probability of evolutionary processes giving rise to humans is low, apparently because the vast majority of relevant possibilities are possibilities in which evolutionary processes occur but human beings do not appear. But, of course, this intuitive suggestion will not do; for (presumably) there are infinitely many possible worlds, and it makes no sense to talk about halves, or majorities, or any other proportion of an infinite set. Perhaps some progress could be made by defining the objective probability of a proposition p on evidence e and background assumptions b in terms of the 'infinitary analogue' of the proportion of (e & b)-worlds which are also p-worlds.[7] But what exactly that analogue would be is far from clear.

For this reason, I propose for purposes of exposition to leave the notion of objective probability as an unanalyzed primitive. I take it that our intuitive grasp of the notion is sufficient to permit evaluation of the probability claims that play load-bearing roles in Plantinga's argument; and I also think that, in places where controversy might arise, an analysis of the notion of objective probability would offer little help in resolving the controversy. However, when it comes time to suggest modifications to the argument, I will for dialectical reasons recommend changes that remove from the argument any reference to objective probability.

As should be clear from Chapter 1, I assume that everyone trusts at least one source of evidence even in the absence of evidence in favor of its reliability. I also assume that everyone is prima facie justified in trusting the sources they treat as basic. Obviously enough, then, I am committed to the claim that the belief that our basic sources are reliable is both justified and not based on evidence (not even non-propositional evidence).[8] Furthermore, I would go so far as to say that one *can* be justified in treating *any* source as basic—at least until one's

---

[7] Cf. Plantinga (1993: 144–51, 161–3).

[8] This claim is controversial. For example, Michael Bergmann (2002) suggests that our justification for believing that our cognitive faculties are reliable comes from nonpropositional evidence; and he also attributes this view to Thomas Reid. But I take it that one

research program runs aground in self-defeat. But different people treat different sources as basic; thus, I think it is probably a mistake to say, as Thomas Reid does, that it is a 'first principle . . . that the natural faculties, by which we distinguish truth from error, are not fallacious' (1983: 275). The truth in the neighborhood is that it is a first principle that the sources of evidence we happen to treat as basic are reliable. But I see no reason to believe that there is a fixed set of natural faculties such that, for everyone, it is a first principle that those faculties are reliable. To say this is to say that everyone shares a research program; but, if the history of philosophy is any guide, this latter claim is false.

Still, what is important to recognize is that, though we can be justified in trusting a source even in the absence of evidence in favor of its reliability, such prima facie justification is defeasible. We can acquire evidence that leads us to take ourselves to be justified in believing that one of the sources we treat as basic is unreliable, or that it is not properly trusted in the absence of evidence for its reliability. In such a case, our research program defeats itself. When that happens, we are not justified in treating as basic *all and only* the sources treated as basic by that research program. We must move to a new research program, either by adding some basic sources or by subtracting some. In the case of intuitionism, this will probably involve a move either to naturalism or to supernaturalism.

Finally, my argument rests on certain assumptions about what intuitions will be common among intuitionists. For example, I assume that nobody will have the intuition that, necessarily, for any evidence one might have against the general reliability of rational intuition, it is always rational to treat intuition as a basic source of evidence. I also assume that nobody will have the intuition that it is a necessary truth that natural evolutionary processes will produce human organisms with reliable cognitive faculties. No doubt other such assumptions lurk in my argument as well. I cannot list them all; nor do I think that they are all strictly true. Some people have unusual intuitions, and I have no business ruling that out a priori. Still, I believe that most readers of this book will conform to the assumptions. Those who do not *might* accept intuitionism without being

---

consequence of the argument in the first section of Ch. 1 is that this assumption could not possibly be true for *all* of the sources we trust. Recognizing evidence as such requires a prior disposition to trust something as a source of evidence; but not all such dispositions can be evidentially based, else we have an infinite regress.

committed to any of the consequences that I will attribute to intuitionism; but my argument is not addressed to them.

3. The Evolutionary Argument against Atheism

We are now ready to discuss Plantinga's argument against atheism.[9] The bare skeleton is as follows. Let R be the proposition that the sources of evidence we treat as basic are reliable.[10] Let A be the proposition that there is no such being as God or any other supernatural designing agent. Let E be the proposition that human beings are the products of evolutionary processes. Let us also adopt the convention that where p is a proposition, B_p is the belief that p is true. Thus, B_R is the belief that R is true, and $B_{A\&E}$ is the belief that A & E is true. Then:

(8.1) The sensible attitude to take toward the objective conditional probability of R on A & E is to believe that $P(R/A \& E)$ is low or inscrutable.

(8.2) One who believes A & E and who believes that $P(R/A \& E)$ is low or inscrutable has a defeater for B_R.[11]

(8.3) Therefore: One who believes A & E and sensibly reflects on $P(R/A \& E)$ has a defeater for B_R.

(8.4) Having a defeater for B_R gives one a defeater for all of one's beliefs.

---

[9] See Plantinga (1991; 1993, ch. 12; 1999; 1994). See also Plantinga (2002) for replies to criticism of the argument.

[10] In Plantinga's discussions, R is the proposition that our cognitive faculties are reliable. But to which faculties is R supposed to refer? Intuitionists and naturalists, for example, can agree that, in some sense, we have a 'faculty of intuition' (i.e. we have a capacity for having conscious episodes that satisfy the definition of intuition). But they disagree about whether intuition is reliable. Do they also then disagree about R? That depends on whether R is supposed to be (*a*) the proposition that *whatever faculties human beings have* are reliable, or (*b*) a proposition like *those faculties that I treat as basic are reliable*. Since R is not, in the context of the present argument, supposed to be highly controversial, I think that it is most sensibly interpreted along the lines suggested in (*b*).

[11] Plantinga's own version of the argument includes the premise that the defeater acquired by reflecting upon $P(R/A \& E)$ cannot be defeated; hence, later premises talk not about the consequences of having a *defeater* for B_R but rather about the consequences of having an *undefeated* defeater for B_R. Since I am assuming that defeaters cancel one another out, so that one can never have a belief or experience that counts as a *defeated* defeater, the premise that the defeater for B_R cannot be defeated is implied by 8.2. For if the defeater for B_R could be defeated, then it would be possible to believe that $P(R/A \& E)$ is low or inscrutable without having a defeater for B_R, contrary to 8.2.

(8.5) Therefore: One who believes A & E and sensibly reflects on P(R/A & E) has a defeater for $B_{A \& E}$.

(8.6) Therefore: It is irrational for one who sensibly reflects upon P(R/A & E) to believe A & E.

(8.7) But: It is also irrational to believe A and not to believe E.

(8.8) Therefore: It is irrational for one who sensibly reflects upon P(R/A & E) to believe A.

Putting meat on the skeleton is just a matter of defending premises 8.1, 8.2, and 8.4. Plantinga seems to take 8.7 for granted; but given his target, and the current state of science, this seems reasonable. Critics have challenged each of the premises except 8.7; but for present purposes, I will leave most of those challenges and Plantinga's defenses of premises 8.1 and 8.4 undiscussed.[12]

What I want to focus on is premise 8.2. My own opinion is that this premise is the real crux of the argument, and that the main weaknesses of the argument lie in Plantinga's defense of it. In the end I will show how the weaknesses might be avoided. Thus, the conclusion of this section will be that if controversies over premises 8.1 and 8.4 can be resolved in Plantinga's favor, his argument for the claim that the conjunction of A and E is self-defeating is successful. More importantly, however, once it is clear how to shore up premise 8.2, it is easy to build a similar but much more convincing argument for the conclusion that intuitionism is self-defeating unless it warrants belief in a cosmic designer.

Summarizing his own defense of premise 8.2 as it appeared in *Warrant and Proper Function* (1993), Plantinga writes:

I argued [for 8.2] by analogy. Among the crucially important facts, with respect to the question of the reliability of a group of cognitive faculties, are facts about their *origin*. Suppose I believe that I have been created by a Cartesian evil demon who takes delight in fashioning creatures who have mainly false beliefs (but think of themselves as paradigms of cognitive excellence): then I have a defeater for my natural belief that my faculties are reliable. Turn instead to the contemporary version of this scenario, and suppose I come to believe that I have been captured by Alpha-Centaurian superscientists who have made me the subject of a cognitive experiment in which the subject is given mostly false beliefs: then, again, I have a defeater

---

[12] For a suitable variety of such challenges, along with Plantinga's replies, see Plantinga (1994) and the articles referred to therein, as well as the articles and Plantinga's reply in Beilby (2002).

for R. But to have a defeater for R it is not necessary that I believe that in fact I *have* been created by a Cartesian demon or been captured by those Alpha-Centaurian superscientists. It suffices for me to have such a defeater if I have considered those scenarios, and the probability that one of those scenarios is true is inscrutable for me—I cannot make any estimate of it, do not have an opinion as to what the probability is. It suffices if I have considered those scenarios, and *for all I know or believe* one of them is true. In these cases too I have a reason for doubting, a reason for withholding my natural belief that my cognitive faculties are reliable. (Plantinga 1994: 11–12)

Contrary to what some critics have suggested, the idea here is *not* that the bare possibility of our having been created by a Cartesian demon or captured by Alpha-Centaurian superscientists provides us with a defeater. Obviously such possibilities are genuine; but they are remote. Not only do we not believe that we are victims of such skeptical scenarios, but we take their objective probability to be very low. However, if we did believe that some skeptical scenario *s* were true (as the naturalist believes A & E), we clearly would have a defeater for B_R; and presumably at least part of the reason is that $P(R/s)$ is low. Hence the analogy. Moreover, Plantinga says, even if we took the objective probability of *s* to be inscrutable, we would still have a defeater for B_R. This seems right. If you do not even think it is *unlikely* that you are the victim of some skeptical scenario, how could you be justified in believing that your faculties are reliable? But notice that, in this case, $P(R/s)$ is *not* inscrutable. So how are we supposed to get analogical support for the claim that those who believe that a defeater for B_R issues from believing both that A & E is true and that $P(R/A \& E)$ is inscrutable? I take it the answer is something like this: $P(s)$ would be inscrutable only if the probability of R on our total evidence about the origin of our cognitive faculties were inscrutable. Thus, if we acquire a defeater for B_R upon coming to believe that $P(s)$ is inscrutable, so too (by analogy) we should acquire a defeater for B_R upon coming to believe both that A & E is true and that $P(R/A \& E)$ is inscrutable.

Still, it is not immediately clear how much weight to assign to Plantinga's analogies. The reason, as critics have pointed out, is that there appear to be alternative analogical cases that do not support premise 8.2.[13] For example: I believe, on the testimony of my very reliable grandmother, that she worked in a parachute factory during

---

[13] For objections in this neighborhood, see Merricks (2002) and van Cleve (2002). See also Otte (2002) and Plantinga's discussion of the 'Perspiration Objection' in Plantinga (1994).

the Second World War. But, upon reflection, I see that the objective probability of this being true on the evidence that she is an American old enough to have been alive during the Second World War is very low. Do I have a defeater for my belief that my grandmother worked in a parachute factory? Clearly not. I win free nachos at a local fast food store. I believe that I have won fairly—that, for example, the nacho lottery was not rigged in my favor by an unknown benefactor. But, upon reflection, I find that the objective probability of my fairly winning on the evidence that I am a customer at the store is completely inscrutable. (I have no idea what proportion of customers win free nachos. Maybe everyone does; maybe one in a million do.) Do I have a defeater for the belief that I have won fairly? Again, clearly not. In some cases, obviously enough, conditional improbability does not issue in defeat; and neither does inscrutability of conditional probability.

For reasons that will become clear shortly, I do not really believe that the cases just described actually succeed as counterexamples to premise 8.2. But it is not immediately obvious *why* they do not; and, unfortunately, Plantinga offers no clear way of settling the issue. He has given no principled way of determining whether any of the above cases (mine or his) are 'relevantly analogous' to the naturalist's situation with respect to R, A, and E. We have our intuitions; but the argument is dialectically weakened by the fact that people's intuitions about which cases are relevant and which cases are not seem to diverge dramatically. This problem would disappear if there were some general principle such that (*a*) we found the principle itself strongly intuitive, (*b*) we could see premise 8.2 as resting on the principle, and (*c*) we could see the various analogical cases as putative illustrations of or counterexamples to the principle. But this is a remedy that Plantinga himself does not offer. He emphasizes that the mere fact that p is improbable on q does not all by itself imply that B_p is defeated for someone who believes q and sees the relevant conditional improbability. But nowhere does he tell us what, in addition to conditional improbability, is necessary or sufficient for defeat. Indeed, he explicitly denies having any general principle in mind.[14] The argument is *nothing more than* an argument from analogy. Fair enough; the argument is what it is. But as such it is considerably less conclusive than an argument whose central analogies

---

[14] Plantinga (2002, p. 11, sect. IV).

are undergirded by a clearly articulated general principle that can be tested by searching for counterexamples.

I hope to remove this weakness in Plantinga's argument by proposing a plausible general principle that will support a suitably modified version of premise 8.2 while not contradicting what I take to be common intuitions about the various analogical cases described above. The general principle that I propose is the following:

> (GP) Let p be a proposition believed by S not on the basis of evidence, and let Z be the set of S's beliefs and experiences. Then: S has a defeater for B_p if, but not only if, S sees that (a) there is a belief or experience ε in Z such that S's rational degree of confidence that p in light of ε is not high, and (b) there is no belief or experience ε^* in Z such that S's rational degree of confidence that p in light of ($\varepsilon \,\&\, \varepsilon^*$) is high.

On this, several comments are in order.

First, I assume (naturally enough) that the roles of ε and ε^* might be played by beliefs and experiences either singly or in groups. Thus, even where I talk of finding 'a' belief or experience ε^*, it is to be understood that doing so might *really* be a matter of finding multiple beliefs or experiences to play that role.

Second, I assume for purposes here that whenever conditions (a) and (b) hold with respect to a belief, we can see that they hold. No doubt this assumption is false; but making it will simplify the following discussion without substantially affecting the argument or its conclusion. Where I speak of GP implying that we have defeaters, it should be obvious anyway from my account of defeaters that, strictly speaking, GP implies that we have defeaters only if conditions (a) and (b) are *recognized* as being satisfied. So making the assumption simply prevents me from having to include the qualification repeatedly.

Third, GP makes no reference to objective probability. Perhaps objective probability has some role to play in the background of GP. For example, it might be that our assessments of objective probability somehow explain or are explained by some of our assessments of rational degree of confidence. But I make no assumptions about what this connection might be. However, it does seem that we have a clearer intuitive grasp of the notion of rational degree of confidence than we do of the notion of objective probability, and that our assessments of the former are less slippery and controversial than our assessments of the latter. It is for this reason that I make use of the notion in GP, and it is also for this reason that I will ultimately recast Plantinga's argument in terms of rational degree of confidence.

Fourth, it might appear that GP could be more simply formulated as follows: S has a defeater for B_p if, but not only if, S's rational degree of confidence that p in light of all the members of Z taken together is not high. However, I opt against this formulation because it is doubtful that one could entertain all of the members of Z at once. Thus, I suspect that there simply is no such thing as the rational degree of confidence that p in light of all the members of Z, since p could not possibly be considered and assessed in light of *all* those members.

Fifth, I assume — as seems obvious — that, for any propositions p and g one's rational degree of confidence that p in light of $B_{g\,\&\,p}$ will be no higher than one's rational degree of confidence that p in light of B_g. Also, I assume that, where r is a proposition believed solely on the basis of p, one's rational degree of confidence that p in light of $B_{g\,\&\,r}$ is no higher than one's rational degree of confidence that p in light of B_g.

Sixth, note that the sort of defeater that results from the satisfaction of conditions (a) and (b) in GP is an *undercutting defeater*. In particular, it is the sort of undercutting defeater one has when one takes oneself to be justified in believing that a belief she holds not on the basis of evidence can rationally be believed only if it is supported by evidence. Moreover, this seems to be the sort of defeater that Plantinga's original argument offered for B_R. Plantinga does not assert that A & E counts as evidence in support of the proposition that our faculties are *unreliable*. But he also does not think that A & E counts as evidence against the truth or veridicality of the evidence upon which B_R is based (for he does not think that B_R is held on the basis of evidence). Thus, plausibly, the idea is supposed to be that our seeing that P(R/A & E) is low or inscrutable is evidence that B_R is no longer rationally held in the absence of evidence in its favor. But, Plantinga says, it is impossible to acquire evidence in favor of B_R; hence, the defeat is final.

Finally, GP is in accord with our intuitions about skeptical scenarios. Let s be a proposition to the effect that some skeptical scenario obtains (e.g. we are brains in vats, in the clutches of a Cartesian demon, or whatever). Most philosophers take it for granted that our initial rational degree of confidence that not-s is very high. So do I; and, given this assumption, GP does not imply that we have a defeater for not-s. Since we have a high initial rational degree of confidence that not-s, and since most of us have no beliefs or experiences that diminish our rational degree of confidence that not-s, our rational degree of confidence that not-*s* in light of any of our beliefs and experiences will always be high. However, it *is* possible to acquire a defeater for not-*s*. For example: Morpheus tells you that you are a victim of the Matrix. He tells you that your (real) body is lying in a vat of nutrients, your brain is connected to a large supercomputer (the Matrix), and none of your current sensory experiences are veridical—all are just the result of your brain's interaction with the Matrix. He then gives you a pill, after which you have experiences that seem to be experiences of your becoming disconnected from the Matrix and experiencing Reality for the first time. Later, however, you realize that taking the pill might have brought about just the opposite. Perhaps you were not connected to any Matrix, but the pill rendered you unconscious and Morpheus himself connected you to something like the Matrix so that all of your *current* experiences are nonveridical. Now, I should think, being a victim of a skeptical scenario is a live option. You have had genuine experiences to the effect that the truth of some such scenario is not at all a remote possibility. In light of those experiences, and in light of your realization that you cannot now tell whether, upon taking the pill, you left the Matrix, or entered the Matrix, or embarked upon some other sort of colossal and still-persisting hallucinatory experience, your rational degree of confidence that you are not now in some Matrix-like scenario is not high. Furthermore, it is plausible to think that none of your other beliefs or experiences could possibly raise your rational degree of confidence in that proposition. Intuitively, then, you have a defeater for your belief that you are not now in some Matrix-like scenario. Accordingly, you also have a defeater for B_R—or, at any rate, for B_R specified to whatever sources (like sense perception and memory) are called into question by the Matrix scenario.[15]

I turn now to the question of how GP bears upon the various analogical cases cited for and against 8.2. Consider first the case where you assign high or inscrutable probability to the hypothesis that you are the victim of a Cartesian evil demon or to the hypothesis that you are in the clutches of an Alpha-Centaurian superscientist. I do not know whether there is any *necessary* connection between assigning high probability to *p* and being unable to be rationally highly confi-

---

[15] Plantinga (2002) lists some other ways in which you might acquire a defeater for the belief that you are not a victim of a skeptical scenario and hence also a defeater for BR (or some suitably restricted version thereof). For example: you might come to believe that you are insane, or that you have ingested an unreliability-inducing substance. In each of these cases too GP yields the right result.

dent that not-p. But it seems clear that as Plantinga has set up his examples, you have beliefs and experiences which make it impossible to be highly rationally confident (even in light of your other beliefs and experiences) that you are not in the clutches of a Cartesian demon or an Alpha-Centaurian superscientist. Accordingly, you have beliefs and experiences which make it impossible (even in light of any other beliefs and experiences you might have) to be highly rationally confident that R is true. By GP, then, you have a defeater for B_R; and, as in the Matrix scenario described above, this is intuitively the correct answer.

However, GP does not imply that I have a defeater for the beliefs that take center stage in the two apparent counterexample cases. Let g be the proposition that my grandmother worked in a parachute factory; let w be the proposition that I have won free nachos in the fast food store's nacho lottery. For one thing, neither B_g nor B_w is initially held in the absence of evidence. Thus, it follows immediately that GP does not imply that I have defeaters for those beliefs. Even ignoring this, however, there is a second reason why GP does not imply that I have defeaters. Admittedly, my rational degree of confidence that g in light of just my belief that my grandmother is an American old enough to have lived during the Second World War is low. Likewise, my rational degree of confidence that w in light of just my belief that I am a customer at the fast food store is low. But in both cases I have other beliefs and experiences in light of which my rational degree of confidence in each of g and w is high, even when those beliefs and experiences are considered in conjunction with the original ones. In the first case, I believe that my grandmother is reliable and that she told me that she worked in a parachute factory. In the second case, I have free nachos in hand and no beliefs or experiences that even so much as suggest that an unknown benefactor might have rigged the nacho lottery in my favor. Thus, again, GP does not imply that I have defeaters for these beliefs. Similar remarks apply to all of the other counterexample cases that I am aware of that appear in the literature.

But if GP is true, then a suitably modified version of premise 8.2 is secure. Suppose that one's rational degree of confidence that R, given just A & E, is not high. (Though defense of this claim is not required to show that GP supports a modified version of 8.2, we may pause to note that it is fairly intuitive. Even if we start with a rationally high degree of confidence that R, it seems clear that reflection upon what A & E imply about the production of our cognitive faculties ought to undermine our confidence that R, even if it does not generate the belief that our faculties are *un*reliable.) On this assumption, we will have a defeater for R *unless* we have in our cognitive repertoire some other belief or experience ε^* such that our rational degree of confidence that R in light of $B_{A \& E \& \varepsilon^*}$ is high. But what could that be? It is certainly *possible* to have beliefs and experiences that do the job required by ε^*. Perhaps it seems to you to be a necessary truth that R; or perhaps it seems to you that you are the star of the universe and so it is nomologically necessary that R will be true of you. Then you will escape defeat. But most of us do not have such beliefs, and those who do have other rationality problems to contend with. For those who have a normal stock of beliefs, once one's rational degree of confidence that R is diminished by A & E, there seems to be nothing left to elevate it again.

Note that finding a belief or experience ε^* such that one's rational degree of confidence that R in light of $B_{A \& E \& \varepsilon^*}$ is higher than one's rational degree of confidence that R in light of $B_{A \& E}$ on its own is not the same as finding evidential support for R. In fact, I take it that the very supposition that R admits of evidential support will lead to self-defeat. The reason is that R is a proposition attributing reliability to our *basic* sources of evidence—sources that we trust even in the absence of evidence for their reliability. Thus, if we acquire evidence in support of R, we at the same time acquire evidence *against* the claim that the sources we treat as basic are rationally treated as basic. (I assume that most of us have a research program according to which it is irrational to believe, in the complete absence of evidence, something that can, in principle, be supported by evidence.) So, upon pain of self-defeat, we should resist the temptation to think that we might acquire evidential support for R. Nevertheless, we *can* have beliefs or experiences ε and ε^* such that, though one's rational degree of confidence that R in light of ε is low, one's rational degree of confidence that R in light of $\varepsilon \& \varepsilon^*$ is high. In that case, belief in R will not be ultimately defeated by attention to ε; but neither will it be evidentially based on or supported by ε^*.

(I did admit earlier that it might make sense to speak of a source or a research program as being *self-supporting* or *self-justifying*; and so too it might make sense to say the same of B_R.[16] But, as I also indicated, I say that a source of evidence or a belief is self-justifying just in case (*a*) the source is appropriately trusted or the belief appropriately held in the absence of evidence for its reliability, and (*b*) trusting the source or

---

[16] Ch. 1, Sect. 1; Ch. 3, Sect. 1.2.

holding the belief does not result in self-defeat. Thus, finding a suitable ε^* such that one's rational degree of confidence that R in light of $B_{A\,\&\,E}$ is high is precisely what is required for R to turn out to be self-justifying in my sense; but ε^* will not in any way confer epistemic justification upon or serve as an evidential basis for R.)

We may observe in passing that, if the foregoing is correct, then it is relatively clear why one common strategy of responding to Plantinga's argument is ineffective. Some critics point out that even if P(R/A & E) is low or inscrutable, the naturalist may have another belief B_O in her evidential repertoire such that P(R/A & E & O) is high.[17] But once we see that rational degree of confidence rather than probability is what is at stake, the irrelevance of this fact becomes readily obvious. Perhaps there is some O such that P(R/A & E & O) is high. But it is very difficult to find some O such that, though one's rational degree of confidence that R in light of $B_{A\,\&\,E}$ is low, one's rational degree of confidence that R in light of $B_{A\,\&\,E\,\&\,O}$ is high. Again, people with unusual beliefs might have an unusual story to tell that supplements the regular evolutionary story about our origins; and that supplemental story *s* might be such that their rational degree of confidence that R in light of $B_{A\,\&\,E\,\&\,s}$ is rather high. Normal people, however, seem not to have any such supplemental story to tell. (Again, we are assuming with Plantinga that the standard evolutionary story, E, is such that rational degree of confidence that R in light of A & E on its own is low.) Thus, they seem to have no way of avoiding defeat.

So, given that $B_{A\,\&\,E}$ diminishes one's rational degree of confidence that R, and given that we have no supplemental story to add to A & E in order to restore our rational degree of confidence that R, GP implies that anyone who believes A & E has a defeater for B_R. If this is right, then Plantinga's argument can be recast as follows:

(8.1*) One who sensibly reflects upon A & E's bearing upon R will see that the rational degree of confidence that R in light of $B_{A\,\&\,E}$ is not high.

(8.2*) One who believes A & E and who is such that her rational degree of confidence that R in light of $B_{A\,\&\,E}$ is not high has a defeater for B_R.

(8.3*) Therefore: One who believes A & E and sensibly reflects upon A & E's bearing upon R has a defeater for B_R.

---

[17] See e.g. Ginet (1995) and O'Connor (1994).

(8.4*) Having a defeater for B_R gives one a defeater for all of one's beliefs.

(8.5*) Therefore: One who believes A & E and sensibly reflects upon A & E's bearing on R has a defeater for $B_{A\,\&\,E}$.

(8.6*) Therefore: It is irrational for one who sensibly reflects upon A & E's bearing upon R to believe A & E.

(8.7*) But: It is also irrational to believe A and not to believe E.

(8.8*) Therefore: It is irrational for one who sensibly reflects upon A & E's bearing upon R to believe A.

GP supports 8.2*. Thus, if GP is correct, premise 8.2* is secure and those who would resist the evolutionary argument against atheism must look elsewhere to do so. Specifically, they must argue that our rational degree of confidence that R in light of $B_{A\,\&\,E}$ is neither low nor inscrutable, or that having a defeater for B_R does not amount to having a defeater for everything else one believes.[18] I believe that both of these claims are false and that the evolutionary argument is sound; and I think that, if the argument is sound, then it shows that any research program (naturalism included) that gives rise to evidence for A & E is self-defeating. However, I will not attempt to defend these stronger conclusions here. My focus, rather, is on intuitionism; and much weaker premises in conjunction with GP are sufficient to show that, unless it warrants belief in a cosmic designer, intuitionism is self-defeating.

4. Against Intuitionism

Consider an intuitionist who believes that human cognitive faculties are not the products of intelligent design. Such a person will be committed to A; and, given the current state of science and the lack of any plausible nontheistic alternative to evolutionary theory, she will also be committed to E. But now what should she think about the thesis (RI) that intuition is a generally reliable source of evidence?

Let us assume that RI is initially believed not on the basis of evidence, and let us examine the rational degree of confidence one might have that RI in light of $B_{A\,\&\,E}$. Plantinga, as we have seen, holds that there is no reason to think that it is likely that evolution would select for truth-tracking faculties. In fact, he goes further: he argues

---

[18] Fales (2002), Fitelson and Sober (1998), Fodor (1998), and Ramsey (2002) all argue in support of the former. In support of the latter, see van Cleve (2002).

that there is good reason to think it likely that evolution *would not* select for truth-tracking faculties. He defends this claim mainly by pointing out that there are many ways in which a system of cognitive faculties might be adaptive without being truth-tracking. Systematically false beliefs in combination with systematically misguided desires might produce adaptive behavior; beliefs or their content might be epiphenomenal so that their falsity would have no maladaptive effects; and so on. If his arguments are sound, then they are sufficient to establish the claim that the rational degree of confidence one might have in *either* R or RI in light of $B_{A \& E}$ is not high.

Critics responding to this part of Plantinga's argument have tended to press for the conclusion that the probability of (and hence, we may assume, the rational degree of confidence that) R on A & E *is* high.[19] Such arguments are most plausible when they are marshaled in defense of the claim that our beliefs and their contents are not epiphenomenal and, despite possibilities to the contrary, the best explanation for the adaptiveness of nonepiphenomenal beliefs is that they tend to track the truth. Especially in the case of sensory beliefs, mathematical beliefs, logical beliefs, and paradigmatic conceptual truths, there is a persuasive case to be made for the conclusion that we (or our ancestors) would probably not have lived long enough to survive and reproduce without those beliefs having a general tendency to be true. It is possible that we (or they) have managed to survive with mostly false beliefs by having systematically misguided desires; but, say the critics, such a possibility seems very remote.

But even if we go along with the critics and concede that our rational degree of confidence that R in light of $B_{A \& E}$ is high, we face special problems when we turn our attention to intuition. The reason is that, whereas Plantinga's critics can point to reasons for thinking that natural selection might favor sensory reliability, and reliability in the domain of logic, mathematics, and elementary conceptual truths, it is extremely hard to see how natural selection could possibly favor the reliability of rational intuition. That is, it is hard to see how evolutionary processes could select for cognitive faculties in which the bare appearance of necessity is a generally reliable indicator of genuine necessity. Consider natural laws. As we saw in Chapter 6, some take the laws to be metaphysical necessities; others take them to have a degree of necessity that is intermediate between brute

---

[19] See Fales (2002), Fitelson and Sober (1998), Fodor (1998), and Ramsey (2002).

regularity and metaphysical necessity; and others deny that there is any necessity to the (alleged) laws at all. In philosophical circles this debate is of some interest; but from an evolutionary point of view, how could having true beliefs on this topic possibly matter? So long as one gets the relevant regularities right, from a fitness point of view it seems wholly irrelevant whether one also happens to believe that some of the regularities are also necessities. Similarly, believing mathematical falsehoods, logical falsehoods, and conceptual falsehoods might result in failure to survive and reproduce. But how could there be any evolutionary advantage associated with having true beliefs about the modal status of these propositions? So long as one believes that $2 + 2 = 4$ will *always* be true, it does not seem to matter whether one also believes that it is *necessarily* true. Moreover, there seems to be no evolutionary advantage associated with having true beliefs about many of the other propositions that appear to us to be necessary. For example, my intuitions report that each of the following propositions is necessarily true: that no two material things occupy the same place at the same time, that removing one grain from a heap never leaves one with a nonheap, that if Socrates exists he is able to think, that no one is morally responsible for something they were forced to do, that torturing small children is morally wrong, that propositions exist, that it is possibly true that a necessary being exists, and that the axioms of the S5 modal system are true. There are many who share my intuitions on these matters, but there are at least as many who do not; and from an evolutionary point of view, it seems not to matter one bit who is correct. Thus, since it is hard to see any reason why natural selection should favor—or even how it *could* favor—generally reliable intuitions over unreliable ones, it seems clear that our rational degree of confidence that RI in light of $B_{A \& E}$ must be very low.

In sum, then, we have no reason to think that evolutionary processes could give rise to creatures that have reliable rational intuitions and, apparently, good reason to think that they could not. Thus, attention to the bearing of A & E upon RI should greatly diminish our rational degree of confidence in RI. Still, GP does not yet imply that we have a defeater for RI; for we might have some other belief or experience ε^* such that our rational degree of confidence that RI in light of $B_{A \& E \& \varepsilon^*}$ is high. But in fact, as in the case of R, it is hard to see what the relevant ε^* might be. Again, one might have unusual beliefs: one might think that RI is a necessary truth, or one might believe that one is the star of the universe. But normal people seem to be left without any supplemental story to tell.

It may be tempting to think that some sort of appeal to intuition's track record might help. Let SI be the proposition that reliance on intuition has proven enormously successful with respect to reaching the truth, at least in your own case if not in the case of others. Now suppose you believe SI. You might then think that, in light of $B_{A\&E\&SI}$, your rational degree of confidence that RI is rather high. If this is right, then GP would not imply that you have a defeater for RI. (An analogous move might be made in the case of R.) But, in fact, this move is misguided. The reason is as follows. Either your belief that SI is based on evidence or it is not. If it is based on evidence, then it is possible to have evidential support for RI. But if RI can be supported by evidence, then surely it is irrational to accept RI in the *absence* of evidence in its favor. (Again, it seems irrational to accept a proposition without evidence which admits of evidential support.) Thus, it follows that RI is not rationally treated as a basic source of evidence, and so intuitionism still turns out to be self-defeating, albeit for different reasons. On the other hand, if SI is not supported by evidence, then it appears that one's rational degree of confidence that SI in light of $B_{A\&E}$ will match one's rational degree of confidence that RI in light of $B_{A\&E}$. But then it is hard to see how one's rational degree of confidence that RI in light of $B_{A\&E\&SI}$ could be any higher than one's rational degree of confidence that RI in light of $B_{A\&E}$ alone. Intuitively, if $B_{A\&E}$ on its own calls *both* RI and SI into question, then one cannot rationally appeal to SI as a supplemental story to restore one's high degree of confidence that RI is true. (And, of course, the same applies to the analogous move in the case of R.)

What has just been said is sufficient to show that attention to intuition's track record will not help the intuitionist avoid self-defeat. But we should also note that, in fact, attention to intuition's track record seems seriously to hurt the intuitionist's prospects for escaping self-defeat. The reason is that evidence about intuition's track record seems to provide prima facie evidence against RI. Thus, attention to intuition's track record only *further* diminishes one's rational degree of confidence that RI. Rational degree of confidence that RI in light of $B_{A\&E}$ is low; rational degree of confidence that RI in light of $B_{A\&E\&t}$ (where t is a proposition describing intuition's sorry track record) is even lower. The evidence here is familiar. We find that a lot of our intuitions lead us into straightforward contradiction. We find that we often disagree with others about intuitions outside the domain of logical, mathematical, and conceptual truths. We find that our puzzles are perennial, and our disagreements often persistent and intractable. Argument and careful reflection lead us to discover a variety of new conditionals, but they go relatively little distance toward helping us to resolve our disagreements and to provide authoritative solutions to our puzzles. A survey of the history of philosophy reveals that intuition-based theorizing has an extremely poor track record with respect to producing anything like the progress and consensus we find in the empirical sciences. Rather, what we seem to find is strong evidence apparently in support of the conclusion that very many people now and throughout history have had very many false intuitive beliefs. On the surface, this looks like persuasive evidence against the truth of RI.

Granted, this view of the history and success of intuition-based theorizing is controversial. But, in fact, the controversy seems only to underscore my point. Witness, for example, the following exchange. Commenting on George Bealer's (1996*b*) defense of intuition, William Lycan writes:

There is a *corner* in which the philosophical track record is good: logic. Otherwise, the history of philosophy is a disgusting mess of squabbling, inconclusion, dogma and counter-dogma, trendy patois, fashionable but actually groundless assumptions, vacillation from one paradigm to another, mere speculation, and sheer abuse. Nothing in that sordid history can be called *progress*, except what derives directly from developments in logic or in science, and consensus has always been limited to what are really very small groups of people confined in small geographical regions over short periods of time. If we use consensus production as our yardstick, then . . . we find that as between science, common sense, and philosophy, science and common sense do very well while philosophy comes in a pathetically weak third. (Lycan 1996: 149)

In response, Bealer has this to say:

Professor Lycan believes that intuition is extremely unreliable and that intuition-based philosophy differs from science and common sense in that the latter lead to consensus whereas philosophy does not. I completely disagree. The on-balance reliability of our elementary concrete-case intuitions is without question one of the most impressive facts about human cognition. And on the matter of consensus, there is significant agreement on a great many points in philosophical logic, philosophy of language, metaphysics, and epistemology. (E.g., the 'is' of existence vs. the 'is' of predication; knowledge vs. justified true belief; and on and on.) (Bealer 1996*c*: 163)

In this debate, I side with Lycan; and, though admittedly it does not prove *much* on its own, the clear and vehement difference of intuitions displayed here—intuitive disagreements about what counts as *progress, success,* and *consensus,* for example—seems only to support Lycan's point.

Notice that in saying that the track record evidence seems to go against intuition, I am not arguing from the mere fallibility of intuition for the unreliability of intuition. Rather, I am merely pointing out that the apparently *widespread* and *uncorrectable* fallibility of intuition is evidence in light of which our rational degree of confidence in RI is diminished. Nobody doubts that our intuitions are fallible; and almost nobody thinks that mere fallibility is evidence of unreliability. But there is a crucial difference between the fallibility that afflicts (say) perception and memory and the fallibility that plagues intuition. In the case of memory and sense perception, it is usually possible to learn not only *that* you have been misled but also to learn specifically the proposition(s) with respect to which you were misled. So, for example, you do not normally learn that you have been hallucinating without also learning that specific visual or auditory experiences were hallucinatory rather than veridical. Similarly, you do not normally learn that you have misremembered the facts without at the same time learning the particular facts that were misremembered. In the case of intuitions, however, matters are different. In most cases, we learn that *someone's* intuitions are fallible (by observing that ours contradict theirs); but we have no way of discovering *whose* intuitions went wrong. In cases of paradox, we do learn *whose* intuitions are wrong (it's ours that are wrong, if we are in fact appreciating the paradox); but we do not learn *which* intuitions went wrong. Do we give up the proposition that it's impossible that one grain of sand make the difference between a heap and a non-heap? Or do we give up the proposition that there are no heaps composed of exactly one grain of sand? Or do we give up the proposition that there are heaps? We may have opinions; but we cannot really be said to *learn* which one to give up in the way that we learn (say) that we remembered Mel Gibson's last word in *Braveheart* incorrectly by rewinding the tape in the VCR and watching the scene over again.[20]

---

[20] Of course, one might have a strong intuition that some disagreement or apparent paradox is to be resolved in a certain way; and one might insist that having this intuition *is* learning how the paradox is to be resolved. But the point is that this sort of 'learning' isn't the *obvious* and *publicly confirmable* sort we find in the case of empirical disputes.

The force of these considerations might be more easily appreciated if we imagine a parallel case arising in connection with vision. Suppose we found that, in most of the visual circumstances we share with other people (i.e. circumstances in which we and our peers have the same regions of spacetime within our visual fields), we are in agreement with many people about our visual beliefs but in disagreement with many others. Several of us say we see an elephant; several others say they do not; several of us say that we see something blue, several others say they see something red; etc. Suppose further that there is no vision-independent way of resolving the disagreement. As far as we can tell, we are employing the same concepts, but we are all isolated from one another so that our visual circumstances are the *only* circumstances we share. What would be a rational response? What should we think about RV (the thesis that vision is reliable) in light of this evidence? It seems clear that our rational degree of confidence that RV is greatly diminished by this evidence—*unless* we have some way of fleshing out the picture that explains the disagreement we observe in a way compatible with RV. For example, we might believe that our apparent disagreement is illusory—that, contrary to appearances, it really *is* the case that we are employing different concepts. Or we might believe that others are victims of a vision-impairing disease whereas we are not. If so, then perhaps we have found a relevant ε^* such that our rational degree of confidence that RV in light of observed disagreement plus ε^* remains high. (Note that, in the cases just described, ε^* would again not be part of our evidential basis for accepting RV. Rather, it would just serve to prevent B_{RV} from being defeated.)

Of course, the same goes for RI. But the relevant difference is that intuitionists who accept A & E seem not to have a story to tell that predicts and explains the widespread disagreement we find about matters of intuition. Furthermore, even if they did, that would only show that the rational degree of confidence that RI in light of $B_{t\,\&\,s}$ (intuition's sorry track record plus the supplemental story) is high. It would *not* show that the rational degree of confidence that RI in light of $B_{A\,\&\,E\,t\,\&\,s}$ is high. The latter would remain low, and, as we have already seen, it appears that (at least for people with normal beliefs and intuitions) nothing can be done to elevate it. Thus, by GP we are still left with a defeater for B_{RI}.

So, intuitionists who accept A & E have a defeater for B_{RI}. Intuitionists for whom belief in a cosmic designer is warranted, however, may not, for (depending on what else they believe about the cosmic designer) attention to their beliefs about the origins of their cognitive faculties may not diminish their rational degree of confidence that RI. The same is true for intuitionists with unusual beliefs or intuitions. For example, if it appears to you to be a necessary truth that intuition is reliable, or if it appears to you to be a necessary truth that evolutionary processes will conspire to render *your* intuitions reliable even if no one else's are, then you will probably avoid self-defeat. Of course, this is not to say that accepting the belief that there is a designer or having unusual beliefs or intuitions is, *all by itself,* sufficient to stave off defeat. But if the argument of this section is sound, it is a minimal requirement.

5. Counterargument

I do not expect that anyone who is not already a skeptic about intuitions will be persuaded to embrace the thesis that intuition is generally unreliable. But it is important to keep in mind that I am not really recommending such a move. I have not argued for the conclusion that it is generally irrational to believe that intuition is reliable. Perhaps (depending on what evidence is available) it is irrational for many, or even most, people to believe that intuition is reliable. But all I am strictly committing myself to is the claim that proponents of A & E who have normal intuitions, and probably anyone else who recognizes intuition's poor track record, cannot rationally treat intuition as a *basic* source of evidence.

In the present section I will buttress the argument of the previous section by examining what I take to be the most persuasive considerations on behalf of the claim that intuition is reliable. I will argue that none of these considerations undermine the argument; at best, all they offer is nonintuitive evidence that intuition is reliable in certain restricted domains. This latter conclusion cannot save intuitionism for reasons we have already discussed; but it could be damaging to the argument of Part II if the domain in which intuition is demonstrably reliable turns out to include IMP-propositions. Thus, I will also argue that even if the arguments in support of the restricted reliability of intuition are sound, they are of no use to a naturalist since the relevant domains do not include IMP-propositions.

Defenders of the evidential value of intuitions (variously construed) typically make one or more of the following claims on their behalf:

(a) It is incoherent to argue for the conclusion that intuition is unreliable, for in making the argument, one must inevitably appeal to intuitions (Bealer 1993, 1996b; Bonjour 1998; Nagel 1997; Pust 2000).

(b) Standard objections to treating intuitions as evidence (specifically, appeals to the demonstrable fallibility of intuition) apply equally to sense perception and memory. Thus, either skepticism about intuition is arbitrary, or rejecting intuition as a basic source of evidence on these grounds leads to other forms of skepticism (Bealer 1993, 1996b; Bonjour 1998; Nagel 1997; Pust 2000; Sosa 1998).

(c) There is positive evidence that intuition is reliable with respect to some propositions (such as truths of logic and mathematics) (Bealer 1987, 1996a,b,c, 1998, 1999; Goldman and Pust 1998; Katz 1998).

The first two claims are important because they might be taken somehow to undermine the argument of Section 4 of the present chapter. The third is important because of the threat it might pose to the argument of Part II of this book. I will discuss each in turn.[21]

5.1. Incoherence

Several philosophers have argued that those who would deny that intuitions are reliable must inevitably rely on intuition in order to support that denial. For example, according to George Bealer (especially 1993) they must rely on intuitions about 'starting points'. In order to distinguish between reason and sense perception, they must rely on intuitions about which conscious episodes count as examples of each. They must rely on intuitions about what constitutes evidence, and on intuitions about the relationship between evidence and knowledge. They must rely on intuitions about what it takes to undermine a putative source of evidence. And so on. Thus, if we assume that intuition in general is unreliable, then any argument

---

[21] Some make the claim that intuition is self-justifying (see e.g. Hales 2000 and Tidman 1996). However, I have already explained the sense in which I think intuition is self-justifying and the sense in which it is not (Section 3 above), so I will not discuss that claim here.

against intuition will defeat itself. On the other hand, if we assume that *these* intuitions are reliable, then intuitionism is self-supporting since, according to Bealer, many of the conscious episodes that we (intuitively) take to be intuitions satisfy the (intuitively plausible) standards that must be met by a putative source of evidence in order for it reasonably to be regarded as reliable. Roughly similar arguments are made by Bonjour (1998), Nagel (1997), and Pust (2000).

Of course, I have not really attempted to argue that intuition is unreliable; so, strictly speaking, even if it is true that it is incoherent to argue for the unreliability of intuition, that conclusion will not damage my argument. Still, the basic point, if sound, might apply to my argument. Clearly the same considerations that suggest that intuition must be appealed to in an argument against the reliability of intuition will also suggest that intuition must be appealed to in an argument for the conclusion that we have good evidence that intuition is unreliable, or in an argument for the conclusion that proponents of A & E have an undercutting defeater for RI. But then one might think one would have to assume RI in order to be persuaded by these arguments; and, if Bealer is right, once we assume RI, we will find that intuition is self-supporting.

I have two responses to this modified line of argument. The first is that it is not at all clear that employing standards of evidence, distinguishing between intuitions and sense perceptions, and the like can be done only on the basis of *intuitions*—conscious episodes not involving memory, inference, or sense perception, in which a proposition seems *necessarily* to be true. I see no reason to think that the appearance of necessity plays any role in our distinguishing intuitions from sense perceptions. It can seem to me that a conscious episode satisfies my concept of an intuition or sense-perceptual experience without it seeming to me to be necessary that the episode satisfies that concept. Furthermore, I see no reason to think that the appearance of necessity *must* come into play as evidence when one argues for the conclusion that intuition is not to be trusted. In fact, as I argued in Chapter 1, it seems clear that we can be (and, indeed, must be) justified in employing standards of evidence—treating certain kinds of arguments as good and others as bad, trusting certain kinds of experience as evidence and others as nonevidence, and so on—even in the absence of evidence (intuitive or otherwise) that our standards are reliable.

The second response is that, contrary to what Bealer claims, starting with the assumption that intuition is reliable will not inevitably lead us to the conclusion that intuition is self-supporting. In fact, the argument in Section 4 is aimed precisely at showing that, depending on what other assumptions we hold, starting with the assumption that intuition is reliable will sometimes lead to self-defeat.

5.2. The Threat of Skepticism

Perhaps the most commonly raised consideration against intuition-ism is the fact that psychological research as well as the prevalence of paradox and persistent disagreement on philosophical issues all bear strong testimony to the fact that intuitions are fallible. Thus, not surprisingly, one of the points most frequently made in defense of intuitionism is that global skepticism looms large if one takes fallibil-ity as decisive evidence of untrustworthiness. Sense perception and memory are demonstrably fallible, but few really take seriously skep-ticism about *those* faculties. Thus, if we behave differently upon learning that intuition is fallible, then either we are arbitrarily treating our other faculties as privileged, or else we are employing a standard which, if consistently applied, will lead us directly into skepticism.

It is important to note, however, that the mere fact that intuition is fallible is *not* here being treated as decisive evidence against its reli-ability. In fact, it is not even being treated as prima facie evidence against its reliability. What counts against RI is rather the fact that (a) intuition seems to be *very* fallible, (b) there is in most cases no intuition-independent way of correcting intuitional error, and (c) our rational degree of confidence that RI in light of $B_{(a) \& (b) \& A \& E}$ is low, and we have no belief or experience ε^* such that our rational degree of confidence that RI in light of $B_{(a) \& (b) \& A \& E \& \varepsilon^*}$ is high. If all of this were true with respect to sense perception and memory, then skepticism would indeed loom large. Indeed, the point of Plantinga's argument is that our diminished rational degree of confidence that R in light of $B_{A \& E}$ alone is sufficient to raise the specter of skepticism for someone who believes A & E. But this, as I have already indicated, is a consequence I am happy with.

5.3. Evidence in Support of RI

The last decade has generated quite a bit of work in support of the conclusion that rational intuitions are reliable at least in certain restricted domains. In most cases, what occupies the foreground is an account of how intuitions *could* be reliable that entails that they *are* reliable under certain conditions in certain restricted domains. In the background (whether explicitly acknowledged or not) there is typically some sort of empirical evidence available for the conclusion that we satisfy the relevant conditions in the relevant domains. Uniformly, however, the evidence only supports the generally uncontroversial conclusion that intuition is reliable in the domain of mathematical truths, logical truths, and conceptual truths.

I say that this latter claim is uncontroversial because even hardline empiricists are willing to concede that (*a*) paradigmatic examples of mathematical, logical, and conceptual truths are *at least* believed by us with maximal confidence, even if they do not appear to be necessary, and (*b*) our beliefs about such propositions are generally reliable. What is in dispute is *how* those beliefs could be reliable and whether the appearance of necessity is *in general* rationally treated as a basic source of evidence. The attempt to draw a coherent and satisfying analytic–synthetic distinction was an attempt to explain how these beliefs could be reliable in a way that would satisfy empiricist scruples. Many are now pessimistic that such a distinction can be drawn. But recent work in defense of the reliability of intuition has produced other explanations of how we might be reliable in the (admittedly ill-defined) domain the empiricists were trying to demarcate. Furthermore, as we will see shortly, insofar as it is plausible to think that evidence does justify us in thinking that we are reliable in that domain, it is also plausible to think that the relevant evidence is empirical. Thus, I am prepared to concede for the sake of argument that there are good arguments available in support of the conclusion that intuition is reliable within the domain of mathematical, logical, and conceptual truths; and I am also prepared to concede that naturalists can take advantage of those arguments. But even so, there seem to be no arguments available that will enable them to establish the reliability of intuition outside the domain of mathematical, logical, and conceptual truths. Some examples will be instructive.

George Bealer (especially 1996*a*, 1998) argues that the reliability of our intuitions is just a consequence of what is involved in *possessing a concept determinately*. A full and precise explanation of determinate concept possession requires a fair amount of technical apparatus which would take us rather far afield; but the upshot is just that *possessing a concept determinately* involves understanding some proposition in which that concept occurs in a mode which is *by definition* such as to give rise to reliable intuitions about the concepts that occur in the proposition. Thus, giving evidence that our intuitions are reliable in some domains will just be a matter of giving evidence for the claim that we in fact possess some of our concepts determinately. Bealer's view is that we do not need evidence of the reliability of intuition in order to be justified in trusting it as a prima facie source of evidence. But he also makes a point of saying that it is clearly possible to possess concepts determinately and that the concepts involved in *elementary propositions*—which are apparently just obvious conceptual truths and simple truths of logic and mathematics—are the most likely candidates for being concepts that we possess determinately. His own view seems to be that intuition offers our primary evidence for the claim that we possess these concepts determinately. But that seems implausible. At any rate, it doesn't seem to *me* to be a necessary truth that the mode in which I possess these concepts satisfies Bealer's definition of determinateness. On the contrary, it seems that if I have any evidence at all that could confer justification on my belief that I possess these concepts determinately, it is just the empirically discoverable fact that my intuitions in the domain of elementary mathematical, logical, and conceptual truths are widely shared and not plagued by the problems of disagreement, poor track record, and paradox that beset our intuitions in other domains. This is not to say that I *endorse* the claim that this evidence confers justification on my belief that I possess these concepts determinately. It is just to say that empirical evidence seems to be the only evidence I have that might have a decent shot at doing so.

Alvin Goldman and Joel Pust (1998) defend a view very similar to Bealer's. They write:

The concept associated with a predicate 'F' will have many dispositions, but among them are dispositions to give rise to intuitive classificational judgments such as 'example e is (is not) an instance of F.' Thus, it is not only possible, but almost a matter of *definition*, that if the concept possessor were fully informed about the relevant features of e, then if e satisfied the concept he expresses through 'F', his intuitive response to the question of whether e satisfies this concept would be affirmative; and if e did not satisfy the concept he expresses through 'F', then his intuitive response to the question of whether e satisfies this concept would be negative. In other words, a concept tends to be manifested by intuitions that reflect or express its content. (Goldman and Pust 1998: 188)

Notably, Goldman and Pust do *not* take intuitions to involve the appearance of necessity. Thus, they appear to be committed to thinking that our evidence for propositions about whether our concepts apply to hypothetical cases is something *other* than the appearance of necessity. They also do not seem to understand concepts in quite the way Bealer does. For Bealer, concepts seem to be mental contents that can be possessed more or less determinately by various different people. For Goldman and Pust, on the other hand, concepts are apparently types of mental states that might be instantiated in other minds but do not, in any case, seem to be possessed in varying degrees of determinacy. Nevertheless, the appearance of necessity is generally in attendance when we make what Goldman and Pust take to be intuitive judgments; hence, evidence for the reliability of Goldman–Pust-intuitions will constitute evidence for the reliability of Bealer-intuitions in the domain of concept application. Furthermore, despite differences in their notions of concept possession, the Goldman–Pust account has roughly the same implications as Bealer's account about what it would take to give evidence for the reliability of our intuitions in a domain. We have evidence for the reliability of intuition in some domain just in case we have evidence that we have fully understood the relevant features of the examples to which we are applying our concepts. But, as before, the empirical facts about the patterns of disagreement and paradox will support, at best, the conclusion that we have the requisite full understanding in examples involving conceptual truths and truths of logic and mathematics.

Whereas Bealer and Goldman and Pust take the reliability of our intuitions to be grounded in our understanding or possession of concepts, Jerrold Katz takes it to be grounded in our grasp of properties.[22] He writes:

The notion of intuition that is relevant to our rationalist epistemology is that of an immediate, i.e., noninferential, purely rational apprehension of the structure of an abstract object, that is, an apprehension that involves absolutely no connection to anything concrete.... It is also crucial to the notion of intuitions in our sense that intuitions are apprehensions of structure that can reveal the limits of possibility with respect to the abstract objects having the structure. Intuitions are of structure, and the structure we apprehend

---

[22] I have listed Bealer in connection with Goldman and Pust because of the superficial resemblance: both take intuitions to be grounded in possession of *concepts*. But it is important to notice that insofar as Bealer seems to treat concepts as *mental contents* rather than *types of mental states*, his view is apparently closer to Katz's.

shows us that objects with that structure cannot be certain ways. (Katz 1998: 44–5)

Why think that we can directly apprehend the properties of abstracta? According to Katz, the reason we should think this is that often there is no other explanation for how we can know the relevant truths. Thus:

There are cases in which we can eliminate everything but intuition as a possible explanation of how it is known that a premise or a step in a proof has no counterexample. In cases like the compositeness of four, the pigeon-hole principle, the indiscernibility of identicals, and the ambiguity of 'I saw the uncle of John and Mary' or the well-formedness of 'The cat is on the mat,' there is no explanation other than intuition for the fact that ordinary, unsophisticated people, without expert help, immediately grasp the truth. (Katz 1998: 45)

One might be tempted to respond by pointing out that the view advocated by Goldman and Pust seems to offer a fairly reasonable alternative. Perhaps it is not our direct apprehension of the properties of an abstract object that explains our knowledge of such truths, but only our facility with the relevant concepts (construed as types of mental states). Perhaps we know the properties of abstract objects only mediately. One might think that first we come to possess our concepts in the right way, then later we learn in some other way— perhaps through some sort of indispensability argument—that the relevant abstract objects exist and satisfy our concepts; and finally we *infer* (rather than intuit) that various abstract objects have the properties we take them to have.

But this sort of reply underestimates the power of Katz's argument. On Katz's view, one of the main reasons for believing in abstracta is that it is impossible to account for the certainty and appearance of necessity that attaches to our knowledge of apparently abstract truths without supposing that the truths in question are really about abstract objects that are indeed necessarily the way they are. But if he is right, and if we are in fact justified in this way in believing that abstract objects exist, it becomes extremely implausible to suppose that our knowledge of the properties of abstract objects is mediated through our knowledge of concepts. Why should we be so lucky as to have concepts that mirror the structure of abstract objects if we are not somehow able directly to grasp their structure? The supposition that we have been so lucky is otiose. It makes much more sense just to believe that we have some faculty whereby we are able directly to intuit truths about abstract objects.

Goldman and Pust raise the obvious initial objection against Katz's view:

The chief difficulty for this approach comes with the assumption that intuition is a basic evidential source, a source of information about universals. Is there any reason to suppose that intuitions could be reliable indicators of a universal's positive and negative instances (even under favorable circumstances)? The problem is the apparent 'distance' or 'remoteness' between intuitions, which are dated mental states, and a non-physical, extra-mental, extra-temporal entity. How could the former be reliable indicators of the properties of the latter? ... Some philosophers ... might reply that abstractness per se does not exclude causal relations. Nonetheless, we certainly lack any convincing or even plausible story of how intuitions could be reliable indicators of facts concerning universals. (Goldman and Pust 1998: 185)

But this objection is misguided. Katz *does* have a story about how intuitions are reliable indicators of facts concerning universals. The story is just that intuitions are immediate apprehensions of the structure of universals. If it be argued that this is not much of a story, the same argument can be leveled against proponents of the view advocated by Goldman and Pust. Why is it any *more* informative to say that the reliability of our intuitions follows *by definition* once we understand what it is to grasp a *concept* than to say that the reliability of our intuitions follows *by definition* once we understand what it is to grasp a *property*, or *universal*? One might reply that at least the mentalistic story has the advantage of grounding intuitions in something we are already committed to. We know that we can grasp concepts (somehow); but one might wonder about whether we can grasp universals. But this is precisely where Katz's argument, if sound, has its strongest bite. If the inference to the best explanation is sound, we do know that we can somehow discover the properties of abstract objects. The only question is whether our knowledge of the properties of abstract objects is mediate (presumably through our concepts) or immediate. At this point in the dialectic the problem of apparent 'distance' is no reason to embrace the mentalistic view.

A better way to object, in my opinion, is to question Katz's inference to the best explanation. The explanans according to Katz is the 'special certainty' and 'apparent necessity' of formal truths. Katz acknowledges that it is hard to give an account of what the special certainty consists in; but he insists that it is 'an objective feature of those [propositions]' and is 'different from the subjective certainty we have about our beliefs in them'. Furthermore, he claims that it is not really necessary to give an account of it. The reason:

Even empiricists like Mill and Quine who deny the existence of necessary truth acknowledge that mathematical and logical truths have a special certainty, as is clear from the fact that they recognize the obligation to provide an empiricist explanation of it. (Katz 1998: 65)

But do they really? We may concede that they both acknowledge that the truths of logic and mathematics have a 'special certainty' about them that is different from the certainty that attends our beliefs about nonlogical, nonmathematical propositions. But do they also acknowledge that the special certainty is an *objective feature* of those propositions, *different from the subjective certainty* we have about our beliefs about them? I see no evidence that they do. As I understand Quine, his view is that the certainty of mathematical and logical truths just *is* our believing them with maximal confidence. There is nothing more to it. But if this is right, it starts to look like Katz is stacking the deck in his favor. It is easy to account for subjective certainty without positing abstract objects. We simply say that it is an artifact of our cognitive construction, a reflection of the fact that the propositions in question are believed with maximum strength, or the fact that they are the very scaffolding on which our theories are built, or the fact that we simply cannot imagine their falsity even if it is strictly possible. But to suppose that there is also some objective certainty that demands explanation is to raise the bar significantly, and illegitimately. Part of what is in dispute between those who believe that we can immediately apprehend the structure of abstract objects and those who do not is whether the truths of mathematics and logic really do possess anything like 'objective certainty' or, what comes to the same thing, objective necessary truth. Simply to assume that they do without argument is to come very close to begging the question against those who deny that there is any reason to posit abstract objects or to suppose that we have a faculty for grasping the properties of abstract objects. At any rate, it seems flatly wrong to assert, as Katz does, that the assumption is not at all controversial and that denying it is simply '... stonewalling ... in the face of such a wide recognition of the "palpable surface differences between the deductive sciences of logic and mathematics, on the one hand, and the empirical sciences ordinarily so-called on the other" '. (Katz 1998: 65).

But suppose Katz's assumption is correct: truths of logic and mathematics really do enjoy a kind of objective certainty. Suppose further that he is right in thinking (a) that we need to believe in abstract objects in order to account for this, and (b) that this licenses the belief that we have a faculty whereby we can immediately apprehend the structure of abstract objects. What follows? Interestingly, if the assumption that formal truths enjoy a special kind of objective certainty can indeed be defended in a way that will satisfy naturalistic scruples (as Katz apparently thinks it can when he declares it uncontroversial), then Katz has offered a straightforwardly *scientific* argument both for belief in abstract objects and for belief in a faculty whereby we can directly apprehend the properties of abstract objects. The argument is scientific because it is an inference to the best explanation (indeed, on Katz's view, it is an inference to the *only* explanation) for an empirically detectable phenomenon (namely, the phenomenon of objective certainty). What more could a naturalist ask for in the way of scientific justification for believing in abstracta and a reliable faculty for knowing abstracta? Inference to the best explanation is well respected; and we have already conceded that one can have scientific justification for believing things that are not directly empirically testable.[23]

As in the case of Goldman and Pust, Katz's arguments are not explicitly aimed at showing that rational intuition as it is being understood here is a reliable source of evidence in any domain. But since (as Katz himself argues) the appearance of necessity generally attends our beliefs about formal truths, his arguments, if sound, do succeed in establishing that rational intuition is reliable, at least in the domain of mathematical and logical truths. Furthermore, as we have already noted, the evidence he cites is plausibly construed as empirical evidence.

So, in light of the foregoing, there is some reason to think that we can have support for the conclusion that rational intuition is reliable in some domains—particularly in the vaguely bounded domain of

---

[23] Furthermore, Katz has also offered a gift to the theist. Katz has provided no reason to think that nontheistically directed evolutionary processes could possibly select for creatures who are able to apprehend reliably and directly the properties of abstract objects. Indeed, it seems impossible to offer such an account for the simple reason that there seems to be no way human beings could possibly acquire such a faculty apart from having been designed with one. The properties of abstract objects are not the sorts of things that one could latch on to by accident. But if that is right, then the success of Katz's argument provides the resources for a rather persuasive argument for theism (or something relevantly like it).

mathematical, logical, and conceptual truths. But do we now have any reason for thinking that our intuitions about IMP-propositions are reliable? Clearly not, for two reasons.

First, as we saw in Chapter 4, it is neither plausible nor helpful (with respect to explaining how we might acquire justified IMP-beliefs) to locate IMP-propositions in the domain of mathematical, logical, or conceptual truths. Second, the arguments discussed above offer no independent evidence that our intuitions are reliable with respect to IMP-propositions, and a little reflection reveals that we have quite convincing evidence that our intuitions are *not* reliable in that domain. For example, it is quite clear that IMP-propositions are not the proper objects of a faculty reliably aimed at grasping formal structures. Are they derivable from propositions about the applicability of our concepts to hypothetical cases about which we are fully informed? Perhaps; but we have no evidence that they are. The reason is that there is much disagreement about the truth of IMP-propositions (split not only along realist–antirealist lines, but also along the lines of different intuitions about what properties are essential to what kinds of objects). Thus, the evidence would seem to be that either we are not fully informed about the relevant hypothetical cases, or else the propositions in question simply are not derivable from propositions about the applicability of our concepts to hypothetical cases. Furthermore, the same evidence speaks against the idea that we 'determinately possess' the concepts involved in IMP-propositions and that assenting to IMP-propositions is rationally required of anyone who determinately possesses the relevant concepts. Of course, the appearances here might be illusory. It might be that those of us who disagree about particular IMP-propositions are all displaying reliable intuitions but about *different* concepts; or it might be that everyone who disagrees with my or your beliefs about IMP-propositions is irrational. But absent some reason to think such things, it seems that the right response is to distrust our intuitions about IMP-propositions.

In sum, then, a close look at some of the most prominent recent attempts to defend the evidential value of intuition reveals that (*a*) they are not aimed at defending the reliability of intuition outside the general domain of logical, mathematical, and conceptual truths and (*b*) they do not offer the resources for supporting the belief that our intuitions about IMP-propositions are reliable.

5. Conclusion

I have argued in this chapter that (for people with normal intuitions) intuitionism is self-defeating unless it warrants belief in a cosmic designer. I have also argued that none of the defenses of the evidential value of intuition available in the literature in any way counts against this conclusion. At best, all these defenses manage to do is to support the thesis that we have empirical evidence in favor of the belief that our intuitions are reliable in the domain of logical, mathematical, and conceptual truths. But not only does this fail to save intuitionism from self-defeat; it also fails to offer refuge to a naturalist who is casting about for some way to avoid giving up RMO, materialism, and ROM.

9

Supernaturalism

I want atheism to be true and am made uneasy by the fact that
some of the most intelligent and well-informed people I know
are religious believers. It is not just that I do not believe in God,
and, naturally, hope that I'm right in my belief. It's that I hope
there is no God! I do not want there to be a God; I do not want
the universe to be like that.... My guess is that this cosmic
authority problem is not a rare condition and that it is responsible for much of the scientism and reductionism of our
time.

(Thomas Nagel, *The Last Word*, 1997)

It is no secret that religious belief—particularly belief in the omnipotent, omniscient, and omnibenevolent God of traditional Judeo-
Christian theism—is frequently greeted with scorn and hostility in
academic circles. One often gets the impression that it is philosophical naturalism and the roaring success thereof that motivates the
scorn and hostility. The common view seems to be that, because
the methods of science are so successful and other methods are
not, the only sensible thing to do is to be a naturalist. But once
naturalism has been adopted, there is no room for belief in the God
of traditional theism since (as we have so far assumed) the methods of
science do not legitimate belief in God. As Steven Weinberg intimated
at a recent conference on naturalism, belief in God is, from the point
of view of naturalism, on a par with belief in fairies.[1]

The idea that naturalism is the only sensible methodological choice
for people of our day seems to be the primary motivation behind
remarks such as the following:

[1] Baylor Naturalism Conference, Baylor University, Apr. 2000.

We cannot use electric lights and the radio and, in the event of illness, avail ourselves of modern medical and clinical means and at the same time believe in the spirit and wonder world of the New Testament. (Bultmann 1941: 4)

It is absolutely safe to say that if you meet someone who claims not to believe in evolution, that person is ignorant, stupid or insane (or wicked, but I'd rather not consider that). (Dawkins 1989)

The view in both cases seems to be that scientific evidence automatically trumps all other evidence (or at least evidence from all religious texts), and that anyone who thinks otherwise is irrational. However, we observed as early as the Introduction of this book that, in fact, there is absolutely no rational basis for claiming that naturalism is the only sensible methodological choice. Moreover, we have also observed that naturalism is saddled with a variety of consequences that many of us will find extremely unpalatable. This does not, of course, show that it is objectively irrational to accept naturalism; but it does provide some pragmatic reason (the only sort of reason that counts in choosing a research program) to reject it. In light of this, one is tempted to agree with Nagel in thinking that it is hostility toward religion that motivates naturalism rather than the other way round.

Be that as it may, the fact is that, if the arguments in the foregoing chapters are sound, one must embrace a research program that legitimates belief in *some* sort of supernatural being if one wishes to avoid the consequences of naturalism laid out in Part II. Admittedly, belief in the God of traditional theism is *not* required (or at least not obviously so); but apparently something close will be required. As we saw in Chapter 6, having warrant for believing a pragmatic theory of truth might indirectly suffice to provide us with epistemic justification for some of our IMP-beliefs; but pragmatic theories of truth carry a commitment to near-theism. Alternatively, having warrant for believing in a supernatural designer who has endowed us with empirically detectable proper functions might also provide us with justification for some of our IMP-beliefs. Or we might be able to have justified IMP-beliefs if we have warrant for believing that there is a supernatural being who has somehow managed to ensure that our intuitions will track the truth under appropriate conditions, and who has also given us a means to tell in some cases (including cases involving MP-beliefs) when we or others are not tracking the truth in our intuitions. Or we might be able to have justified IMP-beliefs if they are transparently implied by the content of something like divine revelation. But the question is what could possibly justify us in believing that the right sort of supernatural being exists, or that this being has done the sorts of things we must suppose to have been done in order for us to avoid the consequences we want to avoid.

In the first two sections of this chapter I will consider ways in which either the methods of science or rational intuition might be thought to support, independently of religious experience, belief in the sort of being in which we would have to be able to believe in order to avoid the unpalatable consequences of naturalism. My goal here is not to treat these matters in detail, but only to gesture at possible lines of argument and familiar concerns about them. If any of those lines of argument are sound, then the door is open for either naturalism or intuitionism to find a way around the consequences attributed to naturalism in Part II. However, the main point of this chapter is to show that, even if rational intuition and the methods of science do not support belief in the right sort of supernatural being to solve our problems, still there might be viable (i.e. non-self-defeating) research programs that will give rise to evidence in support of such beliefs, and embracing these research programs is no less rational than embracing naturalism. Here too my remarks will be programmatic. Properly drawing out the ontological consequences of various forms of supernaturalism would require another book. But I hope to say enough in this chapter to make at least plausible the idea that some form of supernaturalism *might* succeed where naturalism has failed at saving ontological views like RMO and ROM which many of us are strongly inclined to accept.

1. Scientific Evidence

One of the most familiar arguments for God's existence is the Argument from Design. Typically, the argument begins with the observation that the world *appears* to be the product of intelligent design and invites us to infer that the world has *in fact* been designed. The invitation is usually reinforced by an analogy. As William Paley points out, if we were to stumble across a watch, we would automatically assume that it is the product of design, and we would do so because watches bear the marks of design—intricacy, complexity, and so on. But natural objects bear those same marks. Hence the analogy: as in the case of the watch, so too in the case of the cosmic machine, we ought to infer the existence of a designer. But, the argument proceeds, a world as complex as ours could only be designed by a being very much like the God of traditional theism. Therefore, the argument concludes, it is reasonable to think that the God of traditional theism exists.

This is a venerable argument. But it can be resisted. In fact, it is now widely held that one cannot infer the existence of a designer from the mere appearance of design. The reason is that, thanks in large part to Darwin and to more recent work in cosmology and other disciplines, we now have detailed scientific theories that explain how the universe and its inhabitants could have come to be as they are even apart from the existence of any sort of cosmic designer. Of course, not everyone is convinced that such explanations are adequate.[2] Furthermore, not everyone is convinced that the mere availability of nontheistic explanations is enough to undermine the Argument from Design. After all, even if it is *possible* that a complex world bearing the marks of design come into existence as a result of purely chance processes, by all accounts it is extremely *unlikely* that it do so. Thus, many think that even if the contemporary scientific stories are fully capable of explaining the origin and development of our world, the sheer improbability of things happening in the way described by those stories is enough to make it reasonable to believe that our world is the product of intelligent design.

Often this last point is made and defended by way of appeals to the appearance of 'fine tuning' or 'specified complexity'.[3] For example, many have observed that various laws of nature and physical constants are such that, had they been even slightly different, life could not have arisen in the universe. Thus (apparently against all odds) the universe seems to have been *fine tuned* for the existence of life. But, obviously enough, improbability alone does not warrant an inference to design. If someone throws in a full poker hand and draws a royal flush to beat a king-high straight flush when all her money is on the line, we will probably suspect foul play (i.e. design). But the improbability of the outcome alone is not what leads us to suspect design; for the probability of drawing a royal flush at that time is precisely the same as the probability of drawing any of a variety of other poker

---

[2] See e.g. Behe (1996) and Denton (1985).
[3] See e.g. Collins (1999) and Dembski (1998, 1999, 2000).

hands. According to some philosophers, what makes us suspect design is the fact that the outcome is not only 'complex' (i.e. improbable) but also 'specified' in some sense. What makes us suspect design is not the *mere* fact that the person drew an improbable hand (that would have happened anyway), but the fact that she drew exactly the sort of improbable hand needed to win the game. So too, some say, the fine tuning of the universe is not only a highly complex (vastly improbable) outcome, but also a specified outcome (since it is precisely the sort of outcome we need in order to be here). Thus, they conclude, as in the case of the royal flush, we are warranted in suspecting design.

Much as I am intuitively attracted to this line of argument, I do not think that it has yet been developed in enough detail. The crucial sticking point is the notion of 'specification'. What, exactly, is the difference between unspecified complex outcomes and specified ones? Currently, the most thorough answer to this question appears in the work of William Dembski (1998, 2000). According to the simplified definition in Dembski (2000), an outcome, or an event E, is 'specified' by a pattern D just in case background information K has been identified that satisfies the following two conditions:[4]

CINDE: Under the assumption that E occurred by chance, K provides no information about E (i.e. K is conditionally independent of E)

TRACT: The task of constructing D from K is doable (or, as complexity theorists would say, 'tractable').

By way of explaining these conditions, Dembski writes:

CINDE is a probabilistic condition, stating what probabilistic properties K must possess if K is to be suitable for eliminating chance in explaining E. TRACT is a complexity-theoretic condition, stating what complexity-theoretic properties K must possess if K is to be suitable for eliminating chance in explaining E. Probabilistically, K must leave whatever probabilities we assign to the event E untouched. Complexity-theoretically, K must render the task of constructing the pattern D tractable, or doable. (Dembski 2000: 265)

In his more detailed account Dembski (1998) emphasizes that, according to CINDE, *any* information J generated by K must be conditionally independent of E. In other words, CINDE is satisfied only if $P(E/H \& J) = P(E/H)$, where H is a hypothesis according to which E

---

[4] Dembski (2000: 264–5).

happened by chance. He also makes it clear that a 'pattern' is supposed to be 'any description that corresponds uniquely to some prescribed event' (1998: 136), and he adds the following condition to the definition of 'specification':

DELIM: D delimits E.

Roughly, DELIM requires that the occurrence of the event E entail the occurrence of the event uniquely corresponding to D.

There are various questions to be raised about this definition;[5] but for now let us simply focus on the question of how it is to be applied. Consider our poker example. Suppose we assign values as follows:

E = the event of player P drawing a royal flush at a time when she needs to win.

K = information about the relative rankings of poker hands; information about the hands held by other players (Q, R, and S); information detailing P's motive and opportunity for engaging in foul play (a lot of money is on the line; she has cards up her sleeve; etc.); information about P's shady character and history of cheating at cards; information to the effect that, unless foul play occurred, we should not have expected P to win this hand.

D = the English-language description of E.

As we have set things up, it is trivial that D delimits E. Thus, DELIM is satisfied. But when we turn our attention to CINDE and TRACT, matters immediately become much more difficult. Consider CINDE. Is the probability of E on H (the chance hypothesis) equivalent to the probability of E on H & K? That depends in part upon whether H already takes account of facts about what cards are already in play at the time of P's draw. The probability of drawing a royal flush when no cards are in play is very different from the probability of drawing a royal flush when three other players are holding specific hands. Suppose H does not include this information. Then CINDE is not satisfied since information about the hands that is contained in K renders $P(E/H \& K)$ different from $P(E/H)$. Thus, E is not specified by the above information, even though, intuitively, the information in K is surely enough to warrant a 'design inference'. On the other hand, suppose H does include this information. Now, does it also include

---

[5] For some of these questions, see Fitelson *et al.* (1999).

information about P's opportunity (i.e. about her having rigged the deck, or having placed cards up her sleeve)? After all, the probability of drawing a royal flush when you have rigged the deck is much different from the probability of drawing a royal flush when you have not. Again, if H does not include this information, then CINDE will not be specified; if it does, then we can ask about how much more of the information in K is built into the chance hypothesis.

No doubt the problem here is just that I have not chosen the right values for D, H, and K. But that is precisely the worry: it appears that, even in relatively simple cases, we will face serious difficulty in assessing CINDE because we will face serious difficulty in finding values for D, H, and K that seem intuitively (and relatively uncontroversially) to be *the* right values. I suspect the same will be true of TRACT. Furthermore, the difficulty isn't just due to the fact that it is difficult to detect design. In the present case, design is rather easy to detect. But if it is hard to assign values to D, H, and K in the easy cases, how much more difficult will it be in hard cases—where E is the existence of life, or the existence of cosmic fine tuning, or some such thing? Here the presence of design is highly controversial; and it is not at all clear what will count as 'relevant background information', or how much of the relevant scientific theories (plus supplemental assumptions) will be included in the details of H. Dembski and others assert that specified complexity is rampant in science. Dembski (1999, 2000), for example, points to the sort of 'irreducible complexity' heralded by Michael Behe (1996) as evidence of design; Stephen Meyer (2000) cites that, along with apparent fine tuning and a variety of other examples. But nowhere do we find a rigorous argument to the effect that, in each of these cases, we can assign clear and relatively uncontroversial values to D, E, H, and K in such a way as to satisfy all of the conditions in Dembski's analysis of specification. But something like that is what we need if the appeal to 'specified complexity' is going to deliver what its proponents say it can deliver.

Of course, this is only a sketch of an objection; and I have not shown that what I say needs to be done cannot be done. If it can be, then here lie the resources for a scientific argument for the existence of a supernatural designer. The argument would be scientific because, on the assumption that (*a*) 'specified complexity' can be defined in a precise and unproblematic way, (*b*) the apparent fine tuning of the universe actually constitutes specified complexity so defined, and (*c*) specified complexity is an empirically detectable property, our inference to the existence of a designer would be precisely the same sort of empirically based inference that investigators of insurance fraud use when they determine that an accident did not happen by accident, that teachers use when they detect plagiarism, and so on. If this sort of argument were sound, naturalism itself might have the resources for avoiding the consequences attributed to it in this book. At any rate certain arguments in this book would be blocked if it turned out that naturalists could justifiably believe that the universe is the product of design; and if those arguments were blocked, it would be much more difficult to defend the conclusions that I have defended.

2. Intuitive Evidence

Most of the traditional arguments for the existence of God (the ontological argument, the cosmological argument, the moral argument, etc.) make explicit appeal to rational intuitions. For example, consider the following very simplified expression of the well-known modal version of the ontological argument:[6]

(2.1) Necessarily: God exists only if it is necessarily true that God exists. (Premise)

(2.2) Possibly: God exists. (Premise)

(2.3) Possibly: It is necessarily true that God exists. (From 2.1, 2.2)

(2.4) For any proposition p, if it is possible that p is necessarily true then p is necessarily true. (Premise, provable in S5)

(2.5) Therefore: It is necessarily true that God exists. (From 2.3, 2.4)

Notoriously, at least two of the noninferred premises (2.2 and 2.4) are justifiable, if at all, exclusively on the basis of intuition. Similarly, the cosmological argument incorporates the premise that there cannot be an infinite regress of causes, and the moral argument incorporates both the premise that there are absolute moral values and the premise that there could be absolute moral values only if there is a divine being. But, plausibly, if these premises are justified at all, they are justified on the basis of intuition.

---

[6] For a fuller statement, see Plantinga (1974, ch. 10). See also Oppy (1995) for a survey of modal and other versions of the ontological argument.

The trouble with theistic arguments resting on intuition unaided by religious experience, however, is that we have good reason to doubt that our intuitions about the crucial premises of these arguments are reliable. (They lie outside the domain of mathematical, logical, and conceptual truths, and squarely in the domain of otherwise problematic propositions.) After all, even if intuition supports all of the premises of one of these arguments, it will not automatically follow that intuition also supports the thesis that our cognitive faculties are not the products of undirected evolutionary processes. This is because it doesn't obviously follow from the mere fact that God exists that he is also our designer. Perhaps he gave the job to an incompetent subordinate; or perhaps he behaved like the God of deism, winding up the universe at the beginning and then stepping back to watch it unfold without his interference. But if intuition does not support the thesis that we were designed, then nothing supports it (unless we also take religious experience as a basic source), in which case we are again left with a defeater for the reliability of intuition and hence a defeater for the evidence that grounds our belief in God.

Furthermore, even if we thought that intuition somehow indirectly supported the thesis that we are the products of divine design, still we must reckon with the fact that there is much disagreement over nonlogical, nonmathematical, and nonconceptual truths, the fact that our intuitions about such truths often run aground in incoherence, and the fact that there seems to be no empirical evidence in favor of the claim that intuition is reliable outside the domain of logical, mathematical, and conceptual truths. All of this might be taken as support for the claim that, even if we *are* the products of divine design, the divine design plan does not include reliable rational intuitions outside the domain of mathematical, logical, and conceptual truths. If that is right, however, then again we are left with a defeater for the evidence that grounds our belief in God.

At minimum, then, what we need to avoid defeat (under the terms specified in GP) are beliefs or experiences (intuitive or otherwise) which imply not only that God designed our cognitive faculties, but also that he has somehow ensured that our faculties will be reliable at least with respect to the premises of the argument(s) that we believe on the basis of intuition. It is difficult to see how this might go in people with 'normal' intuitions apart from religious experience. But I see no way of ruling it out. Thus, though I think it unlikely that anyone will have intuitive warrant for believing in God (i.e. warrant that rests on the evidential value of intuitions unaided by religious experience), I am also not prepared to rule out the possibility.

3. Religious Experience

The point of the foregoing sections has been to show that one cannot simply dismiss without argument the possibility that one might have scientific or intuitive evidence for the existence of God. But suppose it is impossible to have such evidence. In that event it would appear that some brand of supernaturalism offers the only real hope of avoiding the consequences of naturalism.

Supernaturalism is a research program which treats at least the methods of science and religious experience as basic sources of evidence. I have deliberately left open the question whether supernaturalism treats intuition as a basic source because, as we saw in Chapter 8, embracing theism or the evidential value of religious experience is not all by itself sufficient to defeat the reasons we have for thinking that intuition cannot rationally be treated as a basic source of evidence.

It is an understatement to say that the term 'religious experience' is used in a wide variety of ways to cover a wide variety of phenomena. Among the phenomena that have been variously labeled 'religious experience' are visions apparently of religious figures or objects (such as the Virgin Mary or the Holy Grail), auditory experiences apparently of persons of religious significance (God, angels, saints, and so forth), impressions of overwhelming peace and joy, impressions of being in communion with the divine or with the universe, firm convictions of the truth of various propositions with religious content, phenomena in which a person seems to herself to be speaking to God in a language she does not understand, and so on. In light of this, my own definition of religious experience—as an apparent direct awareness of either (*a*) the existence, character, or behavior of a divine mind, or (*b*) the fact that one of one's own mental states or a testimonial report communicated by others has been divinely inspired—is highly circumscribed. However, I think it is reasonable to offer such a circumscribed definition since many of the experiences just described (along with others commonly or naturally characterized as religious experiences) may just as easily be characterized as perceptions or intuitions with religious content. Only those characterizable as putative direct awarenesses of the divine mind or divine inspiration seem to belong in a *sui generis* category.

Given this understanding of religious experience, however, it should be clear that not just any 'version' of supernaturalism will manage to avoid either self-defeat or the consequences of naturalism. Clearly one *might* have religious experiences in which one takes oneself to be directly aware of a rather unimpressive divine mind— one that does not belong to a being capable of designing the world and endowing us with proper functions, or of knowing all truths, or of ensuring that our intuitions track the truth. Treating such experiences as basic sources of evidence would qualify one as a supernaturalist; but one would not thereby have embraced a brand of supernaturalism capable of avoiding the consequences of naturalism.

To avoid those consequences, what one needs is not just supernaturalism all by itself, but supernaturalism in conjunction with actual religious experiences that one takes to be experiences of a being relevantly like the God of traditional theism (i.e. a being who is very powerful, very knowledgeable, capable of designing the universe in such a way that human beings have cognitive faculties that track the truth in important domains of metaphysics and morality, not malicious in desiring to deceive us, and so on). This might seem to be a tall order; and one might be tempted to conclude that, if the arguments of this book are sound, very few people could ever hope to avoid the ontological consequences of naturalism since very few people have religious experiences that they take to be experiences of a being relevantly like the God of traditional theism. And perhaps this is correct. On the other hand, we should note that many theists hold (in accord with remarks in the first chapter of Paul's epistle to the Romans) that in fact *everyone* has some experience or other that they recognize as an experience of the God of traditional theism, but many people suppress those experiences. This is hardly the sort of claim that will be greeted with warm enthusiasm by the opponents of theism. Nevertheless, if the sentiment expressed by Nagel in the epigraph of this chapter is at all widely shared, it is at least easy to see *why* people might be inclined to suppress such experiences. Furthermore, the truth or falsity of the claim is hardly one that we are in a position to assess apart from something like divine revelation. (Your only evidence apart from divine revelation about whether I am suppressing a religious experience is my testimony. But, even if I am scrupulously honest, there is no more reason to think that I will give reliable testimony about what experiences I am suppressing than there is to think that I will be able reliably to introspect the facts about what experiences I am suppressing. And it seems extremely implausible to think that I am generally reliable at detecting the experiences that I am actively suppressing.) In any case, annoying as the claim might be, it is one that must be entertained in the present context since it rebuts the idea that the arguments of this book *automatically* commit us to thinking that many people in fact could not avoid the consequences of naturalism even if they embraced supernaturalism. By the lights of the apostle Paul and many other theists, embracing supernaturalism and refraining from suppressing the experiential evidence that everyone has for the existence of God will in fact be sufficient for having warrant for believing in God.

But is warranted belief in God enough? Probably not all by itself. To avoid the ontological consequences of naturalism, it appears that we need not only belief in God but also some reason to think that God has ensured a reliable connection between what is theoretically useful for us to believe and what is true, or that God has endowed biological organisms with empirically or intuitively detectable proper functions, or that God has endowed us with the ability to form reliable IMP-beliefs on the basis of intuition and to be able to tell at least in some cases when cognitive conditions are suitable for the reliable exercise of such intuitions. Any of this, however, would require some substantive theology (along with, perhaps, some substantive metaphysics).

Still, the door is open, and I believe that certain very common versions of supernaturalism do in fact manage to avoid the consequences of naturalism. For example, many people apparently have religious experiences that they take to be direct awarenesses of God's having inspired (or of God's testifying to the general reliability of) the message contained in the scriptures shared in common by Judaism and Christianity. And many of the same people take it that the message contained in those scriptures includes a variety of moral and metaphysical truths. Furthermore, many take it that among the truths explicit in or implied by this message are the following: that God created and designed the world; that God regarded the world as a world containing material objects of various familiar sorts even before there were any human beings to conceive of those objects; that among the things God created are minds other than our own; that God created human beings in his image with cognitive faculties whose purpose is to enable human beings reliably to discover the truth about various moral, metaphysical, and empirical matters; that human cognitive faculties—in particular, human intuitions about morality and metaphysics—have become corrupted as a result (both direct and indirect) of sin; and that the damage is correctable and, in fact, gradually comes to be corrected over time as one reflects on the truths contained in the scriptures and as one develops a relationship with God. If all of this is right (and, of course, not every theist thinks that it is), then at least one version of supernaturalism pretty clearly contains the resources to save RMO and ROM, and also to justify the evidential value of intuition in a variety of domains. The only claim that still must go is materialism, but historically that has never been especially important, or even plausible, to those who are likely to find this story to be true.

I expect the objection that the evidential value of religious experience is susceptible to many of the same objections leveled against the evidential value of intuition. After all, just as there is a problem about metaphysical pluralism (diversity among the metaphysical intuitions of human beings) so too there is a problem about religious pluralism. Those who take themselves to have religious experiences differ widely in the behavior and characteristics they are willing to attribute to the mind or minds that they take their experiences to be experiences of; and the theories built on the basis of purported religious experience vary as widely as the theories built on the basis of intuition. Furthermore, the reliability of religious experience does not obviously admit of corroboration from other sources. Why, then, do we not have a defeater for the evidential value of religious experience as I have argued that intuitionists do for the evidential value of intuition?

As I see it, the relevant difference between the two cases is that, at least in some instances, the theories built on the basis of religious experience have the resources both to predict and to explain the pattern of disagreement that one actually discovers and also the resources to provide evidence for the conclusion that one's own circumstances are not circumstances in which relying on religious experience (or other sources treated as basic) is likely to lead to error. In other words, some theories built on religious experience have a supplemental story s to tell such that one's rational degree of confidence that religious experience is reliable in light of $B_{t\,\&\,s}$ (where t is a proposition describing religious experience's sorry track record) is high. Disagreement with others only provides a defeater (by the lights of GP) when this condition is not met.

To see why, just consider again our analogous case with respect to vision: You find that many of those around you have visual beliefs that contradict yours. Further, you find that each of these people, like yourself, can find many others whose visual beliefs corroborate their own, despite the fact that they also can find many whose visual beliefs contradict theirs. Finally, there is no vision-independent way of resolving the matter. Again, it seems that if, upon sufficient reflection in accord with the standards taken for granted by your research program, you find that you have a story to tell that explains why the population of human beings might divide into groups some of whose visual beliefs are generally true and others of whose visual beliefs are generally mistaken (though often in the same way), and if you also have a story to tell that locates you in the group of people whose visual beliefs are generally true, then you do *not* have a defeater for RV, the thesis that vision is reliable. Or, at any rate, you don't have a defeater by the lights of GP. As far as GP is concerned, it is perfectly sensible for you to accept RV and to keep trusting your visual faculties. Likewise, it may *also* be perfectly sensible for those who disagree with you to keep trusting their visual faculties, even though everyone has beliefs arising out of their own research programs that imply that many other people are badly mistaken. The same, I think, goes for intuition and religious experience. It's just that, in the case of intuition unaided by religious experience (or by 'unusual' intuitions), there is no story to be told that explains the pattern of disagreement and allows any of us to locate ourselves among a group of people for whom the appearance of necessity is generally a reliable indicator of truth.

I realize that in the minds of many philosophers, even in the minds of many theists, the way I have suggested for saving RMO and ROM will seem rather quaint. But in light of the arguments presented in this book, I am entirely convinced that some supernaturalistic story along the lines presented above offers our only hope of saving RMO, and perhaps also our only hope of saving ROM. That, to my mind, is pretty powerful reason to take seriously at least the *prospect* of some such story being true, even if, in the end, one cannot bring oneself to accept it.

4. Conclusion

The subtitle of this book suggests that one of its main goals is to draw out some of the more interesting ontological consequences of naturalism. This I have done, though clearly I think that those consequences apply to research programs other than naturalism. Nevertheless, naturalism deserved center stage because, though ultimately I reject it, I think that in fact naturalism is the most viable research program apart from a brand of supernaturalism that warrants belief in a suitably developed version of traditional theism. Intuitionism is self-defeating; and most of the nontheistic religions that have a coherent concept of divinity do not recommend belief in a mind of whose existence, behavior, or characteristics we could be directly aware. Thus, as I see it, the consequences of naturalism just are the consequences of the supposition that our world and we ourselves are undesigned.

References

ALSTON, WILLIAM (1993), *Reliability of Sense Perception* (Ithaca, NY: Cornell University Press).

—— (1978), *Universals and Scientific Realism*, 2 vols. (Cambridge: Cambridge University Press).

—— (1980), 'Naturalism, Materialism, and First Philosophy', repr. in Moser and Trout (1995: 35–46).

—— (1983), *What is a Law of Nature?* (Cambridge: Cambridge University Press).

ANNAS, JULIA (1988), 'Naturalism in Greek Ethics', *Proceedings of the Boston Area Colloquium in Ancient Philosophy*, 4: 149–71.

—— (1989a), *Universals: An Opinionated Introduction* (Boulder, Colo.: Westview Press).

—— (1989b), *A Combinatorial Theory of Possibility* (Cambridge: Cambridge University Press).

ARMSTRONG, DAVID (1997), *A World of States of Affairs* (Cambridge: Cambridge University Press).

AYERS, MICHAEL (1981), 'Locke versus Aristotle on Natural Kinds', *Journal of Philosophy*, 78: 247–72.

—— (1998), 'Theories of Knowledge and Belief', in Garber and Ayers (1998: 1003–61).

BAKER, LYNNE (1997), 'Why Constitution is not Identity', *Journal of Philosophy*, 94: 599–621.

—— (2000), *Persons and Bodies* (Cambridge: Cambridge University Press).

BEALER, GEORGE (1987), 'Philosophical Limits of Scientific Essentialism', *Philosophical Perspectives*, 1: 289–365.

—— (1993), 'The Incoherence of Empiricism', repr. in Wagner and Warner (1993: 163–96).

—— (1996a), 'On the Possibility of Philosophical Knowledge', *Philosophical Perspectives*, 10: 1–34.

—— (1996b), 'A Priori Knowledge and the Scope of Philosophy', *Philosophical Studies*, 81: 121–42.

—— (1996c), 'A Priori Knowledge: Replies to William Lycan and Ernest Sosa', *Philosophical Studies*, 81: 163–74.

—— (1998), 'Intuition and the Autonomy of Philosophy', in DePaul and Ramsey (1998: 201–40).

—— (1999), 'A Theory of the A Priori', *Philosophical Perspectives*, 13: 29–56.

BEDAU, MARK (1992), 'Where's the Good in Teleology?', *Philosophy and Phenomenological Research*, 52: 781–806.

BEDAU, MARK (1993), 'Naturalism and Teleology', in Wagner and Warner (1993: 23–51).

BEHE, MICHAEL (1996), *Darwin's Black Box* (New York: Touchstone).

BEILBY, JAMES (ed.) (2002), *Naturalism Defeated? Essays on Plantinga's Evolutionary Argument against Naturalism* (Ithaca, NY: Cornell University Press).

BERGMANN, MICHAEL (1997a), 'Internalism and Externalism and the No-Defeater Condition', *Synthese*, 100: 399–417.

—— (1997b), 'Internalism, Externalism, and Epistemic Defeat', Ph.D. diss., University of Notre Dame.

—— (2000a), 'Externalism and Skepticism', *Philosophical Review*, 109: 159–94.

—— (2000b), 'Deontology and Defeat', *Philosophy and Phenomenological Research*, 60: 87–102.

—— (2002), 'Commonsense Naturalism', in Beilby (2002: 61–90).

—— (unpublished), 'A Dilemma for Internalism'.

BLACKSON, THOMAS (1992), 'The Stuff of Conventionalism', *Philosophical Studies*, 68: 65–81.

BONJOUR, LAURENCE (1998), *In Defense of Pure Reason* (Cambridge: Cambridge University Press).

BOORSE, CHRISTOPHER (1976), 'Wright on Functions', *Philosophical Review*, 85: 70–86.

—— (unpublished), 'Functions: A Current Scorecard'.

BOUWSMA, O. K. (1948), 'Naturalism', *Journal of Philosophy*, 45: 12–21.

BOYD, RICHARD (1988), 'How to be a Moral Realist', in G. Sayre-McCord (ed.), *Essays on Moral Realism* (Ithaca, NY: Cornell University Press), 105–35.

—— (1991), 'Realism, Anti-Foundationalism, and the Enthusiasm for Natural Kinds', *Philosophical Studies*, 61: 127–48.

BRANDT, RICHARD (1990), 'The Science of Man and Wide Reflective Equilibrium', *Ethics*, 100: 259–78.

BÜCHNER, LUDWIG (1891), *Force and Matter; or, Principles of the Natural Order of the Universe with a System of Morality Based Thereon*, 15th edn. (New York: Peter Eckler).

BUFORD, THOMAS (1970), *Essays on Other Minds* (Chicago: University of Illinois Press).

BULTMANN, RUDOLF (1941), 'New Testament and Mythology: The Problem of Demythologizing the New Testament Proclamation', repr. in his *New Testament and Mythology* ed. and trans. Schubert Ogden (Philadelphia: Fortress Press, 1984), 1–43.

BURGE, TYLER (1998), 'Computer Proof, A Priori Knowledge, and Other Minds', *Philosophical Perspectives*, 12: 1–37.

BURKE, MICHAEL (1994), 'Preserving the Principle of One Object to a Place: A Novel Account of the Relations among Objects, Sorts, Sortals, and Persistence Conditions', repr. in Rea (1997: 236–72).

BUTTERFIELD, HERBERT (1959), *Origins of Modern Science: 1300–1800* (New York: MacMillan).

CARTER, WILLIAM R., and JOHN E. BAHDE (1998), 'Magical Anti-realism', *American Philosophical Quarterly*, 35: 305–25.

CHALMERS, DAVID (1996), *The Conscious Mind* (Oxford: Oxford University Press).

CHANDLER, HUGH (1971), 'Constitutivity and Identity', repr. in Rea (1997: 313–19).

CHIHARA, CHARLES, and JERRY FODOR (1965), 'Operationalism and Ordinary Language', *American Philosophical Quarterly*, 2: 281–95.

CHURCHLAND, PAUL (1979), *Scientific Realism and the Plasticity of Mind* (Cambridge: Cambridge University Press).

——(1988), *Matter and Consciousness*, rev. edn. (Cambridge, Mass.: MIT Press).

COLLINS, ROBIN (1999), 'A Scientific Argument for the Existence of God: The Fine-Tuning Design Argument', in Michael J. Murray (ed.), *Reason for the Hope Within* (Grand Rapids, Mich.: Eerdmans), 47–75.

COMTE, AUGUSTE (1974), *The Essential Comte*, selected from *Cours de philosophie positive*, ed. Stanislav Andreski, trans. Margaret Clarke (New York: Barnes & Noble Books).

CORTENS, ANDREW (1999), *Global Anti-realism: A Metaphilosophical Inquiry* (Boulder, Colo.: Westview Press).

CRAIG, WILLIAM LANE, and J. P. MORELAND (eds.) (2000), *Naturalism: A Critical Approach* (London: Routledge).

CRANE, TIM, and D. H. MELLOR (1990), 'There is No Question of Physicalism', *Mind*, 90: 185–206.

CUMMINS, ROBERT (1975), 'Functional Analysis', *Journal of Philosophy*, 72: 741–65.

CURLEY, EDWIN (1992), 'Rationalism', in Dancy and Sosa (1992: 411–15).

DANCY, JONATHAN and ERNEST SOSA (1992), *Companion to Epistemology* (Oxford: Basil Blackwell).

DANIELS, NORMAN (1979), 'Wide Reflective Equilibrium and Theory Acceptance in Ethics', *Journal of Philosophy*, 76: 256–82.

——(1980), 'Reflective Equilibrium and Archimedean Points', *Canadian Journal of Philosophy*, 10: 83–104.

DANTO, ARTHUR (1967), 'Naturalism', in Paul Edwards (ed.), *The Encyclopedia of Philosophy*, vol. v (New York: MacMillan and Free Press), 448–50.

DARWIN, CHARLES (1996), *On the Origin of Species*, ed. Gillian Beer (Oxford: Oxford University Press).

DAWKINS, RICHARD (1989), Review of *Blueprints: Solving the Mystery of Evolution*, *New York Times*, 9 Apr.

—— (1996), *The Blind Watchmaker: Why Evidence of Evolution Reveals a Universe without Design* (New York: Norton).

DEMBSKI, WILLIAM (1998), *The Design Inference* (Cambridge: Cambridge University Press).

—— (1999), *Intelligent Design* (Downers Grove, Ill: InterVarsity Press).

—— (2000), 'Naturalism and Design', in Craig and Moreland (2000: 253–79).

DENNES, WILLIAM (1944), 'The Categories of Naturalism', in Krikorian (1944: 270–94).

DENTON, MICHAEL (1985), *Evolution: A Theory in Crisis* (Bethesda, Md.: Adler & Adler).

DePAUL, MICHAEL (1986), 'Reflective Equilibrium and Foundationalism', *American Philosophical Quarterly*, 23: 59–69.

—— and WILLIAM RAMSEY (eds.) (1998), *Rethinking Intuition* (Lanham, Md.: Rowman & Littlefield).

DEVITT, MICHAEL (1991), *Realism and Truth*, 2nd edn. (Oxford: Basil Blackwell).

—— (1998), 'Naturalism and the A Priori', *Philosophical Studies*, 92: 45–65.

DEWEY, JOHN (1902a), 'The Evolutionary Method as Applied to Morality, I: Its Scientific Necessity', *Philosophical Review*, 11: 107–24.

—— (1902b), 'The Evolutionary Method as Applied to Morality, II: Its Significance for Conduct', *Philosophical Review*, 11: 353–71.

—— (1909), 'The Influence of Darwinism on Philosophy', repr. in Hickman and Alexander (1998: 39–45).

—— (1917), 'The Need for a Recovery of Philosophy', repr. in Hickman and Alexander (1998: 46–70).

—— (1929a), *Experience and Nature*, 2nd edn. repr. in Dewey (1981: 3–396).

—— (1929b), *The Quest for Certainty*, repr. in Dewey (1984: 1–258).

—— (1940), 'Nature in Experience', repr. in Hickman and Alexander (1998: 154–61).

—— (1943), 'Antinaturalism *in Extremis*', repr. in Hickman and Alexander (1998: 162–72).

—— (1948), *Reconstruction in Philosophy*, enlarged edn. (Boston: Beacon Press).

—— (1952), 'The Development of American Pragmatism', repr. in Hickman and Alexander (1998: 3–13).

—— (1981), *John Dewey: The Later Works, 1925–1953*, ed. Jo Ann Boydston, vol. i: *1925* (Carbondale, Ill.: Southern Illinois University Press).

—— (1984), *John Dewey: The Later Works, 1925–1953*, ed. Jo Ann Boydston, vol. iv: *1929* (Carbondale, Ill.: Southern Illinois University Press).

—— SIDNEY HOOK, and ERNEST NAGEL (1945), 'Are Naturalists Materialists?', repr. in Ryder (1994: 102–21).

DEWEY, ROBERT (1977), *The Philosophy of John Dewey* (The Hague: Martinus Nijhoff).

DOEPKE, FRED (1982), 'Spatially Coinciding Objects', repr. in Rea (1997: 10–24).

DUPRÉ, JOHN (1981), 'Natural Kinds and Biological Taxa', *Philosophical Review*, 90: 66–90.

—— (1993), *The Disorder of Things* (Cambridge, Mass.: Harvard University Press).

EDEL, ABRAHAM (1946), 'Is Naturalism Arbitrary?', *Journal of Philosophy*, 43: 141–52.

ELDER, CRAWFORD (1989), 'Realism, Naturalism, and Culturally Generated Kinds', *Philosophical Quarterly*, 39: 425–4.

—— (1992), 'An Epistemological Defense of Realism about Necessity', *Philosophical Quarterly*, 42: 317–36.

—— (1994), 'Laws, Natures, and Contingent Necessities', *Philosophy and Phenomenological Research*, 54: 649–67.

—— (1995), 'A Different Kind of Natural Kind', *Australasian Journal of Philosophy*, 73: 516–31.

—— (1996*a*), 'On the Reality of Medium-Sized Objects', *Philosophical Studies*, 83: 191–211.

—— (1996*b*), 'Contrariety and "Carving Up Reality"', *American Philosophical Quarterly*, 33: 277–89.

ERESHEFSKY, MARK (ed.) (1992), *The Units of Evolution* (Cambridge, Mass.: MIT Press).

FALES, EVAN (2002), 'Darwin's Doubt, Calvin's Calvary', in Beilby (2002: 43–60).

FITELSON, BRANDEN, and ELLIOTT SOBER (1998), 'Plantinga's Probability Arguments against Evolutionary Naturalism', *Pacific Philosophical Quarterly*, 79: 115–29.

—— CHRISTOPHER STEPHENS, and ELLIOTT SOBER (1999), 'How Not to Detect Design—Critical Notice: William A. Dembski, *The Design Inference*', *Philosophy of Science*, 66: 472–88.

FODOR, JERRY (1998), 'Is Science Biologically Possible', in his *In Critical Condition: Polemical Essays on Cognitive Science and the Philosophy of Mind* (Cambridge, Mass.: MIT Press), 189–202.

FOGELIN, ROBERT (1997), 'Quine's Limited Naturalism', *Journal of Philosophy*, 94: 543–63.

FOLEY, RICHARD (1987), *The Theory of Epistemic Rationality* (Cambridge, Mass.: Harvard University Press).

FORREST, PETER (1996), *God without the Supernatural: A Defense of Scientific Theism* (Ithaca, NY: Cornell University Press).

GARBER, DANIEL, and MICHAEL AYERS (eds.) (1998), *The Cambridge History of 17th Century Philosophy*, 2 vols. (Cambridge: Cambridge University Press).

GIBBARD, ALLAN (1975), 'Contingent Identity', repr. in Rea (1997: 93–125).

GIBSON, ROGER (1987), 'Quine on Naturalism and Epistemology', *Erkenntnis*, 27: 57–78.

GIERE, RONALD (1999), *Science without Laws* (Chicago: University of Chicago Press).

—— and RICHARD WESTFALL (1973), *Foundations of Scientific Method: The Nineteenth Century* (Bloomington: Indiana University Press).

GINET, CARL (1995), 'Comments on Plantinga's Two Volume Work on Warrant', *Philosophy and Phenomenological Research*, 55: 403–8.

GOLDMAN, ALVIN (1999), 'A Priori Warrant and Naturalistic Epistemology', *Philosophical Perspectives*, 13: 1–28.

—— and JOEL PUST (1998), 'Philosophical Theory and Intuitional Evidence', in DePaul and Ramsey (1998: 179–200).

GOODMAN, NELSON (1978), *Ways of Worldmaking* (Indianapolis: Hackett).

GREGORY, FREDERICK (1977), *Scientific Materialism in Nineteenth Century Germany* (Dordrecht: Reidel).

GRIFFITHS, PAUL (1993), 'Functional Analysis and Proper Functions', *British Journal for the Philosophy of Science*, 44: 409–22.

HAACK, SUSAN (1992), 'Pragmatism', in Dancy and Sosa (1992: 351–7).

HACKING, IAN (1991*a*), 'A Tradition of Natural Kinds', *Philosophical Studies*, 61: 109–26.

—— (1991*b*), 'On Boyd', *Philosophical Studies*, 61: 149–54.

HALES, STEVEN (2000), 'The Problem of Intuition', *American Philosophical Quarterly*, 37: 135–47.

HAMPTON, JEAN (1998), *The Authority of Reason* (Cambridge: Cambridge University Press).

HELLER, MARK (1990), *The Ontology of Physical Objects* (Cambridge: Cambridge University Press).

HERSCHEL, JOHN (1987), *A Preliminary Discourse on the Study of Natural Philosophy* (Chicago: University of Chicago Press).

HICKMAN, LARRY, and THOMAS ALEXANDER (1998), *The Essential Dewey*, vol. i: *Pragmatism, Education, Democracy* (Bloomington: Indiana University Press).

HILL, CHRISTOPHER (1991), *Sensations: A Defense of Type Materialism* (New York: Cambridge University Press).

HOBBES, THOMAS (1989), *Metaphysical Writings* (La Salle, Ill: Open Court).

Hookway, Christopher (1988), *Quine: Language, Experience, and Reality* (Oxford: Polity Press).

Hull, David (1965), 'The Effect of Essentialism on Taxonomy: Two Thousand Years of Stasis', repr. in Ereshefsky (1992: 199–226).

—— (1973), 'Charles Darwin and Nineteenth Century Philosophies of Science', in Giere and Westfall (1973: 115–32).

Hume, David (1978), *Treatise of Human Nature*, ed. L. A. Selby-Bigge, 2nd edn. (Oxford: Oxford University Press).

—— (1980), *Dialogues concerning Natural Religion*, ed. R. Popkin (Indianapolis: Hackett).

James, William (1907), 'Pragmatism's Conception of Truth', *Journal of Philosophy and Scientific Methods*, 4: 141–55.

—— (1956), *The Will to Believe and Other Essays in Popular Philosophy* (New York: Dover).

Jordan, Jeff (1996), 'Pragmatic Arguments and Belief', *American Philosophical Quarterly*, 33: 409–20.

Katz, Jerrold (1998), *Realistic Rationalism* (New York: MIT Press).

Kim, Jaegwon, and Ernest Sosa (eds.) (1995), *Companion to Metaphysics* (Oxford: Basil Blackwell).

King, Jeffrey (1994), 'Can Propositions be Naturalistically Acceptable?', *Midwest Studies in Philosophy*, 19: 53–75.

Kitcher, Philip (1992), 'The Naturalists Return', *Philosophical Review*, 101: 53–114.

—— (1993), 'Function and Design', *Midwest Studies in Philosophy*, 18: 379–97.

Koons, Robert (1998), 'Teleology as Higher-Order Causation: A Situation-Theoretic Account', *Minds and Machines*, 8: 559–85.

—— (2000a), 'The Incompatibility of Naturalism and Scientific Realism', in Craig and Moreland (2000: 49–63).

—— (2000b), *Realism Regained* (New York: Oxford University Press).

Kornblith, Hilary (1993), *Inductive Inference and its Natural Ground* (Cambridge, Mass: MIT Press).

—— (1994), 'Naturalism: Both Metaphysical and Epistemological', *Midwest Studies in Philosophy*, 19: 39–52.

Krikorian, Yervant (ed.) (1944), *Naturalism and the Human Spirit* (New York: Columbia University Press).

Kvanvig, Jonathan (1986), *The Possibility of an All-Knowing God* (New York: St Martin's Press).

Kvanvig, Jonathan (ed.) (1998), *Warrant in Contemporary Epistemology* (Lanham, Md.: Rowman & Littlefield).

Lakatos, Imre (1970), 'Falsification and the Methodology of Scientific Research Programmes', in Lakatos (1970: 8–101).

LAKATOS, IMRE (1978), *The Methodology of Scientific Research Programmes*, ed. J. Worrall and G. Currie (Cambridge: Cambridge University Press).

LANGE, FREDERICK (1879), *History of Materialism*, tran. E. C. Thomas, 3 vols., 2nd edn. (London: Trübner).

LANGTON, RAE, and DAVID LEWIS (1998), 'Defining Intrinsic', *Philosophy and Phenomenological Research*, 58: 333–45.

LEITER, BRIAN (1998), 'Naturalism and Naturalized Jurisprudence', in Brian Bix (ed.), *Analyzing Law: New Essays in Legal Theory* (Oxford: Clarendon Press), 79–104.

—— (2002), *Nietzsche on Morality* (London: Routledge).

LEVIN, MICHAEL (1997), 'Plantinga on Functions and the Theory of Evolution', *Australasian Journal of Philosophy*, 75: 83–98.

LEWENS, TIM (2000), 'Functions Talk and the Artefact Model', *Studies in the History and Philosophy of the Biological and Biomedical Sciences*, 34: 95–111.

LEWIS, DAVID (1971), 'Counterparts of Persons and their Bodies', repr. in Lewis (1983: 47–54).

—— (1983), *Philosophical Papers*, vol. i (New York: Oxford University Press).

—— (1986), *On the Plurality of Worlds* (New York: Blackwell).

LYCAN, WILLIAM (1996), 'Bealer on the Possibility of Philosophical Knowledge', *Philosophical Studies*, 81: 143–50.

McDOWELL, JOHN (1995), 'Two Sorts of Naturalism', in Rosalind Hursthouse, Gavin Lawrence, and Warren Quinn (eds.), *Virtues and Reasons* (Oxford: Clarendon Press), 149–79.

MADDY, PENELOPE (1996), *Realism in Mathematics* (Oxford: Clarendon Press).

MAUND, BARRY (2000), 'Proper Functions and Aristotelian Functions in Biology', *Studies in the History and Philosophy of the Biological and Biomedical Sciences*, 34: 155–78.

MELANDER, PETER (1997), *Analyzing Functions: An Essay on a Fundamental Notion in Biology* (Stockholm: Almqvist & Wiskell).

MELNYK, ANDREW (1994), 'Inference to the Best Explanation and Other Minds', *Australasian Journal of Philosophy*, 72: 482–91.

—— (1997), 'How to Keep the "Physical" in Physicalism', *Journal of Philosophy*, 94: 622–37.

MENN, STEPHEN (1998), 'The Intellectual Setting', in Garber and Ayers (1998: 33–86).

MERRICKS, TRENTON (2001), *Objects and Persons* (Oxford: Clarendon Press).

—— (2002), 'Conditional Probability and Defeat', in Beilby (2002: 165–75).

MEYER, STEPHEN (2000), 'Evidence for Design in Physics and Biology: From the Origin of the Universe to the Origin of Life', 53–111 in Michael

Behe, William Dembski, and Stephen Meyer (eds.), *Science and Evidence for Design in the Universe* (San Francisco: Ignatius Press).

MILL, JOHN STUART (1875), *A System of Logic, Ratiocinative and Inductive, Being a Connected View of the Principles of Evidence, and the Methods of Scientific Investigation*, 9th edn. (London: Longman's, Green, Reader, & Dyer).

—— (1889), *An Examination of Sir William Hamilton's Philosophy*, 6th edn. (London: Longman's).

MILLIKAN, RUTH (1984), *Language, Thought, and Other Biological Categories* (Cambridge, Mass.: MIT Press).

—— (1989), 'In Defense of Proper Functions', *Philosophy of Science*, 56: 288–302.

MILLS, EUGENE (1998), 'The Unity of Justification', *Philosophy and Phenomenological Research*, 58: 27–50.

MOSER, PAUL (1985), *Empirical Justifiation* (Boston: Reidel).

—— and J. D. TROUT (eds.) (1995), *Contemporary Materialism* (New York: Routledge).

—— and DAVID YANDELL (2000), 'Farewell to Philosophical Naturalism', in Craig and Moreland (2000: 3–23).

MURPHY, A. E. (1945), Review of *Naturalism and the Human Spirit*, *Journal of Philosophy*, 42: 400–17.

NAGEL, THOMAS (1997), *The Last Word* (New York: Oxford University Press).

NEANDER, KAREN (1983), 'Abnormal Psychobiology', Ph.D. thesis, La Trobe University.

—— (1991), 'Functions as Selected Effects: The Conceptual Analyst's Defense', *Philosophy of Science*, 58: 168–84.

NIELSEN, KAI (1996), *Naturalism without Foundations* (Amherst, NY: Prometheus Books).

NISSEN, LOWELL (1997), *Teleological Language in the Life Sciences* (Lanham, Md.: Rowman and Littlefield).

NOONAN, HAROLD (1988), 'Reply to Lowe on Ships and Structures', *Analysis*, 48: 221–3.

NOZICK, ROBERT (1993), *The Nature of Rationality* (Princeton: Princeton University Press).

O'CONNOR, TIMOTHY (1994), 'An Evolutionary Argument against Naturalism?', *Canadian Journal of Philosophy*, 24: 527–40.

OPPY, GRAHAM (1995), *Ontological Arguments* (Cambridge: Cambridge University Press).

OTTE, RIC (2002), 'Conditional Probabilities in Plantinga's Argument against Naturalism', in Beilby (2002: 135–52).

PALEY, WILLIAM (1963), *Natural Theology: Selections* (Indianapolis: Bobbs-Merrill).

PAPINEAU, DAVID (1993), *Philosophical Naturalism* (Oxford: Basil Blackwell).

PARGETTER, ROBERT (1984), 'The Scientific Inference to Other Minds', *Australasian Journal of Philosophy*, 62: 158–63.

PAUL, L. A. (2001), 'Essentialism', Paper presented at the Second Annual Bellingham Summer Philosophy Conference.

PEIRCE, C. S. (1878), 'How to Make Our Ideas Clear', repr. in N. Houser and C. Kloesel (eds.), *The Essential Peirce* (Bloomington: Indiana University Press), 124–41.

PETTIT, PHILIP (1992), 'The Nature of Naturalism II', *Proceedings of the Aristotelian Society*, suppl. vol. 66: 245–66.

PLANTINGA, ALVIN (1967), *God and Other Minds* (Ithaca, NY: Cornell University Press).

—— (1974), *The Nature of Necessity* (New York: Clarendon Press).

—— (1982), 'How to be an Anti-realist', *Proceedings and Addresses of the American Philosophical Association*, Sept. 1982.

—— (1991), 'An Evolutionary Argument against Naturalism', *Logos*, 12: 27–49.

—— (1993), *Warrant and Proper Function* (New York: Oxford University Press).

—— (1994), 'Naturalism Defeated', http://www.homestead.com/philof religion/files/alspaper.htm

—— (1999), 'Reid, Hume, and God', in Thomas Hibbs and John O'Callaghan (eds.), *Recovering Nature* (Notre Dame, Ind.: University of Notre Dame Press), 201–27.

—— (2002), 'Reply to Beilby's Cohorts', in Beilby (2002: 204–76).

—— and PATRICK GRIM (1993), 'Truth, Omniscience, and Cantorian Arguments: An Exchange', *Philosophical Studies*, 71: 267–306.

POLAND, JEFFREY (1994), *Physicalism: The Philosophical Foundations* (Oxford: Clarendon Press).

POLLOCK, JOHN (1987), 'How to Build a Person', 109–54 in James Tomberlin (ed.), *Philosophical Perspectives*, vol. i: *Metaphysics* (Atascadero, Calif.: Ridgeview).

—— (1995), *Cognitive Carpentry* (Cambridge, Mass.: MIT Press).

—— and JOSEPH CRUZ (1999), *Contemporary Theories of Knowledge* (Lanham, Md.: Rowman & Littlefield).

POST, JOHN (1998), 'Critical Notice of Ruth Millikan's *White Queen Psychology and Other Essays for Alice*', *Philosophy and Phenomenological Research*, 58: 233–7.

PRICE, H. H. (1938), 'Our Evidence for the Existence of Other Minds', repr. in Buford (1970: 133–76).

PRIOR, ELIZABETH (1985), 'What is Wrong with Etiological Accounts of Biological Function?', *Pacific Philosophical Quarterly*, 66: 310–28.

PUST, JOEL (2000), *Invitations as Evidence* (New York: Garland).

PUTNAM, HILARY (1976), 'Realism and Reason', repr. in Putnam (1978: 123–38).

—— (1978), *Meaning and the Moral Sciences* (Boston: Routledge & Kegan Paul).

—— (1981*a*), *Reason, Truth, and History* (New York: Cambridge University Press).

—— (1981*b*), 'Why there is not a Ready Made World', repr. in Putnam (1983: 205–28).

—— (1983), *Realism and Reason* (New York: Cambridge University Press).

—— (1992), *Renewing Philosophy* (Cambridge, Mass.: Harvard University Press).

QUINE, W. V. (1951), 'Two Dogmas of Empiricism', repr. in Quine (1980: 20–46).

—— (1960), *Word and Object* (Cambridge, Mass.: MIT Press).

—— (1968*a*), *Ontological Relativity and Other Essays* (New York: Columbia University Press).

—— (1968*b*), 'Epistemology Naturalized', in Quine (1968*a*: 69–90).

—— (1976), 'Whither Physical Objects', 437–504 in R. Cohen, P. K. Feyerabend, and M. W. Wartofsky (eds.), *Essays in Memory of Imre Lakatos*, (Dordrecht: Reidel).

—— (1978), 'Goodman's *Ways of Worldmaking*', repr. in Quine (1981: 96–9).

—— (1980), *From a Logical Point of View*, 2nd edn. (Cambridge, Mass.: Harvard University Press).

—— (1981), *Theories and Things* (Cambridge, Mass.: Belknap/Harvard University Press).

—— (1992), *The Pursuit of Truth* (Cambridge, Mass.: Harvard University Press).

—— (1995*a*), *From Stimulus to Science* (Cambridge, Mass.: Harvard University Press).

—— (1995*b*), 'Naturalism; or, Living within One's Means', *Dialectica* 49: 251–62.

RAMSEY, WILLIAM (2002), 'Naturalism Defended', in Beilby (2002: 15–29).

RATNER, JOSEPH (1951), 'Dewey's Conception of Philosophy', in Schilpp (1951: 47–74).

RAWLS, JOHN (1951), 'Outline for a Decision Procedure in Ethics', *Philosophical Review*, 60: 177–97.

RAWLS, JOHN (1971), *A Theory of Justice* (Cambridge, Mass.: Harvard University Press).

—— (1975), 'The Independence of Moral Theory', *Proceedings and Addresses of the American Philosophical Association*, 48: 5–22.

—— (1980), 'Kantian Constructivism in Moral Theory: The Dewey Lectures 1980', *Journal of Philosophy*, 77: 515–72.

REA, MICHAEL (1995), 'The Problem of Material Constitution', *Philosophical Review*, 104: 525–52.

—— (ed.) (1997), *Material Constitution: A Reader* (Lanham, Md.: Rowman & Littlefield).

—— (2000*a*), 'Naturalism and Material Objects', in J. P. Moreland and William Lane Craig (eds.), *Naturalism: A Critical Analysis* (London: Routledge), 110–32.

—— (2000*b*), 'Theism and Epistemic Truth Equivalences', *Noûs*, 34: 291–301.

—— (2000*c*), 'Constitution and Kind Membership', *Philosophical Studies*, 97: 169–93.

REID, THOMAS (1983), *Inquiry and Essays*, ed. Ronald Beanblossom and Keitta Lehrer (Indianapolis: Hackett).

ROSENBERG, ALEX (1996), 'A Field Guide to Recent Species of Naturalism', *British Journal for the Philosophy of Science*, 47: 1–29.

RUSSELL, BERTRAND (1948), 'Analogy', repr. in Buford (1970: 3–8).

RYDER, JOHN (1994), *American Philosophic Naturalism in the Twentieth Century* (Amherst, NY: Prometheus Books).

SALMON, N. (1981), *Reference and Essence* (Princeton: Princeton University Press).

SCHAFFNER, KENNETH (1993), *Discovery and Explanation in Biology and Medicine* (Chicago: University of Chicago Press).

SCHILPP, PAUL ARTHUR (1951), *The Philosophy of John Dewey*, 2nd edn. (New York: Tudor).

SCHMITT, FREDERICK (1995), 'Naturalism', in Kim and Sosa (1995: 343–5).

SCHRÖDINGER, ERWIN (1964), *My View of the World* (Cambridge: Cambridge University Press).

SCHWARTZ, STEPHEN (1977), *Naming, Necessity, and Natural Kinds* (Ithaca, NY: Cornell University Press).

SEDLEY, DAVID (1982), 'The Stoic Criterion of Identity', *Phronesis*, 27: 255–75.

SELLARS, ROY WOOD (1922), *Evolutionary Naturalism* (Chicago: Open Court).

—— (1944*a*), 'Is Naturalism Enough?', *Journal of Philosophy*, 41: 533–44.

—— (1944*b*), 'Does Naturalism Need Ontology?', *Journal of Philosophy*, 41: 686–94.

SELLARS, WILFRID (1963), 'Empiricism and the Philosophy of Mind', in his *Science, Perception, and Reality* (London: Routledge & Kegan Paul), 127–96.

SHOEMAKER, SYDNEY (1980*a*), 'Causality and Properties', repr. in Shoemaker (1984: 206–33).

—— (1980*b*), 'Properties, Causation, and Projectibility', in L. J. Cohen and M. Hesse (eds.), *Applications of Inductive Logic* (Oxford: Oxford University Press), 291–312.

—— (1984), *Identity, Cause, and Mind* (Ithaca, NY: Cornell University Press).

SIDELLE, ALAN (1989), *Necessity, Essence, and Individuation: A Defense of Conventionalism* (Ithaca, NY: Cornell University Press).

SIDER, THEODORE (1996), 'All the World's a Stage', *Australasian Journal of Philosophy*, 74: 433–53.

—— (2001), *Four-Dimensionalism* (Oxford: Clarendon Press).

SOBER, E. (1980), 'Evolution, Population Thinking, and Essentialism', repr. in Ereshefsky (1992: 247–78).

—— (1993), *Philosophy of Biology* (Boulder, Colo.: Westview Press).

SOSA, ERNEST (1998), 'Minimal Intuition?', in DePaul and Ramsey (1998: 257–70).

STACE, WALTER (1949), 'Naturalism and Religion', *Proceedings and Addresses of the American Philosophical Association*, 23: 22–46.

STUART, MATTHEW (1999), 'Locke on Natural Kinds', *History of Philosophy Quarterly*, 16: 277–96.

SWOYER, CHRIS (1982), 'The Nature of Natural Laws', *Australasian Journal of Philosophy*, 60: 203–23.

THOMSON, JUDITH (1998), 'The Statue and the Clay', *Noûs*, 32: 149–73.

TIDMAN, PAUL (1996), 'The Justification of a Priori Intuitions', *Philosophy and Phenomenological Research*, 56: 161–71.

TYE, MICHAEL (1994), 'Naturalism and the Problem of Intentionality', *Midwest Studies in Philosophy*, 19: 122–42.

UNGER, PETER (1979), 'There are no Ordinary Things', *Synthese*, 41: 117–54.

VAN CLEVE, JAMES (2002), 'Can Atheists Know Anything?', in Beilby (2002: 103–28).

VAN FRAASSEN, BAS (1989), *Laws and Symmetry* (Oxford: Clarendon Press).

—— (1998), 'Science, Materialism, and False Consciousness', in Kvanvig (1998: 149–82).

VAN INWAGEN, PETER (1983), *An Essay on Free Will* (Oxford: Clarendon Press).

—— (1990), *Material Beings* (Ithaca, NY: Cornell University Press).

—— (1993), *Metaphysics* (Boulder, Colo.: Westview Press).

VENDLER, ZENO (1984), *The Matter of Minds* (New York: Oxford University Press).

VITZTHUM, RICHARD (1995), *Materialism* (Amherst, NY: Prometheus Books).

VON MISES, RICHARD (1957), *Probability, Statistics, and Truth* (New York: Dover).

WAGNER, STEVEN, and RICHARD WARNER (eds.) (1993), *Naturalism: A Critical Appraisal* (Notre Dame, Ind.: University of Notre Dame Press).

WHEWELL, WILLIAM (1967a), *History of the Inductive Sciences* (London: Cass).

—— (1967b), *The Philosophy of the Inductive Sciences, Founded upon their History* (New York: Johnson).

WOODFIELD, ANDREW (1976), *Teleology* (Cambridge: Cambridge University Press).

WRIGHT, CRISPIN (1992), *Truth and Objectivity* (Cambridge, Mass.: Harvard University Press).

—— (2000), 'Truth as Sort of Epistemic: Putnam's Peregrinations', *Journal of Philosophy*, 97: 335–64.

WRIGHT, LARRY (1973), 'Functions', *Philosophical Review*, 82: 139–68.

—— (1976), *Teleological Explanations* (Berkeley: University of California Press).

ZIFF, PAUL (1965), 'The Simplicity of Other Minds', repr. in Buford (1970: 177–88).

Index